PSYCHOANALYSIS AND MENTAL HANDICAP

PSYCHOANALYSIS AND MENTAL HANDICAP

EDITED BY
Johan De Groef
and **Evelyn Heinemann**

Translated by ANDREW WELLER

FREE ASSOCIATION BOOKS / LONDON / NEW YORK

First published in Great Britain in 1999 by
FREE ASSOCIATION BOOKS
57 Warren Street, London W1P 5PA

A CIP catalogue record for this book is available from the British
Library

ISBN 1 85343 431 0 pbk; 1 85343 432 9 hbk

Designed and produced for the publisher by
Chase Production Services, Chadlington, OX7 3LN
Printed in the EC by T.J. International Ltd, Padstow

Contents

Notes on Contributors

Colette Assouly-Piquet is a film director and psychoanalyst. She teaches at l'Ecole Normale Supérieure de Fontenay/Saint Cloud and Paris VII. She has published (together with Fr. Berthier-Vittoz) *Regards sur le handicap* (1994).

Paul Berry is a psychologist at the Evangelische Stiftung Neuerkerode, a village for 900 people with mental handicap. He is the author of several publications on the topic of mental handicap.

Claude Boukobza is a psychoanalyst in private practice and at l'Unité d'Accueil Mères-Enfants, Saint Denis (Paris). She has been published in journals such as *Etudes Freudiennes* and is editor of *Les relations précoces mères-enfants et leurs vicissitudes* (1995).

Johan De Groef is an educationalist, a psychoanalyst and Director of Zonnelied, Roosdaal, Belgium (a residential setting and day centre for 140 adults with a mental handicap). He has been published on psychoanalysis and mental handicap in journals such as *Psychoanalyse, Psychoanalytische Perspektieven* and *Le Coq Héron*. He is editor (with E. Heinemann) of *Psychoanalyse und Geistige Behinderung*, M. Grunewald Verlag (1997).

Joost Demuynck is a clinical psychologist and psychoanalyst (ACF-Belgique) in private practice. He is a staff member of t Wit Huis – Spermalie (Loppem) Belgium.

Olivier-Rachid Grim is a physiotherapist working on a doctorate at the EHESS on mental handicap from the viewpoint of a psycho-analytic anthropology. He has been published in *Contraste*.

Evelyn Heinemann is a Doctor of Psychology, a psychoanalyst and professor at the University of Mainz, Germany. She is author of *Agression* (1996) and *Gewalttätige Kinder* (1992) and some ethno-psychoanalytic studies: *Die Frauen von Palau* (1995) and *Mama*

Afrika. Das Trauma der Versklavung (1990). She is also editor (with J. De Groef) of *Psychoanalyse und Geistige Behinderung*, M. Grunewald Verlag (1997).

Cecile Herrou is Director of La Maison Dagobert and chief editor of *Contraste, Enfance et Handicap.*

Simone Korff-Sausse is a psychoanalyst, a Doctor of Clinical Psychology, and teaches at the Université de Paris VII. She has had many articles published in journals such as *Contraste* and *Topique.* She is author of *Le miroir brisé. L'enfant handicapé, sa famille et le psychanalyste* (1996) and co-author of *Trauma et devenir psychique* (1995).

Maud Mannoni (1923–1998) was a psychoanalyst. She was the author of *L'enfant arriéré et sa mère* (1964). She founded L'École experimental, Bonneuil-sur-Marne. (See Chapter 2, this volume.)

Claire Morelle is a Doctor of Psychology and a psychoanalyst. She teaches at the Université Catholique de Louvain. She is in private practice and is also a staff member of the Centre Chapelle aux Champs, Bruxelles. She is author of *Le corps blessé. Automutilation, psychiatrie et psychanalyse* (1995).

Dietmut Niedecken is a psychologist and psychotherapist in private practice. She is a professor of music therapy at the Musikhochschule in Hamburg, Germany. She is author of *Namenlos. Geistig Behinderte verstehen. Ein Buch für Psychologen und Eltern* (1989).

Marc Pattyn is a clinical psychologist and a staff member of Zonnelied, Roosdaal, Belgium. His special area of interest is Szondi, anthropopsychiatry and mental handicap.

Richard Ruth is a psychologist and psychoanalyst in private practice, and a member of the faculty of Trinity College, Washington D.C. and the University of Virginia. He is co-author of *Sometimes You Just Want to Feel Like a Human Being. Case Studies of Empowering Psychotherapy with People with Disabilities* (1995).

Regine Scelles is a Doctor of Clinical Psychology. She teaches at the Université de Tours and has been published in journals such as the *European Journal on Mental Disability, Cahiers du CTNERHI and Dialogue.* She is co-author of *Le handicap en visages. Ed Eres* (1997).

Monique Schneider is a psychoanalyst. Her publications include *La Parole et l'inceste* (1980), *Père, ne vois-tu pas ... ?* (1985), *Le Trauma et la filiation paradoxale. De Freud à Ferenczi* (1985), *La Part de l'ombre – Approche d'un trauma féminin* (1992) and *Don Juan et le procès de la séduction* (1984).

Valerie Sinason is a consultant child psychotherapist in private practice and at the Tavistock Clinic, London and teaches at St George's Hospital Medical School. She is also Honorary Lecturer at the Anna Freud Centre. She is author of *Mental Handicap and the Human Condition. New Approaches from the Tavistock* (1992).

Preface

'Auntie, speak to me! I'm frightened because it's so dark.'
'What good would that do, You can't see me.'
'That doesn't matter; if anyone speaks, it gets light.'

It is with this quotation from Freud's *Three Essays on the Theory of Sexuality* (1905, p.127) that Maud Mannoni begins her book *The Backward Child and His Mother* (1972). Decades later, these words still retain their full significance. Her pioneering work was the first – before Lacan's *Ecrits* (1990) – of the famous series 'The Freudian Field' published by Seuil, Paris.

Since then, only a very few psychoanalysts, like Valerie Sinason, have done pioneering work in this field. In the meantime there have been developments: the Freudian debate continues and the 'nameless' are being brought out of the darkness.

Outside the institutional limits of the psychoanalytic field and without fear of language barriers, twenty-five psychoanalysts from seven different countries have emerged from their quiet isolation. In June 1996, they came together for a three-day conference in Blankenberge, Belgium to exchange ideas on the relation between psychoanalysis and handicap. The work group provides a support structure (in the sense of Winnicott's 'containment'), a forum for exchanging and sharing truths which we hear from our patients.

This work made such an impression on the participants that, without wishing to institutionalise or hypostasise themselves, the lectures were published and biannual conferences were planned for the future in the hope that the issues and questions which had been raised would be followed up. In February 1997, a further two-day conference was held in Paris with the financial support of the European Commission–Association for the Research and Training on Integration in Europe. The articles in this book are contributions from the Belgian and Parisian conferences.

This work group – in line with the psychoanalytic ethic – provides a supportive framework for psychoanalysts, therapists and educationalists. Dialogue is their natural way of working and not just a tool. Individual contributions reflect different psychoanalytic concepts – and perhaps the ethos of specific countries too – of which readers will form their own picture.

Since Maud Mannoni died on 15 March 1998, we also include Claude Boukobza's 'Maud Mannoni and the Retarded Child': In Memoriam Lecture held in June 1998 at the third conference on Psychoanalysis and Mental Handicap, Tavistock Clinic, London.

We would like here to invite you to participate in the discussion and to take part in the next conference. For more information **contact: Johan De Groef, Zonnelied, Kloosterstraat 7, 1761 Roosdaal/Belgium.**

Johan De Groef
Evelyn Heinemann

REFERENCES

Freud, S. (1905) 'Three Essays on the Theory of Sexuality', in James Strachey, ed., *The Standard Edition of the Complete Psychological Works of Sigmund Freud*, 24 vols, London, Hogarth, 1953–73, Vol. 7.

Lacan, J. (1990) *Ecrits: A Selection*, London, Routledge.

Mannoni, M. (1972) *The Backward Child and His Mother*, trans. A.M. Sheridan Smith, New York, Pantheon.

Translator's note

For a long time it was considered that the mentally handicapped were not able to make use of psychoanalytic therapy due to insufficient capacity for insight. These chapters by an international group of practitioners, all involved with psychoanalysis and handicap, bear witness to the great advances being made in the therapeutic treatment of men, women and children with a handicap. I cannot here but outline a few of the ideas and themes which seem to me seminal in these chapters; but, in so doing, I hope to encourage interested readers to discover the richness of these contributions for themselves.

It has not been easy to work on such a range of articles by authors with different specialities, vocabularies and theoretical outlooks. Some of the chapters reflect Lacanian thinking and vocabulary for which there are not always neat equivalents in English. For example 'the real' *(le réel)*, which is not the same as reality, or Lacan's English neologism 'want-to-be' for *'manque à être'*, might well seem odd to anyone unfamiliar with these terms. I have tried not to simplify these difficulties while at the same time being concerned to get ideas in the original texts across in meaningful English. Usually, in such cases I have decided to give the French term alongside the translation to make it clear that this is a technical usage and have added an endnote where it seemed necessary. Translators are notorious traitors. I hope the authors will show forbearance if I have fallen into this trap unwittingly.

At the international conference on Psychoanalysis and Mental Handicap in Paris last year, I think everyone felt handicapped by their linguistic limitations, to a lesser or greater extent. Being deprived of your mother-tongue can be an extremely frustrating, alienating and handicapping experience; an experience of *étrangeté*. Imagine then what it might be like not to be able to speak at all. Of course, the former situation is not at all comparable with a real organic disability, a primary handicap, which may in addition be compounded with a secondary handicap resulting from the attitudes of family or society at large to the original handicap. However, if we want to come to a deeper understanding and acceptance of *difference* (*l'étrangeté de l'autre*), it goes without saying that we need to be more

than a little in touch with our own woundedness, our own handicapped selves.

I have very close friends who have children with a disability and I
know how confrontation with handicap arouses all sorts of difficult
and painful feelings in oneself. As Johan De Groef points out in his
chapter 'Mental Handicaps: A Dark Continent', we all have our own
dark continents, our shortcomings or our own lacks which are
mirrored when we are faced with disability. In *Le miroir brisé* (1996),
Simone Korff-Sausse speaks of how parents faced with a handicapped child are confronted with a deformed mirror image from
which they shy away.

Lacan suggests we all suffer from 'debility' in as far as we do not
want to know (Lacan 1973, Bruno 1986). *Knowing, not-knowing* and
not-wanting-to-know strike me as being key themes in these chapters,
particularly in those of Claire Morelle and Joost Demuynck, but
others as well. Again it is painful not to know; it faces us with our
own vulnerability, chaos and disarray. It feels so much better to have
an answer, if not 'the' answer. Theoretical dogmatism often masks
inner uncertainty which cannot be acknowledged. Bion (1974, p.72),
perhaps more than anyone, emphasised the importance for openness
to the unknown in each individual. He did not advocate the comforts
of knowing. In order to remain open to fresh understanding it is
necessary to maintain a certain attitude of not-knowing. As for not-
wanting-to-know, we only need to listen to ourselves to see how
readily we evacuate uncomfortable perceptions and feelings.

All the chapters bear witness to the suffering caused by trauma,
guilty anxiety and the catastrophic. Trauma is an unexpected shock
for the psyche. Too much pain is numbing. Emotions get frozen and
split-off. Curiosity, intelligence and the capacity to communicate are
inhibited. As Valerie Sinason points out in her book *Mental Handicap
and the Human Condition* (1992), all of us have the tendency to 'go
stupid' under stressful conditions. 'Stupidity' is then seen as a
defence against the pain or grief of trauma. She also points out that
it is important to distinguish between emotional and cognitive intelligence, that people with low IQs do just as well in therapy as others,
and that their IQs can improve considerably as a result of therapy if
some of this frozen potential can be reached and released. In her
chapter on sibling relationships, Regine Scelles explores the effects of
trauma and guilt on the non-handicapped siblings of disabled
children. Monique Schneider's chapter 'Encountering the Real in
Handicap' discusses trauma, guilt and catastrophe with reference to
Goethe's autobiography in which he speaks of the 'monstrous' earthquake in Lisbon which echoes his own experience of family suffering
in childhood (Goethe 1975).

The monstrous aspect of handicap is a central motif: 'When the monster recognises himself in the mirror ... then he will become more human', is the epigraph for Olivier-Rachid Grim's chapter on sexuality and handicap. As he shows through the myth of Priapus and the legend of Cyrano, the physical freak has often been an object of derision in human society. But what of the freak within ourselves? Monstrosity is to be found as much within as without. If we can withdraw our projections and face these dimensions in ourselves we will be less afraid and rejecting of what appears unbearable without. Inside and outside must come together.

Apart from the wide-ranging theoretical contributions in these chapters, many interesting clinical cases are discussed which afford a real insight into the processes that can take place between therapists and patients. The chapters by Evelyn Heinemann, Richard Ruth, Regine Scelles, Paul Berry, Simone Korff-Sausse, Dietmut Niedecken, Marc Pattyn and Valerie Sinason all contain rich clinical material. Fortunately, there is more than a grain of humour in these accounts with some poignant jokes, such as the one about the Nutcracker Suite. The capacity to laugh is surely absolutely life-saving for all concerned at times when such unbearable truths emerge between therapists and their patients.

Beyond the strictly psychoanalytic themes, these chapters touch on many other fields too, such as anthropology, politics, literature, mythology and art. For example, the writings of Kenzaburo Oë such as *Teach us how to Outgrow our Madness* (1989), which explore the relationship between a father and his handicapped son are of particular interest for workers in this field and have inspired the chapters by Colette Assouly-Piquet and Johan De Groef.

The themes of exclusion and integration are never far from the surface and are particularly thought-provoking in the context of modern society which systematically excludes all those who do not fit in with dominant cultural values. Here, I would like to draw attention to the short chapter by Cecile Herrou, the director of an innovatory child care centre, La Maison Dagobert in Paris which welcomes both handicapped and non-handicapped children from the community. She lays stress on the need to push back the barriers of prejudice, fear and hate which perpetuate exclusion in our society. Maud Mannoni, in her chapter, reminds us of the *political* dimensions of handicap, institutionalisation, integration and exclusion and raises important questions about our society at a time when we are in principle moving towards greater political and economic unity.

Finally, I would like to thank Johan De Groef for entrusting me with the translation and editing of these chapters as well as Monique Zerbib and Des Sowerby for their encouragement and help with reading and checking the manuscript, though I bear full responsibility for any shortcomings which may persist.

Andrew Weller

REFERENCES

Bion, W. (1974) *Brazilian Lectures 1*, Rio de Janeiro, Imago Editora.

Bruno, P. (1986) 'A côté de la plaque', *Ornicar?*, 37: 38–65.

Goethe, J.W. (1975) *Dichtung und Wahrheit*, Frankfurt am Main, Inseltaschenbuch.

Korff-Sausse, S. (1996) *Le Miroir Brisé*, Paris, Calmann-Lévy.

Lacan, J. (1973) *The Four Fundamental Concepts of Psychoanalysis*, Penguin, 1979.

Oë, Kenzaburo (1989) *Teach us to Outgrow our Madness*, trans. J. Nathan, London, Serpent's Tail.

Sinason, V. (1992) *Mental Handicap and the Human Condition: New Approaches from the Tavistock*, London, Free Association Books.

1 Words of Greeting: Psychoanalysis and Handicap

MAUD MANNONI

Dear friends, my thoughts are with all of you and I wish you a successful congress. As a contribution, I would like here to share with you some of my thoughts on this subject.

It is erroneous to force a young person 'to accept his handicap' when the disability is mental. The protagonist in Dostoevsky's novel *The Idiot* puts it as follows:

> It may be so that my social contacts are not without troubles and difficulties. Anyway, I have decided to be courteous and straight-forward towards everyone; after all no one will ask more of me. Maybe they too will think of me a child – what do I care. For one or other reason they all see me as an idiot and indeed I have been so ill for a while that I must have looked much of an idiot at that time. But how could I still be like that, now that I myself realise that people take me for an idiot? Whenever I go somewhere, I think: they take me for an idiot, but I really have quite a lot to offer, even if they haven't got a clue.[1]

Far from having to reconcile a young person to his (or her) handicap, as is recommended by some, it is necessary in the case of those who are the most deprived to trust in their own 'genius' (deprived, that is, according to our normative criteria). It is in this way, and only in this way, that a young person with a history of being handicapped and marked by the signifier 'negative score', will find opportunities to break free from it and to build up a decent existence, in his or her own way.

For example, Victor is a twenty-five-year-old who lives in a council flat together with his so-called normal girlfriend. Victor had to give up his job as a waiter because he kept telling his life-story to the clients. He now works as a municipal maintenance man, a solitary job which interests him little. But the discovery of love and the perspective of setting up his own home have worked wonders. They turned this illiterate rebel into a man willing to make up for lost time, searching for both a new identity and other opportunities on the professional level.

It is not easy for an adult who is labelled as handicapped to find his place and to hold down a job. We often tell our youngsters in Bonneuil: 'If you value your job, just act as if you're normal. That's all that will be asked of you.'

However, a young person can only act normal on condition that he can be himself elsewhere, in other more tolerant places, such as the 'circle of friends' we have created in the provinces. The 'quality of life' of those with a serious psychiatric history is much higher there than in Paris or the region of Le Val de Marne. The friendly welcome which allows for people to be different is invaluable.

Much could be said about the harsh fate of farmers nowadays. It is amongst them that we have found the greatest degree of generosity and solidarity in welcoming youngsters with difficulties. Some of them have been able to build up a life in rural surroundings, others have been the silent witnesses of a drama taking place on the land they had learned to love. Many farmers rely on their sons to take things over, but see their heirs go off to the city. When they realise that there is no one to carry on the tradition[2] and that the fruit of generations of sacrifice will be lost, they experience the death of their business as if it were their own death. They wonder what sense their lives have had.

The loss of the land condemns not only the people who live off it, but a whole culture. However, it is exactly in the poorest regions that we have found the greatest conviviality and helpfulness, not to mention the mountains, where shepherds have saved many young people adrift. This knowing of the heart is not acquired through measures of further education introduced by the administration to create 'efficient' host families; exactly the kind of host families in fact, which were declared unfit in Canada some thirty years ago: families abandoning the land and animals to 'benefit' from the handicap.

It is with the small owners, 'the greens', the winegrowers, the poultry keepers, those who use organic farming methods that we work. They are thought to be finished; the future belonging to the farmer-manager. The trend towards city life brings with it, it must be stressed, a regrettable change of mentality. In such a society there is no room for a handicapped person, someone who is 'different', and lives life at slower, 'non-productive' pace.

In the rural world of our grandparents, there is still time to live, to listen, to communicate. A countrywoman, belonging to this disappearing world, took the time to listen to a mute autist: 'Listen to this child, talking to the fire, the plants, the birds; he has so much to say.'

She was full of admiration for his wordless language and learnt to *communicate* with him. The technological changes that Europe is pushing for world-wide bring with them radical changes in attitudes, I would even say a change in our civilisation. It is a schizophrenic and inhuman world which is being constructed nowadays, a world in which the human spirit is diminished by economic value and 'productivism'.[3] In this world of machines and micro computers, there is no more room for the unpredictable. On the contrary, unpredictability and human phantasy disturb.

Psychiatric provision based on unequal access, denounced by Jacques Ruffié, was established between 1986 and 1988. A society with a fast and slow track has also been established in Europe since 1986 with the approval of the 'politicians'.

The Kreisky report (1989)[4] draws attention to the gravity of the situation, untenable in the long term, both from an economic as well as a human standpoint. It is unacceptable that one part of the population should be economically active while another remains inactive and on benefits. This situation can only lead to a social explosion.

The problem of the 'mentally ill' is getting worse with the present economic crisis. There is a tendency to obscure their actual situation by giving them a disablement benefit. However, the issue is more complex, for this category of 'excluded' people requires the most flexible and varied provision available. What really matters for those labelled 'mentally ill' is that they should not be stuck with this label of 'madness' for ever and that they be able to find their identity within a given social setting.

Jacques, thirty years of age, took his diploma as a cabinet maker when he was eighteen. His parents had already sentenced him to 'life-long retirement'. However, he refused this and managed to change his statute as a handicapped minor into that of an adult handicapped person. He then found a normal job which meant the end of his benefit as a disabled person. He even managed to complete three months of military service in Germany. However, his mother's daily calls for news of him finally aroused the General's anxiety. A welfare officer was asked to look after this 'case' (unfortunately meaning the son, not the mother). Army staff were afraid that the family might turn against them and would appeal for benefit based on mental disability. The army feared being held responsible and decided to discharge Jacques as unfit, although he had served to everyone's satisfaction. He was put on the reservists' list and the General himself promised Jacques that France would call on him if the country needed him. Reassured by the proof he had given of his 'normality', Jacques decided to travel from city to city, far from his mother and irksome officialdom.

He wanted to be like Don Quixote, a free man and an adventurer. He lived rather well from small jobs, allowing himself the time to return to the world of salaried employment. He wanted to live like the ancient master craftsmen *(les compagnons du Tour de France)*. He started his 'Tour' in Germany where he had known military life before his mother put him back on the trail of disability. He used our network of friends in France and abroad, and in these convivial circles he was accepted as a craftsman and entitled to his touch of 'madness'.

We have never asked our patients 'to learn to live with their handicap'. On the contrary, we try to help them escape the exclusion created by the attitude of others. It is a question of helping them to truly run their own lives, rather than be robots resigned to exclusion. You cannot work wonders with the severely mentally handicapped, but if you take care of them when they are young you can develop their intelligence, liberate a wisdom of the heart and a way of communicating without words.

It is very important to find a place for them in the network of host families, craftsmen, farmers and friends; a place where they can be accepted and loved, with their own limitations. Meanwhile, the respect they experience as subjects awakens the desire to live up to expectations; they participate, at their own rhythm, in a shared passion for animals, agriculture, and so on.

As for intelligent psychotics, we try to make them combative, with the aim of helping them overcome the rejection which they experience. After all, if it suffices to act normal while preserving a touch of madness, why not? We adapt them to a world where some people defend their own dignity by attributing insanity to others, to those who disturb or tell the truth.

Young people with a history of abnormality have to make a double transition: one from childhood to adulthood and one from the statute of handicapped person to that of a 'normal' person. They have to earn their independence twice over to be allowed to run their own lives and to get jobs. From a pedagogical point of view, this means we have to acknowledge the specific problems of some of these youngsters, instead of denying them. It is exactly this acknowledgement which has to be the instrument of success. This requires the energy of everyone concerned: children, youngsters, social workers, but also volunteers and friends of all sorts. All knowledge is in fact *political* and matters only as a means of struggle. Actually, it is events that speak: 'discourse' *(le discours)*, as Foucault puts it, 'is only the reflection of a truth arising in front of one's eyes'.[5]

But in our academic system everything combines to destroy the truth present in discourse. Attempts are made to master the uncontrollable. Discourse remains stuck in a senseless proliferation. When words no longer carry any weight, and all that is said turns out to be false and full of shallow promises, an individual's despair can be great, indeed. It cannot be predicted with what violence he will respond to discourses in which he cannot believe and which leave him with no way out.

What is most cruelly lacking for the most deprived children, is simply *a place to live*. If only they could find a home in a village which was ready to receive them (offering activities which interest them, for they are children capable of passion and excelling themselves) they could later, as adults, be spared the need for institutionalised psychiatric provision.

A child who, when he becomes an adult, is unable to meet the demands of normal working life should have the choice between a life in which he chooses not to work (while nonetheless providing for his needs) and a life where he can choose his work from a wide variety of activities. In the former case, he will need a minimum of financial assistance to meet his daily needs (but life in the mountains is not expensive and some schizophrenics like it there and are eventually accepted in the local community).

After May 1968,[6] Winnicott asked some questions about the students' revolt and insisted on the necessity of preserving the generation conflict. It appeared to him that adults can learn something from the younger generation but that the latter also need responsible adults who do not abdicate their authority. Confrontation, he used to say, has its own form and should be maintained in order to guarantee freedom of opinion. He added, moreover, that it would not necessarily be a laughing matter (alluding to how, in phantasy, life and death forces are always enacted in the generation conflict).

Our society needs these '*adolescent states*' as much as it needs 'adult wisdom'. The dissident minority (including the insane) raise a question that has to be heard and faced. This question is about their claim for the right to be *different*. How can we give them the means to live without requiring that they be socially rehabilitated?

That is one of the problems of our time.

NOTES

1. Dostoevsky, F. (1975) *The Idiot*, London, Heinemann, p. 71.
2. Bourdieu, P. (1998) *Symbolic Exchange and Death: Theory, Culture and Society*, London, Sage.
3. Cf. Jacob, C. (1994) *La clé des champs*, Paris, Odile Jacob. Le Bourdonnais, Y. (1994) *Des paysans heureux, une révolution en marche*, Paris, Flammarion.

4. Kreisky, B. (1989) *Pour en finir avec le chomage en Europe*, Paris, La Decouverte.
5. Foucault, M. (1981) 'The Order of Discourse', in *Untying the Text: A Post-Structuralist Reader*, Boston, London and Henley, Routledge.
6. Winnicott, D.W. (1968), lecture given during a symposium on the occasion of the 21st meeting of the British Health Association, Newcastle-upon-Tyne, 18 July. Taken up again in *Playing and Reality*, London, Tavistock, 1971, pp.206–7.

2 Maud Mannoni and the Retarded Child

CLAUDE BOUKOBZA

I would like to begin by retracing the journey of Maud Mannoni, as she described it in 1988 in her text, *Ce qui manque à la Vérité pour être dite* (*What the Truth Needs to be Told*).[1] I am aware that in Anglo-Saxon countries, particularly, a biography is usually expected to be an objective work, documented and confirmed by witnesses and buttressed by facts. However, there has been no such work to date with regard to the life and work of Maud Mannoni and, furthermore, it seems much more interesting to me to make her own voice heard with regard to her experience in a way which is similar to what we French analysts call the pass – this working through, in a different way, of one's own analysis and of what has made analysts of us.

Subsequently, since it is the theme of this conference, I shall clarify the originality of her contribution to our understanding, of *L'enfant arriéré et sa mère*[2] which has been translated into English as *The Retarded Child and His Mother*.

Mannoni's journey

Opening her book with the question, 'How does one become an analyst?' Maud Mannoni affirms straight away that the events that marked her life are not without relation to her interest in retarded development and psychosis.

Maud Mannoni was born in 1923. Her mother was of Belgian origin and her father was Dutch. As a diplomat, he was posted to Ceylan, where Maud spent the first years of her life. Her Sinhalese nurse raised her in complete freedom (while her younger sister was entrusted to a stricter French governess). They lived in a large house overlooking the ocean which Mannoni later remembered as a kind of fairytale terrestrial paradise. There she experienced the abundance of

7

a tropical landscape, the pleasure and richness of playing games with the local neighbourhood children, and the plenitude of stories that she heard in Hindi from the nurse and the Hindu porter. It was there, in her early years, that she was brought up speaking English.

When she was six years old, her family had to return to Europe, only to find the bourgeois world in decline. The nurse was not able to follow them there, and Maud experienced this rupture as a terrifying abandonment: 'I couldn't recognize anymore who I was, where I was going', she wrote.

Welcomed initially by her maternal grandparents in Courtrai, Belgium, Maud learned French quickly but she forgot her early English and Hindi. She entered, she said, into a sort of 'affective anesthesia', a mode of defence that she would retain for the rest of her life.

Then, in yet another rupture of both place and language, her parents took her to Amsterdam where she was forced to learn Dutch. From the ages of six to eleven, she lived in total affective solitude feeling, once again, completely anesthetised. 'The words had lost their sense. I unlearned how to speak.'

Her school years, spent in Anvers, left her with memories of boredom and mediocrity. It was her university years that would be truly formative for her. This was paradoxical for the university was closed at the time as a sign of protest against the German invaders. She was thus trained 'on the job' at the psychiatric hospital. Due to the war she experienced great liberty at the hospital, in particular with regard to the care of feebleminded adolescents and psychotics in the suburbs of Anvers. She spent the better part of her time with them outside the hospital in the daylight, in the wilderness, and she staged a travelling theatre with them. Further, with these patients, she favoured the use of the Flemish dialect in order to facilitate the symbolisation of the violence which had been suffered and enacted by these adolescents into words. It was, in fact, a sort of anti-psychiatry experience *avant-la-lettre* (that is, before it was theorised as such).

During the war years, Maud met a young man and fell in love. This first experience of love roused her from the lethargy she had felt, faced with the world, and gave her support. She was further indebted to this young man, himself in analysis with Leuba in Paris, for orienting her towards Maurice Dugautiez. He had trained, together with Fernand Lechat, a small group of original and non-conformist analysts who were not integrated into the Institute of Psycho-Analysis (IPA) until 1946.

At the end of the war, she received a diploma in criminology from the University of Brussels and began to practise psychoanalysis. In 1948, at the age of twenty-five, she was the first to be appointed by the fledgling Belgian Society for Psychoanalysis. Due to this connection, she remained affiliated with the IPA until her death, even when the French Lacanian analysts where excluded from it in 1963. In spite of what seems to have been a precocious professional success, she spoke of having lived through this period in a sort of moral lethargy, and she felt she had been intellectually asleep.

Just as significant for her training as the interruptions in her childhood and her university apprenticeship, were her first two patients who were to 'mark and form' her profoundly. One was a man who had survived the concentration camps and who committed suicide in order to escape the state of dehumanisation into which he had been thrown. The other was a developmentally impaired child whose first drawing was of a headless man walking on a tightrope on top of a precipice. Conscious that analysts had excluded developmental retardation from the field of their preoccupations, she nevertheless took this child into analysis, an analysis which had as its price the death of the mother. 'I would not do anything in the same way today', she said. It is noteworthy, however, that from the very beginning Mannoni was confronted with death, whether it was a patient's death or a death the patient had encountered in his or her environment.

From the heroic war years and post-war years, Maud Mannoni said that she retained the sense of 'having learned alongside ignorant masters'. She was referring to her clinical supervisors who had had none of the clinical experience that she had. It was doubtless the precociousness of her own experience that gave her the confidence she always transmitted to those younger than herself and who were often better, in her judgement, at dealing with psychosis than the more senior analysts.

Intending to work on a thesis in New York, Mannoni stopped off in Paris where she finally stayed. There, she looked for theoretical support in order to articulate the questions that had arisen very early on in her life. Some decisive encounters allowed her 'to come to herself and to know, finally, who she was'.

The first of these encounters was with Françoise Dolto. This was initially a personal encounter, where the young student who had arrived alone in Paris was welcomed with open arms into the Dolto family. Françoise Dolto introduced her to a brilliant ethnologist-psychoanalyst who had just arrived from Madascagar, Octave Mannoni. During the funeral for Maud Mannoni on 3 April, in Paris, Catherine Dolto spoke of the joy that the Dolto children had felt whenever Maud arrived at their house, always ready to play with them and to tell them marvellous stories.

The meeting with Françoise Dolto was also decisive in terms of her own formation. Dolto shook up Mannoni in her theoretical certitudes with regard to mental debility and backwardness. Mannoni

attended the consultations at Trousseau Hospital and discovered a
new approach to mental illness. Dolto introduced her to the dimensions of play, paradox and humour in her relations with patients. She
was particularly attentive to what Ferenczi called the 'context', and
would later develop this concept herself, in 1967, as the 'collective
discourse' which she understood as the discourse in which the child
is taken up even before his birth. In Françoise Dolto's method, the
crux of what is going on in the relation between the mother and the
child is always identified right away. This is also true for the place
which the father comes to occupy in the discourse of the mother.
Mannoni would say later about Dolto that she truly incarnated
psychoanalysis. Françoise Dolto was able to touch, in her dazzling
interventions with child patients, the blindspot of each of the adults
present, who often left disturbed or at least somehow changed by the
experience. Dolto knew, Mannoni tells us, how to introduce into the
analysis a questioning which was always altered in some way by the
experience and which always remained open in the face of desire. She
had the ability to find just the right words to reach each child at
whatever point he could be found and to put into words for him what
she thought the effects of the surrounding family situation were, and
to comment on the intentions of the parental discourse. While Dolto
had an approach towards psychosis from which Mannoni would
eventually break away, Mannoni would nevertheless retain a way of
questioning she had learned from Dolto regarding the mother–child
relationship. Françoise Dolto, emphasised Maud Mannoni, 'was the
only analyst to have a word of her own'. She says in her own words
what Lacan laboriously tried to elaborate on a theoretical plane.
Mannoni reproached her, however, for having left child analysis at a
low ebb in French analytic institutions, 'led by men', and for not
having fought to give child analysis the prominent position that it had
attained in England.

The First Meeting with the Psychoanalyst,[3] with a preface by
Françoise Dolto, testified to the training experience and interventions made in collaboration with her.

The second decisive meeting for Mannoni was with Lacan. She
joined in all his battles and in 1963 started with him, at his request,
a second analysis which enabled her to write her first book L'enfant
arriéré et sa mère (The Retarded Child and His Mother: A Psychoanalytic
Study).[4] 'Without him', she said, 'I would never have found the
words.' In this first book which in 1964 inaugurated, in accordance
with Lacan's will, the collection 'le champ freudien' ('The Freudian
Field'), Mannoni advanced essential ideas which she would continue
to develop: notably, that it is sometimes the child who figures 'a
mother of an abnormal child'. The parents need to bring their word

to the place where the child is heard, and the analyst must be attuned to the collective discourse.

A long collaboration and friendship followed with Lacan. Unlike many analysts of her generation who began to speak 'Lacanian', Maud Mannoni knew how to make use of Lacanian concepts clinically in order to use them with dynamic effect in the cure. And if one looks at the dates of publication, one cannot say for certain what came first – the theoretical advances of Lacan or the clinical discoveries of Françoise Dolto and Maud Mannoni.

It was Lacan who oriented her towards Winnicott, whom she met regularly in London during the 1960s for supervision just at the time he was emerging from his isolation and beginning to be acknowledged as a great clinician. The last conference that Maud Mannoni gave at our association on 8 December 1997 concerned, precisely, her meetings with Winnicott. He taught her, she said, 'to speak of analysis in the language of the every day, staying close to actual clinical experience'. During these meetings, two styles confronted each other: a French one, theorised and at times closed; and an English one that looked for the flaws in concrete experience. This confrontation did not take place without difficulty. Mannoni was also interested in Winnicott's insistence on the need for inventive and friendly institutional places to welcome, in a calm environment, the troubled adolescents' delirium. 'Why do you speak about curing when often it suffices to accompany [to heal] a being in his distress?' It was Winnicott who finally orientated her towards Laing and Kingsley Hall with the malicious intention of shaking up her theoretical certainty. Laing also became a friend. He put her on her guard against the tendency to confuse, on the one hand, accompanying someone in their distress while respecting the moment of necessary rupture and, on the other hand, the preoccupation to cure at all costs.

Certain chapters of her book *L'enfant, sa 'maladie' et les autres (The Child, his 'Illness' and the Others)*[5] were the subject of debate at the Institute of Psycho-Analysis in London. There, Mannoni met the analysts in Winnicott's group who tended in their practice to substitute listening to a discourse, that is, the collective discourse of the family, the plot of a psychotogenic situation, for the conception of developmental stages. The analysts in Winnicott's group maintained that it was to know how to hear in the patient's delirium a truth that those surrounding the patient plug up or deny. The theories of these English analysts were little known in France at the time, at least in the Lacanian milieu, which was cut off from the IPA. Beyond all dogmatism, Mannoni knew how 'to give importance, according to the clinical situation, to the contribution of Lacan as much as that of Winnicott or of Bleger'. All of these theoretical references were useful, but 'it is the patient who must serve as the guide'. Mannoni would take up the question of the function of theory in the field of psychoanalysis in 1979 in *La theorie comme fiction* (*Theory as Fiction*).[6]

From Winnicott, Mannoni retained the notions of holding, which corresponded with the Lacanian notion of the child who perceived himself in the mirror through the gaze of his mother; the transitional and creative space; the true and false self, and the analysis of the analytic situation as a relationship which includes the analyst and the patient.

The apogee of these Franco-British exchanges was the Seminar for the Study of Child Psychoses, organised by Maud Mannoni in Paris in 1967 in which Laing and Cooper participated with Lacan and several French analysts. Winnicott, who had announced his participation, did not attend in the end because he had just been appointed president of the British Society for Psychoanalysis and he feared that his presence would give sanction to the Ecole Freudienne de Paris which was not recognised by the IPA. He did, however, send a paper on schizophrenia. During this seminar 'two universes confronted one another', said Mannoni: 'French certainty regarding a knowledge about madness and the questioning of the English stemming from an identification with the patient.' Lacan concluded the conference, which became an event in the history of the French psychoanalytic movement, by a touching homage to Maud Mannoni and a beautiful text announcing the entry of the occidental world into the field of segregation.

In 1970, Mannoni published Cooper's book, *Psychiatry and Anti-Psychiatry* in the collection 'The Freudian Field' ('Le champ freudien'). This was the only psychoanalytic collection which published a book from the English anti-psychiatry movement.

In 1964, in the service of Dr Helene Chaigeau in Ville-Evrard, Mannoni met with the same type of patients, now adults, whom she had described as children in *The Retarded Child and His Mother*. Only the time that she had spent at Kingsley Hall enabled her to endure the world of the psychiatric hospital. However, she came to the conclusion that psychoanalysis and the practice of sequestering people in a sanctuary or retreat are not compatible. Mannoni tried again in 1967 to introduce a group of analysts into an institution for children, the Institut Medico-Pédagogique of Thiais in the Parisian suburbs. She recounted this experience, which she concluded was a failure, in her text *Le psychiatre, son 'fou' et le psychanalyse*.[7]

These reflections on psychosis and the institution led her to create, in 1969, the experimental School of Bonneuil. Convinced that psychoanalysis had everything to gain from confronting psychiatry and pedagogy and that the analyst must maintain his or her position in the community, Maud Mannoni developed the notion of the

Exploded Institution. Bonneuil is open to the outside world, that is Mannoni encouraged the psychotic children to live among foster families in the countryside, to work with local artisans, and to take trips to foreign countries. (She praised the English educational system.) Many foreign students also arrived to train in her clinic. The word soon got around that what could not be said in one place could now be said somewhere else.

Maud Mannoni fought passionately to create and defend Bonneuil against the administration and also to defend a certain idea of a mental health policy. From then on, her life was dedicated to her work and until the end of her life she fought to safeguard the originality of this specific institutional experience. Three books, *Education Impossible*[8], *Un lieu pour vivre*[9] and *Bonneuil, seize ans apres*,[10] and two films called *Secrète enfance*[11] testify to this experience.

In the 1970s, she travelled a great deal with Octave in Latin America, in particular in Argentina and Uruguay. She aligned herself with South American analysts against the dictatorship and supported them unconditionally. The memory and impact of Maud Mannoni is still felt immensely there even though she had not been there for many years. Many young analysts came to Bonneuil to study. The numerous moving letters of condolence that we received from Latin America since her death testified to this.

In addition to the question of the institution and of the fight against exclusion and segregation, another question pursued Mannoni until the end of her life, the question of writing – something she had a tremendous need for. Something which could not be expressed in words pushed her specifically to write. In her writing, she asked if the trauma and the search for 'the lost language of childhood' pushes writers and poets to write. She looked in particular at the writings of Kipling, Charles Dickens and Anthony Trollope: 'I am looking in certain writers for a knowledge regarding an unknown part of the self.' She finished her work as a writer by reading Virginia Woolf. Her last book, which appeared shortly before her death, *Elles ne savent pas ce qu'elles disent*,[12] is dedicated to the underlying debate, according to Mannoni, between the works of Virginia Woolf and Freud. She wanted to give voice to the words of women which have always been set apart. What follows can be said to be her last words:

[W]oman, for a century now, has tried to rescue the independence of her life from men ... Her truth, she finds it either in identifying with men to the point of alienating her discourse, or looking for a level of being, and re-inventing herself with the other. A woman realizes herself in a creative fashion in marrying rebellion more than the establishment.

L'Enfant arriéré et sa mère (The Retarded Child and His Mother)

This book has a special place in the work of Maud Mannoni. 'It is my first book which I still consider today to be the best one ... the most authentic, the most original', she wrote in *What the Truth Needs to be Told* in 1988. 'It is dedicated to a deceased father, it speaks of the past. It liberated me from my unpaid debts.'

Her tie with developmentally arrested children is paradoxical and strange. In *Le symptome et le savoir (Symptom and Knowledge)*,[13] her doctoral thesis in 1983, Mannoni tells that the place of the retarded child was given to her in her family, as opposed to her younger sister who was considered to be gifted. She felt that she had left her intelligence in India along with her language and the memory of a lost childhood. In Europe, she was a spectator of the other and of herself, insensitive to the goings-on in the world. This book is at the same time an attempt at theorising a rich clinical experience and an elaboration of her personal analysis with Lacan.

As the first book to appear in the collection 'The Freudian Field', two years before Lacan's *Ecrits*, this book has the advantage of showing the trials and errors of analytic work, the failures and the advances. 'Lacan authorized me to articulate a work in progress', she wrote.

THE MOTHER–CHILD TIE

After many years of clinical practice with developmentally arrested and retarded children, Maud Mannoni affirmed that she no longer knew exactly what was the distinction between true and false retardation; a distinction often made in the psychiatric milieu at the time. What interested her more was to look for the meaning that a retarded child had for his (or her) family, in particular, for his mother, and to understand that the child himself gives a meaning to his retardation in relation to the one that is given to him, even and most of all unconsciously, by his parents.

When the child is seriously disturbed and organically marked, the mother feels narcissistically affected by the infirmity of her child and by the finality of the diagnosis given to him. She then engages in a passionate battle for the health of her handicapped child. 'The mother–child relationship will always, in such a case, have an aftertaste of death about it, of death denied, of death disguised usually as sublime love, sometimes as pathological indifference, and occasionally, as conscious rejection; but the idea of murder is there, even if the mother is not always conscious of it.'[14] At the same time, one sees in these mothers a desire to commit suicide insofar as the mother and child in this situation form one unit.

Confronting a husband who is generally indifferent and impotent, the mother looks to doctors for 'a witness that she is at her wits' end; someone who, if necessary, knows that she wants to kill'.[15] She is overwhelmed in a struggle between life and death instincts. With her child who is dependent on her, this mother must 'continue a perpetual gestation, like a bird sitting on an egg that will never hatch'.[16] The situation develops in the same vein, in an exclusively dual mode.

Even though Mannoni was, following this book, heavily reproached for implicating the mother in the child's illness, she nevertheless continued to insist that the child constructs his mother himself 'and induces her to adopt a type of sado-masochistic relation with him'.[17] The mother finds here once again something that she experienced very primitively and furtively, something that was never symbolised. The mother oscillates between an attitude of severe discipline and inattentive, whimsical neglect. The mother of the developmentally arrested child is 'forever fascinated, fashioned, by that in her child which will never take on human shape'.[18]

In the cases of feebleminded children, the decisive diagnosis is usually not made immediately. The effects are therefore different, less radically murderous. When she was consulted, Maud Mannoni chose deliberately not to know about the feeblemindedness but chose rather to go beyond these terms. Her question was rather to try to understand what was disturbed in the mother–child relationship fixating each one in a given role. She maintained that, in the cure of feebleminded children just as in the cure of psychotic children, the family plays a massive role, whether one wants it or not. Moreover, the family values the place assigned to it by the child.

We shall attempt to follow Maud Mannoni's method with regard to the case of Mireille, an eight-year-old girl, who was sent to Mannoni after attempts at re-education had failed. Her IQ was evaluated at 54. She was brought to a psychoanalyst as a last resort.

At the beginning, psychoanalysis was refused by the mother: 'When Mireille is there, I don't get frightened ... If you take Mireille, I won't be able to go on living.'[19] As an echo, the child said, '[T]he little girl does rude things. She was undressed. She was eaten, and the mother became ill because of it.'

These first exchanges, like many others that would follow, showed that Mireille and her mother were indistinguishable from one another. It was thus necessary, first of all, to look for the meaning of the child's symptoms in the parents.

Mireille's father was a high-ranking official in the police force, but actually, at home, it was the mother who laid down the law and ran the show. Mireille's mother was infantile and phobic; she did not exist except as someone glued repeatedly to images of adults who had died one after the other. At the age of twenty, she found herself orphaned and got married in order to find another adult who would protect her from her fear. Later, Mireille would come to play this counter-phobic role for her mother.

At five years old, Mireille was hit by a car. The irruption in reality of a flattened body, at an age when the child had the feeling she was growing up, triggered a psychotic breakdown that was considered by psychiatrists to be a manifestation of feeblemindedness. 'A body is never a body', she said, 'but pieces that go together or don't.'[20] This accident that took place in reality had a traumatic effect on the child: it prevented her from passing through symbolic castration. Furthermore, the interwoven imaginary world between mother and child was quite evident. It was superimposed over the story of a rape which the mother had experienced just before puberty.

When the evolution of the child during the cure enabled her to be more autonomous, the mother wanted to stop the treatment. Mireille commented: 'Mummy wants Mireille like this, so why change?'[21]

She was there to represent everything in her parents which could not be symbolised. This mother who presented herself as 'duty incarnate' was in fact ceaselessly preoccupied with fantasies of rape. Mireille acted out the fantasms of the devouring mother, her perpetual anxiety was the echo of her mother's anxiety. Or, at times, prey to hypomania, Mireille tried to suppress the Other by acting the clown. What was considered by the psychiatrist to be an expression of her feeblemindedness was, in fact, a manifestation of madness in which she sought shelter from any confrontation with the law.

Mireille's fantasies, like those of her mother, were themselves a search for symbolisation, but in the absence of a paternal signifier she remained stranded in a world deprived of sense. Significantly, this atmosphere, which Maud Mannoni considers as psychotogenic, existed even before the child's birth. The primary objective of the cure was to disengage the child's fantasies from mother's. This is what would enable the subject to assume her own history instead of remaining alienated in the history of her mother.

Maud Mannoni maintained that there always exists 'a fundamental misunderstanding between mother and child'.[22] The imaginary child is destined to repair the wounds suffered by the mother in her own childhood. The real child is always disappointing with regard to this fantasmatic image. If the child cannot find another place except one in which he fills up the lack in his mother, he cannot exist for himself.

What is it that the mother want from the child, asks Maud Mannoni. The mother does not know herself. Her demand is the envelope of her lost desire. When, in a certain context, the mother requires her child to be intelligent, this concerns something else that is ignored or unrecognised in herself. The child remains there, like a shadow, and his intelligence is stolen in the desire of his mother. If the child is feebleminded, it is in him that something fails: the illness of the child thus dissimulates the illness of the mother. 'Any study of the feebleminded child remains incomplete unless the meaning of the feeblemindedness is first sought in the mother',[23] concludes Maud Mannoni. Furthermore, she adds that we cannot cure the mother in place of the child. In spite of the efforts of child analysts since Anna Freud's time, we cannot avoid 'the anxious irruption of the parents into the analysis';[24] even if they are sent elsewhere to other analysts, this does not resolve the problem. Thus, although Mireille's father had asked for the address of a psychoanalyst, he could not make up his mind to finally go and see one. 'The child was once again for him and his wife their own account.' This was an assertion that she would take up again and develop at length in *The Child, his 'Illness' and the Others*: 'It is futile to analyze a mother on the basis of her own accounts, when her own accounts *are* the child to such an extent that her perpetual presence is expressed through the child's symptom.'[25] Rather than being an obstacle, the so-called intrusion of the parents in the cure is a major trump. It is the moment in which the parents' murderous fantasies can be given to the child's analyst who, if he (or she) is able to mark them as such, can make these fantasms meaningful for both the parents and the children. The analyst thus functions as a third term, in relation to which the family discourse is redistributed and repositioned differently.

Touching on what Lacan had advanced in 'the direction of the cure',[26] – that the subject awaits to receive from the Other that which is lacking in his word – Mannoni underlined that the subject will articulate his discourse in the field of the analyst. The field of the cure is thus one of neither dialogue nor interpersonal relation but of putting into circulation a discourse that will open the way to the symbolic. In the analysis of children it is through the analyst that the discourse of the parents and the children can circulate from one to the other. This process cannot take place unless the child and the parents are received by the same analyst.

Thus, in the process of Mireille's cure, the mother became pregnant and completely neglected her other children. The father wanted his wife to have an abortion, then tried to suffocate the baby, eventually forcing Mireille's cure to stop: 'You can't offer me sufficient protection against my wife',[27] he said to the analyst who had to bear this anxiety in order for the cure to continue.

It was only on the condition that the analyst was able to bear this anxiety, that a child who had been fused with the mother could disengage and have her own place. 'What does it mean to lose one's parents? Aren't I already losing them, in fact?',[28] asked Mireille.

An analysis runs the risk of stalling when it is confronted with the work of mourning a fundamentally structurating parental image. Maud Mannoni took up the case of Mireille at length in a chapter of *The Child, his 'Illness' and the Others*.[29] She showed that the child could not encounter the madness of the father other than by maintaining her mask of feeblemindedness or madness. Although she had recuperated a normal level of intelligence, Mireille spoke of the difficulty which confronted her: 'I always have to have someone to speak through.'

THE QUESTION OF FEEBLEMINDEDNESS

Maud Mannoni rigorously put into question the distinction between true and false feeblemindedness. With the feebleminded child, not only is intelligence structured to avoid symbolic castration, as well as questions concerning life and death, but it is actually this death itself.

At the beginning of a treatment, it is necessary to leave the issue of IQ and the organic problem in suspension in order to listen to the subject and to grasp, as we have already shown, through his (or her) own discourse and that of his parents, the meaning that the child's feeblemindedness can acquire for himself and for his parents.

If it is difficult for the feebleminded child to speak, it is because he is already spoken of elsewhere. This is the very specificity of his position. If he is treated as a subject, he loses all benchmarks of his identification. 'He no longer knows who he is, or where he is going.'[30] You will recognise there the sentence that Maud Mannoni uses with respect to herself in *What the Truth Needs to be Told*.

The endeavour of psychotherapy uncovers all the child's negativity which is attached to him like a parasite of the mother making all attempts at re-education fail. Once this work is effected, the re-education, if it is desired by the child, can be successful.

Feeblemindedness, according to Maud Mannoni, is different from stupidity which is a neurotic defence. Feebleminded children, without even a change in the level of their test results, can, on the other hand, be perfectly adapted.

If it is not stupidity or failed adaptation, what then is feeblemindedness? In feebleminded children, Maud Mannoni finds factors common with psychotic children:

• the dual situation with the mother
• the rejection of symbolic castration
• the difficulty of acceding to symbols.

This leads her to ask: 'Has not the feebleminded child more to gain from being treated as mentally ill (with hope of recovery) than from being trapped within a form of re-education based on deficient capacity?'[31]

At the end of her study, the notion of feeblemindedness, in a certain sense, disappears. It is not a nosographic category: '[U]nder the label "retardation" one can find the whole spectrum of neurosis, psychosis and perversion.'[32] Furthermore, as psychotic children are being cured earlier and earlier, it seems to me from my own experience – and after a small enquiry conducted with other clinicians without statistical value – that we are seeing far fewer children said to be feebleminded in our clinic.

TRANSFERENCE AND COUNTER-TRANSFERENCE

In studying this question, Mannoni dared to grapple with the questions – in all their freshness – that young analysts ask, while speaking candidly of her own errors and failures.

With oligophrenic children, the analyst often has scruples about taking money from the family without being certain as to whether the patient's condition will improve. If the mother, in her distress, wants to believe in the psychoanalyst, the father is often sceptical, taking the analyst for someone who profits from the misfortunes of others.

Or, the mother may be one who uses the child to prove and to prove to herself that no one can do better than she. The question of the mother's omnipotence and, where appropriate, of the female analyst's, cannot be pushed under the carpet. Either the child is just as badly off in the presence of the analyst as in the presence of the mother and the analyst must personify a compassionate mother, or the child behaves better in the session than at home and the analyst must confront the negative feelings of the mother. If, however, the analyst, in a 'commendable' effort at honesty, declares his impotency, his limits (in a kind of political correctness), this often leads the parents, and usually the father in particular, to interrupt the cure. The analyst thus must sustain whatever negativity there may be in the transference of the parents and not give up on his desire to sustain the analytic work with the child; it is only at this price that he is reliable.

The relation of the analyst to the parents depends on the role assigned to the infant and to this feeblemindedness. The mother needs to make use of the analyst to depress him (or her) instead of herself. The analyst must be able to sustain the depression of the mother, eventually even the risk of suicide often must be confronted so as to be able to conduct the cure of the child. It is then that the father often enters the game to complain, but at a moment when he knows that his complaint carries no risk.

It is therefore the parents who, at the beginning of the analytic work, express the transferential relationship. The analyst must accept and receive this message.

In the event that the child's feeblemindedness is not tolerated by the parents, they put the analyst in the role of the re-educator. Confronted with a strangulating mother, the analyst cannot necessarily give her back her problems. There again, he must serve the role of making her speak of her suffering, playing the role of an 'anxiety sponge' as Françoise Dolto has called it. One cannot oppose this type of mother without risking provoking an unbearable anxiety in the child.

Conducting analysis with children said to be feebleminded implies a certain number of trials for the analyst.

A trial of complete non-satisfaction

The patient for whom the real and the symbolic are confused, who is incapable of creativity and humour, bores the analyst. This shell of mediocrity hides the impotence of the subject, but if one touches it, one touches the mother's lack-of-being. The way out for the child, if it is possible, will involve going through a period of phobia during which he will seek solutions which do not involve the mother. The flat and poor language of feebleminded children is maintained during the cure in the mythopoetic discourse which Maud Mannoni has often been accused of having invented. 'What is wrested from such children is the wrath of the poet or of the gods and it is from this revolt that something can be eventually verbalized',[33] she said, with regard to the case of Mireille.

The risk that the analysis will remain incomplete even if re-adaptation is achieved

While the child may be re-adapted to his social world, further analysis may be needed regarding ideas of death which alone will allow the subject to have access to symbols. However, the feebleminded child personifies, to a certain extent, death. 'He is the living negation.' During the course of the treatment, the analyst must be patient enough to become more dead than the subject himself, so that anxiety can finally manifest itself.

Sometimes the silence of the child serves to maintain a 'secret' of the parents that he is afraid of revealing due to fear of losing them or fear of being lost himself. The whole familial edifice can be put into question and it is from this risk that the analyst protects himself when he declares a child 'cured' or 'incurable' who has not managed to say 'I'.

These are the undeciphered and unexamined difficulties which have allowed these children to be overlooked and excluded from the field of psychoanalysis for so long.

Thus, for Maud Mannoni, what counts in analysis with feeble-minded children, and is just as significant in any analytic work with children, is to look 'beyond what is deficient, for the word that will constitute the child as a subject of his desire'. One must help the child to pass beyond the despair that has constituted him in order to ask the question, 'Who am I?', thereby putting his own destiny, within his intellectual and physical limits, back on track. He can thus access his own history, situate himself in the direction of desire and enter into a symbolic dimension.

Perhaps all of this seems evident to you today. These ideas were, however, at the time that Maud Mannoni developed them, truly revolutionary. While initially formulated with regard to feebleminded children, Mannoni's work opened up a new field in terms of the exploration, understanding and treatment of psychosis, autism, the pathology of the mother–child relationship and the trials of adolescence. Mannoni's life and work paved the way for new methods of understanding the world of the child and his madness. They continue to bear fruit today.

NOTES

1. Mannoni, M. (1988) *Ce qui manque à la Verité pour être dite* [*What the Truth Needs to be Told*], Paris, Denoël.
2. Mannoni, M. (1964) coll. 'Le champ freudien' ['The Freudian Field'], Paris, Seuil.
3. Mannoni, M. (1965) *Le premier rendez-vous avec le psychoanalyste* [*The First Meeting with the Psychoanalyst*], Paris, Denoël-Gonthier.
4. Mannoni, M. (1973) *The Retarded Child and His Mother: A Psychoanalytic Study*, trans. A.M. Sheridan Smith, London, Tavistock Publications; *The Backward Child and His Mother: A Psychoanalytic Study* (1972), trans. A.M. Sheridan Smith, New York, Pantheon.
5. Mannoni, M. (1967) *L'enfant, sa 'maladie' et les autres* [*The Child, his 'Illness' and the Others*], coll. 'Le champ freudien', Paris, Seuil (London, Tavistock).
6. Mannoni, M. (1979), *La theorie comme fiction* [*Theory as Fiction*], coll. 'Le champ freudien', Paris, Seuil.

7. Mannoni, M. (1970) *Le psychiatre, son 'fou' et le psychanalyse*, coll. 'Le champ freudien', Paris, Seuil.
8. Mannoni, M. (1973) *Education Impossible*, coll. 'Le champ freudien', Paris, Seuil.
9. Mannoni, M. (1976) *Un lieu pour vivre*, coll. 'Le champ freudien', Paris, Seuil.
10. Mannoni, M. (1986) *Bonneuil, seize ans apres*, coll. 'L'espace analytique', Paris, Denoël.
11. Mannoni, M. (1979) *Secrète enfance*, Paris, EPI.
12. Mannoni, M. (1997) *Elles ne savent pas ce qu'elles disent* [*Women do not Know what they are Saying*], coll. 'L'espace analytique', Paris, Denoël.
13. Mannoni, M. (1983) *Le symptome et le savoir* [*Symptom and Knowledge*], Paris, Seuil.
14. Mannoni, *The Backward Child*, p.4.
15. Ibid., p.5.
16. Ibid., p.10.
17. Ibid.
18. Ibid., p.13.
19. Ibid., p.56.
20. Ibid., p.57.
21. Ibid., p.58.
22. Ibid., p.62.
23. Ibid., p.65.
24. Ibid., p.91.
25. Ibid., p.55.
26. Lacan, J., (1990) *Ecrits: A Selection*, London, Routledge.
27. Mannoni, *The Backward Child*, p.95.
28. Ibid., p.97.
29. Mannoni, 'Mireille's question', *The Child, his 'Illness' and the Others*, 'Mireille's question', pp.168–92.
30. Mannoni, *The Backward Child*, p.149.
31. Ibid., p.150.
32. Ibid., p.85.
33. Mannoni, *The Child, his 'Illness' and the Others*, p.185.

3 Psychoanalytic Therapy with an Autistic Young Man: A Discussion of Frances Tustin's Theories

EVELYN HEINEMANN

Frances Tustin's Contribution to the Theories on Autism

THE ROLE OF THE MOTHER IN PSYCHOANALYTIC THEORIES ON AUTISM

As psychoanalytic theories consider symptoms to be an expression of inner conflicts mainly developed in childhood, there exists an ongoing misunderstanding that autistic behaviour is a result of the relationship between the mother and the autistic child. Even today, some psychoanalysts like Dornes (1993, p.49) in his much respected book *Der kompetente Säugling (The Competent Baby)*, say that Bettelheim explains the causes of autism in terms of the mother's neglect.

However, if we look at Bettelheim more closely, we can see that he does not in fact say anything like that, although one might get such an impression from his case studies. As the goal of his orthogenic school was to work with severely disturbed children whose parents were unable to be supportive – which is why the children had to be residential – it is tempting to link this parental behaviour to theories on autism.

But Bettelheim writes: 'Fortunately, psychoanalysts are starting to turn away from the idea of the rejecting mother' (1974; my translation). He stresses the similarity of his point of view with that of Anna Freud (1954a, 1954b), namely, that it is not the attitude of the mother but the spontaneous reaction of the child that leads to autism. The child makes the mother responsible for his (or her) difficulties and rejects her: 'Nevertheless, the original reaction and the later autistic behaviour are spontaneous and autonomous responses of the child' (1974; my translation).

Bettelheim (1974) says that it makes no sense to give parents of autistic children the feeling that they are the cause of the illness. However, we need to discover whether experiences cause autism or contribute to it.

Autistic children are convinced that they are threatened by total destruction and that they live in extreme situations. Autism starts with the collapse of communication. Both the outer world which requires action and the inner world which can react, are denied by defence mechanisms. According to Mahler (1972, p.73) there is a 'core deficiency' in the child who is unable to use the symbiotic partner for orientation in the inner and outer world. Mahler points out that contrary to neurotic disorders, autism results from the child's disposition. Tustin (1981, p.29), like Mahler, believes in a disturbance of primary bonding which leads to a hypersensibility in the child, arresting development. She says very clearly:

> Most psychotic children have not experienced coldness, neglect or physical violence from their parents ... These children have retreated to the sensual fastness of their own bodies and have become insulated from outside influences ... Such children become more and more out of touch with any reality which they can share with other human beings. They become increasingly isolated and, in a state of insulation, dominated by their idiosyncrasies and stereotypes. (Tustin 1981, p.11)

The main conditions of this autistic psychosis are confusion and denial. A vicious circle of psychological and physical factors is thus set in train. Since these autistic children presented a picture of being unnurtured, workers who observed them in the early days of studying psychotic children thought that the parents had been cold and neglectful (Tustin 1981, p.11). But Tustin assumes that things are much more complicated than this and that each child must be analysed separately. She examines closely what Mahler simply calls a core deficiency.

THE MYTH OF NORMAL AND PATHOLOGICAL AUTISM

Mahler (1972, p.72ff.) considers autism as a fixation or regression to the first and most archaic stage of extrauterine life which she calls the 'normal autistic stage'. In the autistic stage, the mother seems to be unrecognised. The self cannot distinguish between animate and inanimate objects. That is why Mahler speaks of autism as a primary lack or loss of the ability to distinguish between animate and inanimate objects. Autistic children make no demands on the mother and no attempt to touch her, but they show a certain attachment to toys or other inanimate objects and a compulsive need to preserve the uniformity of stereotyped patterns of behaviour. Children with an autistic defence organisation nevertheless show the ability to proceed to a symbiotic organisation. This indicates that autism is more or less a regression rather than a total lack of libidinal desire for satisfying experiences. Symbiotic defence organisation, says Mahler, is primarily a reaction to separation anxiety which is warded off by defence mechanisms such as non-discrimination, dehumanisation and the denial of perceptions.

In the first period of her work, Tustin was strongly influenced by Mahler's concept of a normal autistic stage. Like Mahler, Tustin (1981, p.6ff.) also assumed that there was a stage of normal autism. She distinguished between normal and pathological autism which she categorised as psychosis.

> Thus, autism is a state in which auto-sensuousness holds sway, attention being focused almost exclusively on body rhythms and sensations. Objects in the outside world may be attended to (often it seems intently and in minute detail) but on close observation it becomes clear that these are experienced as being part of the body or very closely akin to it. People and things outside are scarcely used or seen as having a separate existence. (Tustin 1981, p.3).

Furthermore, she distinguished with reference to Freud (1914, p.142) between primary autism and primary narcissism. Primary autism is characterised by the dominance of sensations as a foundation of the self, whereas primary narcissism is a later stage that is linked with feelings. The normal autistic stage is undifferentiated autosensuality. The child is able to react because of congenital patterns but it has no awareness of itself as a separate self.

However, even at that time, Tustin was aware of the contradiction with the results of normal infant development observations (Lichtenberg, 1983; Stern 1985, 1991).

Babies can co-ordinate perceptions. Normal babies are able and sufficiently flexible to shift from one modality of the senses to another. A baby is able to differentiate the perception of its senses and even co-ordinate these perceptions. It perceives the outer world and wants to perceive it. Allurements attract the baby's interest and are actively sought. This is tremendously different from the way autistic children try to isolate and separate their perceptions.

Finally, Tustin (1991) proposed that we give up the concept of a normal autistic stage. This provides a new basis for research on autism. The concept of a normal autistic stage was a cul-de-sac for research and therapy which, however, does not imply abandoning the more reasonable concepts of symbiosis and separation (Dornes 1993, p.57).

Tustin (1981, p.10ff.; 1991) speaks of autism as a pathological reaction. The child feels its body to be damaged, development is arrested and the hypersensitivity of early childhood remains. Primal bonding is disturbed and either the children refuse bonding (ecysted children) or they live in symbiotic fusion (confused children). Tustin asks how this pathological autistic reaction comes about.

It is the result of organic, metabolic and psychic factors. The primary traumatic feeling is that of being cut off from the mother's body. The mother becomes the 'not-self' mother. Anxiety, despair and terror arise. These feelings are suppressed by denial and confusion (Tustin 1981, p.11ff.; 1991).

Tustin (1981, pp.68, 149; 1991) concentrates on two concepts: black holes and terror. The autosensorial mother, who is experienced as part of the baby's own body, suddenly seems 'to break away like a piece of rock from a rock face'. The child has little or no awareness of being flesh and blood and of being alive. He is not aware of these sensations until he has lost them. They arise at the moment of breakdown and the black hole appears – the black hole of the unknown 'not-me'. Bodily separateness from the mother has left a hole; the ego is full of black holes. The 'not-me' is a wound.

This seems to be a psychosomatic experience, a disorder of the fundamental integration of the senses. These terrors that arise are so bizarre that they can easily be referred to as nonsense by psychotherapists who write about them, says Tustin (1981, p.149).

PSYCHOANALYTIC THERAPY WITH AUTISTIC CHILDREN

The description of psychoanalytic therapies in the literature is largely confined to work with autistic children. Mahler (1972, pp.190ff.) says that therapy is necessary to get the children out of their isolation. If autism is a defence against an earlier symbiotic relationship, therapy has to recreate the symbiosis. The therapist becomes an auxiliary-ego, that is to say, he offers himself as a substitute for the symbiotic object. The child's panic reactions subside when he can profit from the outside world. He should gradually feel more comfortable with the unobtrusive presence of the therapist than without it. The development and extension of independent ego-functions is strived for along with the overcoming of separation anxiety.

The therapeutic aim in Mahler's theory is a corrective symbolic experience. She believes autistic children are very intolerant of groups and thinks that groups have harmful effects on the children.

She works with the so-called three-party plan in the mother's presence. Sessions last about two to three hours.

Bettelheim (1974) stresses the importance of groups and the reflection of counter-transference which he describes as a descent into hell. Children do not give up autism, says Bettelheim, when we offer them satisfaction. They give it up when we succeed in activating them. In contrast to passive patients with whom therapists take a more active approach or to patients who are offered satisfactions during treatment, Bettelheim emphasises the need for patients to be active. 'They returned to life when we succeeded in creating circumstances that made them act in their own name and when we succeeded in responding as a container' (Bettelheim 1974; my translation).

Both Mahler and Bettelheim changed the psychoanalytic setting; Mahler with her concept of the three-party plan. However, with respect to the latter, I have uncertainties concerning method. Should a therapist really offer himself as the symbiotic partner? How can individuation be stressed in the mother's presence? Bettelheim works with the concept of 'environmental therapy', a specific educational and therapeutic setting, which can only be the right choice under certain conditions.

It is Tustin (1981) who shows in the different examples of her work that it is possible to work in a normal child therapy setting with autistic children. Her work on transference, counter-transference and interpretation is based on the normal setting. Tustin explains that:

> The transference situation is different and cannot be established by the use of interpretation alone. The therapist must be more active without letting these active measures take the place of interpretative therapy. (1981, pp.169ff.)

The memory function has to be nurtured because anger, anxiety and terror are the only feelings the child knows. The experience of bonding as well as the differentiation and integration of perceptions must be strengthened. When the child experiences himself as separate from the therapist, he gets the feeling that there are holes in his body and in the outside world. The holes are like monsters and considerable empathy for the intense vulnerability of a body with open holes is required. The secure frame of the setting is necessary to free the child from these feelings. When the body has borders and is controllable, the child starts to develop his cognitive abilities, the integration of his perceptions, and becomes a thinking being. Considerable patience is required from the therapist as well as a capacity to bear the powerful feelings of terror involved.

Tustin worked for thirty years with autistic children and her theories and therapeutic experiences are the richest source for an understanding of autism. With her work, a psychoanalyst who is interested in working with autistic children and adults can learn to understand the therapeutic processes involved.

I would now like to show in the following case study how useful Tustin's theories are and that we can also treat autistic adults within the normal setting of psychoanalytic therapy.

Psychoanalytic Therapy with Mr R.

PREVIOUS HISTORY

Mr R. was diagnosed as autistic when he was three years old. He showed all the typical signs of autism such as echolalia, walking on tiptoe, and a refusal to look at anyone. When he was six years old, he entered a special school for mentally retarded children. At that time, I was working as a special education teacher for children with learning difficulties.

I had not seen him for thirteen years when his mother phoned me and asked for help. In the meantime, I had started working as a psychoanalyst with disabled people in private practice. Mr R. was twenty-two years old and had started to show a number of behavioural problems. The mother interpreted this behaviour as a reaction to his father's sudden death and thought therapy was necessary. I offered Mr R. and his mother an interview.

THE FIRST INTERVIEW

Mr R. and his mother arrived on time. I was surprised that Mr R. immediately looked at me and that there was a marked atmosphere of confidence in the room, as if we had seen each other only a few days before. I asked Mr R. if he knew why his mother thought that he should begin therapy. After a while, because he was unable to reply, his mother answered: 'He thinks that he has no problems. After the death of his father he started to laugh a lot and everyone gets confused when he does this. The sudden death of his father must have hurt him but he cannot show it.' I was shocked that the subject of his father's death was brought up so abruptly and wondered how Mr R. could cope with that.

He remained sitting, showing no reaction. I asked him about his life, his work, his hobbies. He said that he watched television and liked to ride around on buses. I came back to the question of therapy and asked him if he wanted to come for a session once a week. I explained that he could talk about anything he wished in therapy, even his father's death. I told him that he could draw and maybe play a game with me sometimes. He replied cheerfully that he would like to come. His mother was relieved and added that Mr R. had very disturbing rituals when going to bed, that he walked streets in one direction only and that he never took plates back to the kitchen. He was also afraid of enclosed spaces. I told Mr R. that we could talk about all of these things in therapy.

The setting of the first interview was adapted to Mr R.'s problems. He did not think that he had a problem and there was no conscious wish for therapy. His mother, who was a very sensitive person, empathically interpreted her son's behaviour as a defence. Functioning as an auxiliary-ego, she verbalised the problems and aims of therapy. While I was talking to Mr R. I stressed his separateness from the start (like a non-verbal interpretation). From the viewpoint of transference and counter-transference I could feel the deep confidence of those present, but also my shock when the father's death was mentioned so abruptly. The main themes of our work, such as sudden death, closeness and fright, were already visible in the first interview.

THE FIRST SESSION

In the meantime Mr R. had started working in a sheltered workshop. Once again, I explained the nature of the therapeutic setting to Mr R. We agreed that for the first thirty minutes we would talk and that for the last twenty minutes we could play if he wished. Again and again, I asked him questions and he talked a little about his work. Then he drew his room with a big bed. Only one square in the drawing had been filled in: there was an alarm clock which indicated six o'clock, the time of his session.

Drawing number 1: a room with a bed

Since he had drawn a bed, I asked him about his rituals when trying to go to sleep. He said that he made a noise to keep his brother awake. He then asked if there was anyone else coming after him and, if not, could I take him to the bus station? I explained that this was not possible and for the last twenty minutes we played cards.

The rituals of the session helped Mr R. to adhere to the setting. To begin with, it was difficult for him to talk for fifty minutes. In contrast to a classical therapeutic setting I was obliged to talk more than usual and to ask questions continually. I associated to the patient's drawings in his place. Mr R. was gradually able to speak

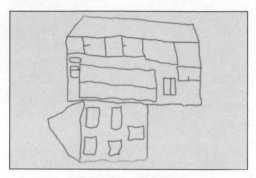

Drawing number 1

about the problems he had with his brother. These were transferred in the session during which he enquired about other patients. Acting as an auxiliary-ego, I took over the ego-functions of associating and speaking, but I also emphasised his individuation by saying that he had to go to the bus station by himself. We can see from the time shown on the alarm clock (six o'clock) that there was transference from the start.

THE NEXT SESSION

Mr R. sat on his chair and I noticed his facial tics. I asked him what he wanted to talk about. He said: 'The builders are on the roof of our house.' Then he said that he would have his own apartment in his mother's house soon. I asked him what he liked best about the apartment. He replied: 'That I will be independent.'

He then drew a house.

Drawing number 2: house with roof

Drawing number 2

I interpreted: 'This is a roof. You have not painted the builders.' Mr R.: 'I can paint them too.'

He drew two builders.

Drawing number 3: house with builders

Drawing number 3

Then he drew his room again; this time there were two people in the room, he and his brother.

Drawing number 4: room with brother

Drawing number 4

Mr R.: 'My brother disturbs me sometimes.'
Me: 'When?'
Mr R.: 'When I listen to CDs.'
Me: 'What kind of CDs?'

Mr R. named a special song. I asked if this song reminded him of anything.

Mr R.: 'Yes, we heard that song when we were four.' I was perplexed and invited him to speak about his father's death. But there was no feeling of grief between us.

This session showed that by interpreting the defence mechanisms of denial and depersonalisation (the roof without the builders) he could talk about his conflict with his brother and father. During the entire therapy these were the only drawings with people in them. My interpretation was made in such a way that he was free to draw the builders or keep his defence. The choice remained with the patient. In unconscious partial identification (counter-transference) I perceived the meaning of the song. I had to force myself to ask questions to overcome his resistance which would have kept us in unhealthy silence, even though this made me rather controlling.

But, as Tustin describes in her work, the therapist must take more active measures than in other therapies.

A FEW WEEKS LATER

Mr R. told me that they had talked about trees in the sheltered workshop. I asked him why he liked plants.

Mr R.: 'Giving water to the flowers and taking off the rotten leaves.' (I thought about life and death)

He drew a tree; it was the ficus plant I had in my therapy room.

Drawing number 5: tree with circles (holes) in the trunk

I asked him about the circles.

Mr R.: 'These are the places in the bark where the bark is a bit thicker.'

Mr R. stood up and looked out of the window: 'The tower was not lit up last time.'

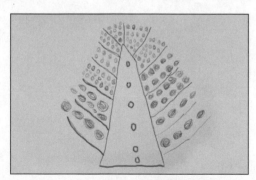

Drawing number 5

Because he often looked out of the window during sessions, I interpreted: 'You like talking about what is going on outside. In therapy, we have to deal with what is going on inside you, too.' He sat down, smiled and said: 'I know.'

His reaction surprised me a lot. He really stopped looking out of the window after my interpretation. When I interpreted his defence – the stereotype displacement of his interest from inside to outside – he could give up this behaviour.

At home, I wondered about the circles in the tree. I thought that the drawing showed that the tree was hurt, as if it had scars. Could the circles be the holes Tustin places so much emphasis on in her work?

THE NEXT SESSION

Mr R. again drew a tree with circles. I took the drawing of the last session and interpreted: 'Maybe the tree-trunk is hurt.' We then talked about the different parts and functions of trees. Mr R. said suddenly: 'Oh, the tree needs bark.'

He painted a brown colour over the trunk with circles (holes).

Drawing number 6: tree with brown bark

Mr R. looked at both trees and said happily: 'This tree is much nicer than the other one.'

Me: 'The tree is protected now.' So fascinated were we with the trees, that we spoke about them until the end of the session, forgetting our game.

Drawing number 6

In this session we reached the core reaction of autism. Mr R. perceived reality and his body (Tustin's theory of holes) as damaged. This meant he projected affects and anxieties about his body (the unknown ego) into reality and reality then became frightening. Through strengthening his cognitive functions, his perception of reality, he found a solution for his affects by himself. Trees are not only hurt, but they also protect themselves with the bark. He was then able to project a positive expectation into reality.

This was only possible by using the therapist as a bridge to reality (not as a symbiotic substitute, as with Mahler). The trees were a symbol for reality, for Mr R.'s body and for the therapist, because he drew the therapist's ficus plant. This was not a purely cognitive process, otherwise the conversation in the sheltered workshop would have had a therapeutic effect, but it did not. Mr R. used the relationship to his therapist and his cognitive knowledge for a change in his perception of reality and of himself. His ego was thereby strengthened.

SOME WEEKS LATER

Mr R. came to the next session very excited. My car was not in its usual place in the parking lot. I interpreted that this alarmed him and explained why the car was not there. Then, I interpreted his defence by saying that perhaps he thought that I was not there. Mr R. said: 'No.'

In this session I tried to interpret his defence of displacing affects from human beings to objects like the car. He was still using denial to protect himself.

THE NEXT SESSION

Mr R. came to the session alarmed. Once again, my car was not in its parking lot. I simply said: 'This alarms you again.'

Mr R: 'I did not think that you were not here.'

Mr R. told me now that he had gone to a musical concert all by himself on Sunday.

Mr R. had internalised my interpretation from the week before. Our dialogue had become an inner dialogue so he expected me to interpret his behaviour as displacement which I did not do in this session. From then on he had to use denial twice to suppress the affect of anxiety over losing the other, which was now linked with me and not the car.

It is very impressive to see how this process of interpretation and internalisation led to a new step towards independence. Insofar as I was then internally present, Mr R. was able to go to a concert by himself.

SOME WEEKS LATER

I was startled to see Mr R. with his mother on my doorstep. Mr R.'s mother explained that she had happened to see Mr R. making huge detours on the way to therapy, because he did not want to use a certain bus line. I asked Mr R. to come in and his mother went home.

In the session I asked Mr R. what it was that frightened him about streets and buses. He replied that bus Number 4, a *'Gelenkbus'* (meaning 'articulated-bus', and which refers to his bodyparts too), once stopped too far away from the pavement and he was afraid of hurting his foot. He liked going along a certain street in one direction only because he could see the city gate as well as the city, whereas he did not like going in the other direction because of the ramp. There was another street he avoided if possible, because it was dark there at night. Once, a noisy lorry went by and frightened him.

Tustin's theory of hypersensitivity and the insecurity of body perceptions could be seen here with its dramatic implications. Noise and unevenness were very frightening. The terror was not just a projection of an insecure mother–child relationship, as we might interpret in a neurotic case; it was what Tustin calls a psychosomatic experience, an organic and psychic disorder of the integration of the senses. The only way he could protect himself against the experience of terror was by ritualised avoidance, but avoidance leads to ego-restrictions so that the verbalisation of these events was a first step towards developing more adequate solutions.

SOME WEEKS LATER

Mr R. started the session with the following words: 'The sixteenth was nice, the seventeenth was not.' I asked what he meant, and Mr R. explained: 'On the sixteenth, a year ago, there were still four of us.'

I understood that he was talking about the anniversary of his father's death and there was a very sad atmosphere between us. After a while, I asked him if he had any idea as to what he could do when he felt so sad. He replied: 'I can go to the graveyard and pray. I can clean the gravestone.' I said that I thought these were very good ideas.

During the conversation his facial tics had almost vanished. On the anniversary of his father's death, he brought the subject up spontaneously, even if in the form of abstract numbers. I could feel in the counter-transference that progress had been made in reducing his defence. I experienced feelings of grief myself in this session. After a period of silence and containment I encouraged him to find more adequate ways of coping with his grief. The unconscious battle was seen in his tics. I tried to strengthen his ego by supporting the solutions he found for himself.

SOME WEEKS LATER

Mr R. said that he was feeling very well now. He could walk streets in both directions. I asked him if he could recall any situations that could explain his behaviour. He said: 'Once I was going out of the house and a boy came up behind me. I started to run.' I asked him about the boy. 'He wanted to beat me. He wanted to drag me into a corner. He wanted to take out a gun, but the gun was not real.' I suggested that perhaps the boy had simply wanted to frighten him, and wondered whether his fear was similar to the experience he had had with the lorry.

Mr R. was frightened by minor incidents such as the boy running up fast behind him. I did not interpret this perception as a projection of oedipal anxiety for instance (the gun as the phallus; it was not a triangular situation). Mr R. tried to cope with his fear of noises (caused by perception disorders) not only through avoidance and rituals but also through turning from passivity to activity. For example, he frightened his mother by turning on the water tap at home. If the other person was frightened, he laughed. The phantasy about the boy contained the projection of his own way of dealing with his fear of noises and unexpected situations (turning from passivity to activity).

THE FOLLOWING WEEKS

There followed a long period during which I had to strengthen Mr R.'s individuation from his mother. He had his own apartment in his mother's house and started to miss meal-times. Sometimes he was late or hung up the phone when she called. His mother was frightened by this. This situation was transferred in therapy for which he was also repeatedly late. I was able to strengthen his wish for autonomy and individuation by not letting him feel guilty, by respecting his coming late without pressure and by interpreting the situation, especially his aggressive feelings that he could not allow for himself. We talked of more adequate forms of resistance too; saying 'no', for instance. His self and ego were thereby strengthened.

SOME WEEKS LATER

Mr R. came with his trouser zip open and explained that he now shaved alone in his apartment. At the end of the session he noticed his zip and felt embarrassed. He closed it and said that he had changed his trousers that morning because there was a hole right beside the zip. He pointed to the spot.

I thought that the theme of identity had come up in the session but I didn't make an interpretation at that point. Perhaps the zip and the hole stood for male and female (phallus or hole)?

THE NEXT SESSION

Mr R. came with a bag. He put it on the table, took something out of it and smoothed the bag flat with his hand. As he did this, I noticed the drawing on the bag.

Drawing number 7: bag with frog and turtle

Drawing number 7

I asked Mr R. if he liked the bag. 'Yes', he answered proudly. I asked him if he had bought the bag by himself, to which he again replied 'Yes.' Then I asked him what he could see on the bag. 'They are kissing each other', said Mr R.

I questioned him about the meaning of the hearts but he did not know what they meant. I said: 'The hearts mean that these two animals like each other. A man and a woman kiss and like each other. But which is the man and which is the woman?' 'The turtle is the man and the frog is the woman,' said Mr R. I was confused, and thought it was the other way round. So I asked him why he thought it was like that. 'Because of the long eye-lashes and turtle's lips', he replied. I thought that this was exactly why the turtle was the woman and asked him which animal he was. 'The turtle', he said immediately. I then asked him if there was perhaps someone he would like to kiss. Going red in the face, Mr R. replied: 'The woman I am working with.'

Part of Mr R.'s confusion was about his sexual identity. Of course, as an autistic man he liked to identify himself with the turtle, but if we look at the last session we can observe a deeper confusion over his sexual identity. Again he uses the therapist as a bridge. He did not mention the name of the woman he was working with until I asked him. As I was working with him too, we can see that he was using the transference to develop libidinal wishes. There was still no oedipal solution; it was two people in a shell (the rainbow circle).

In the next sessions we talked about his feelings towards the woman he was working with in the sheltered workshop and I supported him verbally in his intention to invite her to his apartment (which in fact he never did). Even though I was verbally quite active in therapy, I had to let the patient deal with his reality in his own way. This demanded a lot of patience on my part.

END OF THERAPY

After two and a half years I mentioned the possibility of our ending the therapy. Mr R. was sitting like a stone on his chair. At the end of the session he left his coat behind so I had to call him back. He was overwhelmed and completely unable to cope with the anxiety of separation.

Six months later, after working through his separation anxiety, he came to a session and said that he enjoyed watching movies about doctors on television. He was interested to see whether a patient who had been operated on recovered. He thereby found a way to express his concern about the outcome and end of therapy. He was actively using reality in his search for a solution (as he had done with the trees) – a non-autistic way.

In the last session we both felt very sad but there were other feelings, too. He said it would be nice to have his evenings free now to relax at home (it took him an hour and a half each way when coming to sessions). I felt happy that he was doing so well after all our work in therapy.

Mr R. still comes three times a year 'to say hello' and to talk to me. He still needs to know the therapist is there (a 'background safety': Sandler 1960). My office number, which he keeps in a special book, and the exact details of the next appointment, are very important for him.

The first interview and termination were quite different from what happens in a normal adult therapeutic setting, but I think the therapy in between was normal psychoanalytic work.

The therapy with Mr R. shows that psychoanalytic treatment of an autistic patient is possible. Through transference, counter-transference and interpretation it is possible to understand the psychic processes and inner structure involved. As a therapist I was forced to actively ask questions and to stimulate ego-functioning. Sometimes I felt like an interrogator. I understood this as counter-transference and tried to find a balance between asking questions and remaining silent.

Too much silence would have been destructive. Mr R. slowly gave up some of his defence mechanisms and was able to talk with me for fifty minutes. During the sessions I interpreted everything he said to me, both verbal and non-verbal (scenic understanding; Lorenzer 1983). In accordance with Tustin's findings my work was based mainly on perception disorders, terror, separation anxiety, body sensations, 'holes' in perception and interpretations of defence mechanisms as a protection of the self.

Mr R. reached a point where he felt happy and comfortable in his job, at home, and in his body too – more or less. He has a friend now whom he meets. He has given up most of his rituals, walks streets in both directions, sleeps well and regularly takes care of his father's grave. Of course, there are areas left unresolved – the oedipal stage, for instance – but we must have the patience to accept the patient's own rhythm of development. At present he has to live in his mother's house and work in a sheltered workshop. It will probably be several years before the level of development reached can be adequately assessed, which is why it made sense to terminate therapy at this point. Another possibility would be to change the setting to three times a year. He has the possibility of coming back to therapy for further development. At this point he feels happy with his life which is probably more than we can expect for most of our patients.

REFERENCES

Bettelheim, B. (1974) *The Empty Fortress: Infantile Autism and the Birthday of the Self*, New York.

Dornes, M. (1993) *Der kompetente Säugling. Die präverbale Entwicklung des Menschen*, Frankfurt, Fischer Taschenbuch.

Freud, A. (1954a) 'Psychoanalysis and Education', in *The Psychoanalytic Study of the Child*, 9: 9–13.

Freud, A. (1954b) 'The Widening Scope of Indications for Psychoanalysis', *Journal of the American Psychoanalytic Association*, 2: 607–20.

Freud, S. (1914) 'On Narcissism. An Introduction', in James Strachey, ed., *The Standard Edition of the Complete Psychological Works of Sigmund Freud*, 24 vols, London, Hogarth, 1953–73, Vol. 14, pp.67–102.

Lichtenberg, Jo (1983) *Psychoanalyse und Säuglingsforschung*, Berlin Heidelberg, Springer Verlag.

Lorenzer, A. (1983) 'Sprache, Lebenspraxis und szenisches Verstehen in der psychoanalytischen Therapie', *Psyche*, 37: 97–115.

Mahler, M. (1972) *Symbiose und Individuation. Bd 1: Psychosen im frühen Kindesalter*, Stuttgart, Klett Verlag.

Sandler, J. (1960) 'The background of safety', *International Journal of Psychoanalysis*, 41: 352–6.

Stern, D. (1985) *The Interpersonal World of the Infant. A View from Psychoanalysis and Developmental Psychology*, New York, Basic Books.

Stern, D. (1991) *Tagebuch eines Babys. Was ein Kind sieht, spürt, fühlt und denkt*, München, Piper.

Tustin, F. (1981) *Autistic States in Children*, RKP, London.

Tustin, F. (1991) 'Revised Understandings of Psychogenic Autism', *International Journal of Psychoanalysis*, 72: 585–91.

4   Mental Handicaps: A Dark Continent

JOHAN DE GROEF

> And then, all over again, the same dissatisfactions, the same desires unrealised, Africa the same vast distance away ...[1]

Ever since the Romantic Movement, our culture and its autochthons have been captivated with 'dark continents'. Following the example of the explorer Stanley, Freud described in 'The Question of Lay Analysis' a woman's sexual life as a 'dark continent'.[2] In alignment with this statement, I shall call the phenomenon of a 'mental handicap' an Africa for our human condition.

Dark continents have always had double and ambiguous meanings. On the one hand, we fantasise about them as if they were exotic, sun-drenched resorts and heavenly paradises dating from before the Fall of Man, virginally immaculate. On the other hand, we depict them as disintegrated and infernal places filled with corruption, enticingly perverted.

Dark continents strike us with terror and fascinate us simultaneously. They are 'uncanny' places which, as Freud points out in *The Uncanny*, are not new nor strange to us; on the contrary, they are familiar from time immemorial, although they have become strange to us through a process of repression.

Dark continents appeal to the phantasm of a return to the source of all life, to the primal soil of our existence. Hence, the fear of and fascination for Mama Africa.[3] Hence, the fear of and fascination for everything which is obscure and unclear and which leaves us speechless.

In his novel *A Personal Matter*, Kenzaburo Oë, the Nobel Prize winner for literature in 1994, describes the hesitation, the anger and depression of Bird, a twenty-seven-year-old youth who becomes the father of a handicapped child. No earlier than in the epilogue, he tells how Bird took the decision to save his unfortunate child's life through a series of operations and to take care of its upbringing.

Nauseated (Sartre's *nausée*) by the handicapped child, full of disgust for the baby that was atrophied by a handicap, and hoping that his baby (which still hadn't got a name and was not his son as yet) would die through no action of his own – in fact through his inaction – his mistress reads an episode from his African book (*My Life in the Bush of Ghosts*, by the African author Amos Tutuola):

'Did you read the chapter about the pirate demons?'

Bird shook his head in the dark.

'When a woman conceives, the pirate demons elect one of their own kind to sneak into the woman's house. During the night, this demon representative chases out the real foetus and climbs into the womb himself. And then, on the day of the birth, the demon is born in the guise of the innocent foetus ...'.

Bird listened in silence. Before long, such a baby invariably fell ill. When the mother made offerings in hopes of curing her child, the pirate demons secretly deposited them in a secret cache. These babies were never known to recover. When the baby died and it was time for the burial, the demon resumed its true form, and, escaping from the graveyard, returned to the lair of the pirate demons with all the offerings from the secret cache.

'... apparently the bewitched foetus is born as a beautiful baby so it can capture the mother's heart and she won't hesitate to offer everything she has. The Africans call these babies "children born into the world to die", but isn't it wonderful to imagine how beautiful they must be, even pigmy babies!'[4]

To Bird, Africa means a refuge, a place to run to. If he were an African, he would get rid of his problem of having a handicapped child. The dark continent acts as a fictitious object of his old and new longing.

Our own autochthonous culture defends itself against every other allochthonous culture with the basic mechanism of a negative self-definition to differentiate between its own characteristics and the other's. This implies a bipolar pattern of representation; the two poles being each other's antithesis. Self-image and the image of the Other are intertwined dialectically. Each portrait is, as it were, a self-portrait but like a mirror image. Dark continents photographed by means of a camera obscura.

A succinct anthropological study of common social images of the disabled reveals the same mechanism of negative self-definition. The same general gallery of images apparently has its effect and even seems to be introjected in the imaginary life of all those directly involved. Professionals do not live in an imaginary vacuum either.

Figure 4.1 expands on the portraits of the disabled and of our self-portraits.

IMAGE	*SELF-IMAGE*
angel (of fortune)	person full of worries
spontaneous	inhibited
authentic	
natural	cultural
affectionate	selfish
willing	will of his own
sensitive	insensitive
emotional	rational
monster	human being
animal	
uninhibited and hot-tempered	self-restrained
child	adult
physical anomalies	beautiful
fragile	strong

Figure 4.1 The binary representation of disability

This way of binary representation involves a double mirror relationship: image versus self-image and + versus –. Two remarks are to be made:

First, this mirror relationship would only have an alienating effect if it were not incorporated in a dialectical and historical context. Finding oneself via the deviation of another and therefore alien image, is a process during which a simple contradiction develops and unfolds into a multiplicity of more complex contradictions and correlations. The basic contradiction between self and other, between inside and outside, splits up into multiple contradictions giving rise to fusions;[5] for example, one appropriates the strange image – what was outside now becomes inside – but time and again new images are needed – new outsides – in order to establish oneself from inside.

Second, this mirror relationship strongly emphasises the visual character of the relationship. The visual aspect is, more than any other of the senses, binarily structured. Since the Enlightenment, sight has become a dominant sense (as compared to the sense of hearing, for example) which enabled the world to be organised in clear-cut terms. According to D. Anzieu,[6] it is a sense which brings safety by standing exactly midway between desire and danger. Against this background, it is all the more significant that the use of video as an observational medium catches on as a new therapeutic treatment: perhaps this has something to do with the phantasm of control – something is what it is – and with the fear of dark continents, rather than with the method itself, which provides a framework of interpretation of a certain image: something is what one tells it to be. Psychoanalysis does not grant privileges to the specular position of seeing but hands back its lustre to the position of hearing: the mirror as opposed to the echo (cf. the myth of Narcissus).

Let us return to our gallery of images now. Oddly enough, and actually understandably so, we are faced with the same metaphors which, on the one hand, were used to refer to other 'marginal' sections of the population, for example, savages, jesters, farmers and beggars, and, on the other hand, which were and still are in vogue to denote other strange and so-called primitive cultures and peoples, for example, black people.[7]

This cultural integration mechanism of negative self-definition also seeps through and repeats itself in individual relationships. At the same time, individual variants from our own personal histories exercise their influence. It did not take too long before Freud talked about (counter-)transference and projection. Since Klein and Bion, we can call this negative self-definition projective identification, which illustrates at once how this cultural preconscious mechanism is also inscribed in a psychodynamic process.

Our gallery of images shows that both our culture and its standardised vehicles of culture are assaulted by a feeling of uncanniness (fear and fascination) when they are confronted with the phenomenon of a 'mental handicap'. The more uncanny, the more dire the need for clearly contrasting simple images that are self-evident.

However, one may well ask what is meant exactly by this old, familiar image that has been suppressed and which partially re-emerges when we are confronted with a mental handicap. Which anthropological questions does the continent (and from time to time the contingent) of handicap evoke? Handicap considered as some sort of Sphinx, only this time not asking questions such as 'What walks initially on four, then on two and finally on three legs' (notably a human being) but poses the enigma of the origin of mankind itself?

Speaking in terms of *cultural anthropology*, a 'mental handicap' confronts us with the question as to which processes enable the transition from a natural creature to a cultural creature to take place; in other words, the transition from exogenity (outside a given culture) to endogenity (inside a given culture).

Speaking in terms of *individual psychology*, a 'mental handicap' confronts us with the question 'What is a human being without defects?'[8] Or to put it differently, in a more familiar but more frightening way too 'Is a human being with a defect still a human being?'

Considered that way, it should hardly surprise us that with regard to the phenomenon of being 'handicapped', there exists, on the one hand, a huge fascination for 'natural sciences' such as genetics and biology, so much so that expectations are running too high. To paraphrase Freud: genetics are our fate. On the other hand, it is striking how everyone involved is affected by the phantasy of perfection and completeness. Every defect, lack or shortcoming calls for rectification.

The interest of the remedial educationalist sector in Gentle Teaching, for example, is in this context symptomatic. Aware, as one is, of the trendsetting character of the emancipation in remedial education (that a mentally handicapped person has as many rights as anyone else) it is considered modern that a mentally disabled person with so-called additional psychic disorders is approached as a real person. Only this time from a therapeutic point of view, it is as if one abandons one's own modernising vision. Otherwise it would indeed be impossible to consider this very vision as modern any longer. As I see it, this especially illustrates how *unheimlich* a 'mental handicap' is and remains for an emancipatory kind of remedial education, and to what extent the fact of being a person is questioned.

Be that as it may, for everyone involved, and not forgetting professional carers themselves, Freud's casual remarks in 'The Psychopathology of Everyday Life'[9] remain valid; notably, that in the case he discussed he could not but come to the conclusion that there is a 'death wish with regard to abnormal children'.

Naturally, we react differently[10] towards the phenomenon of a mental handicap. On the one hand, this phenomenon poses a threat to our order and our physical and psychic integrity; on the other hand, it allows us to compensate for our narcissistic lesions through our *furor sanandi* and the effect of over-invested ideals. The caring relationship is more complex than the mirror-like division between the carer and the one who is cared for. Reading Hegel's text 'Master and Slave' be instructive in this respect.

The question might well be raised, 'Who echoes whom and who mirrors whom?'

VITAM INSTITUERE

Portmann wrote that we are born far too early: unsure of our instincts and unfinished (Lacan: *manque-à-être* (want-to-be);[11] Nietzsche: *das (noch) nicht festgestellte Tier*). Our features are both those of nidifugous and nidicolour birds. In fact, we still have to find our place in this world. After a nine-month intra-uterine period, we are premature babies who still have a few years ahead of us in a social uterus before we are capable of taking our first independent faltering steps into the world, into language.

This broken birth structure (another fissure) lays the groundwork for the risk and the opportunity involved in learning. This basic dependence can never be turned into complete autonomy without leaving some trace. The original need of the other can only be mediated and confined symbolically. There is no autonomy without heteronomy.

The history of the development of each human being is comprised of the 'learning process' of joining in a discussion in which one had a place even before one's birth. Before our birth, people talk about us; from our birth on, people talk to us; and around the age of three, the time is right for us, through being talked to, to say in grammatically correct sentences 'I', in reply to the summons which is contained in our being talked to. Previously, we used to speak as others spoke about us (John is a good boy, and so on).

Not until saying 'I' do we assert ourselves as an 'I' towards the other. By saying 'I', the other is delivered from the perpetual repetition of his own speech. Being addressed by one's own name provides for the possibility of dialogue. The 'I' is the pre-eminent mode of speech, the form of life of our culture. It is the entrance fee to our culture, it is our identity card which is handed to us during our upbringing.

It is not merely a genetic process, but a fundamentally structural event, too, in which the three modes of speech – speaking about, speaking to and speaking with one another – leave a permanent mark on our existence.

This being 'talked into' a culture, was called by the Romans *vitam instituere*[12]– 'instituting life'. Culture is the great institution, as it were, to which we are admitted and in which we live and work. In this process, as is explained above, mirrors and negative self-definition play a crucial part.

This summons to respond in our own name when we are addressed is the moment when the remedial educational insertion of each one of us occurs, before any specific remedial educational counselling *strictu sensu*. A human being with his (or her) lack (of being) is put on the right track, in order that he does not go adrift, and is counselled in the institution that we tend to call culture. Acquiring this cultural mentality is the indispensable (remedial) educational project *par excellence*.[13]

HIS MAJESTY THE BABY[14]

According to Legendre, for a biological creature to be considered as a subject in practice, it must be 'instituted'; in other words, it has to be humanised by some kind of marking, a denotation which makes of the individual somebody else. This somebody else is no alter ego nor an appendix of oneself. To Legendre, civilising is an act of dividing an individual (literally: un-divided) to make him/her somebody else. By way of support, the divided subject is given this cultural stick which distinguishes him from the one without a stick – the *imbecillus*.[15]

Why do parents long for children? Children are an extension of their parents. Every parent has to do some mourning, parallel to their children's growing up: the real child is not the child[16] of one's dreams. My child is not my child. Real and unreal become one. It was indeed for good reason that Freud turned this into a theme in his dissertation on narcissism: a child as a projection of oneself and as a stranger at the same time, impossible to appropriate completely.

This dying of the child of our dreams is, however, no once-only event, but an unremitting dialectical process. The child of our dreams does not only have to die but we should be able to keep on dreaming about the deceased and real child too. If we cannot dream about a child anymore, then life ends and there is only survival left. If we are merely capable of dreaming, then there is no more life either but one is drawn into total silence, stagnation, a deadly straitjacket.

Children also have to mourn for the loss and grief they cause their parents as well as themselves. This loss of a time when one was one's own ideal, this mourning over the loss of oneself (which at the same time constitutes a self-discovery) is only possible to the extent that the parents themselves are capable of coping with and passing on this loss, this real expropriation (in this sense a genuine self-gift) and the so-called symbolic violence of acculturation.

THE EXCEPTIONS[17]

The birth of a handicapped child immediately shatters the mirror of so many hopes. We are not given sufficient time to adapt to the other's being different, just as we are not given a chance to come to terms with this expropriation gradually. The other presents himself in utter impudence. Nature, it is experienced, wrongs those parents and that child, without any prospect whatsoever of compensation for this narcissistic lesion.

From an infinitely hard mourning process for the parents and the child, we understand that their histories progress in a typical way. Either handicapped people remain phantasmatically and unconsciously locked in the limbo of the dreamt ideal and the link with reality is severed, or they are crucified by the sheer materialism of an anatomic or physiological reality.

From this point of view, it is not difficult to understand that they are either granted the status of an angel on earth, some kind of extraterrestrial being, or allocated the status of a fallen angel, a devil. In both cases they do not have a proper name; they are nobody, no more than a shadow of the other. At the same moment and in the same way, the time of transitoriness is curbed and a sterile tension-less potentiality of an eternal now arises.

By way of illustration, I shall quote from a highly interesting *document humaine* bearing a title that reflects both tendencies: the crimson earth and the ethereal thin air and what human life is in between.[18]

A mother of a handicapped child wrote:

'At that time I already realised that however big Stijn was to grow, he would always be at this place (mother's belly).' Or: '... she looked more like a living doll than a baby ... brought into the world far too early and too abruptly.'

Here, the dialectics of identification (the entanglement of self-loss and self-finding) have made room for some puppet-like normality and separated feelings of blind trust or distrust towards any other person.

Apparently, a great number of people with a mental handicap are locked into the impossibility of their parents mourning and they identify themselves with a 'melancholic' position, so to speak. It is as if they were sent into exile. The handicapped person waits in front of the gate – outside in the freezing cold – to be admitted to the insti-tuted life. In this postponement of 'institution', he plays the role that we are able to cope with.

The question remains whether we are capable of 'declaring in default' a disabled person on top of his handicap, so as to enable him through this cultural marking to become a partner in everyone's cultural process of labour by the sweat of one's brow (as it was ordered after the Fall of Man and the expulsion from Paradise). The act of 'declaring in default' brings about the entanglement of what is dreamt for and reality through symbolic mediation. It is precisely this entanglement, this intricacy[19] which allows integration in our culture: there is no development without entanglement.

Perhaps this is what Schiller[20] suspected when he wrote that there was some kind of affinity between the genius and the fool, notably that they are both seeking reality and that they are virtually imper-vious to keeping up appearances. Both of them are tuned in to that which still lies fallow and is waiting to be cultivated. Both stand at the side of what is and remains inalienably alien.

THE COLONISATION OF THE DARK CONTINENT: MENTAL HANDICAP

It is exactly because a 'mental handicap' is uncanny to us that we are driven by fear and fascination for this dark continent.

The drive to obtain a clear and intelligible knowledge is so much the stronger. Many a so-called theory functions in this context as projective identification: denial of one's own handicap and not-knowing, which turns into hybrid eclectic constructions.

An established knowledge, either flowing from a theory or a directly experienced or shared feeling, transforms the unknown into something familiar. The unknown is colonised and appropriated.

From psychoanalysis as a method, therapy and theory, which is brilliant in distinguishing knowledge from truth and in questioning established values time and again, grows the consciousness and the experience that the analyst also has to go through his (or her) own mourning process time and again: the client of his dreams must die and make room for the real client through symbolic mediation. Analytical theory itself is finite, is limited in thinking and retains a central place for what cannot possibly be appropriated without leaving a trace.

Over and over again, the analyst's listening implies the acceptance of his own mental handicap.

The phenomenon of a 'mental handicap' is our blind spot, as it were, which accounts for the fact that when looking with one eye only, there is a dead angle in our field of vision.

In a letter dated 28 December 1914, addressed to Frederik van Eeden, Freud wrote (using the term 'feeble-mindedness' for only the third time in his *oeuvre*):

> Psychoanalysis has taught us further that our intellect is a weak and dependent thing, the plaything and tool of our drives and affects, and that we all behave sharp-wittedly or feeblemindedly according to our personal attitudes and resistances.

Just as Odysseus evaded the one-eyed Cyclops, we might argue that a handicapped person uses the same trick to escape from one-eyed looks: he disguises himself as an obedient sheep and calls himself 'nobody'.

NOBODY IS PERFECT

His parents' unbearable mourning incites the handicapped person to strive for identification with this melancholic position: he identifies himself with what is lost; that is, the dreamt ideal, or with the merely physiologically and genetically programmed fragility. He turns into an outsider in the shape of an angel or a fallen angel. This position deprives him of his libidinous body and therefore both his life and death. The concomitant, however, is that he has to rely permanently on something or someone to carry him.

Hence, we can understand why so many handicapped people are so ingenious when it comes to adapting to and fitting in with what is asked of them. They make up for the other's lack as if compensating for the unbearable sadness they caused. Wherever possible, they restore what is lost.

A smile on the face of the one who makes a demand is the most gratifying reward for someone who sees a reflection of himself in a sad look. The idiot smile is a mute witness to both the fear of the aggression that may follow the sadness and an imitation of the mode of existence that is lacking.

In this way, it is perhaps understandable too, that the handicapped person also fits in with the analyst's own questions, that is by reflecting those problems which the analyst is all too familiar with from his own history and which he consequently shows most affinity with through projective identification. Indeed, the melancholic position implies a blended image which precedes all pathological structures – it is some kind of psychopathological zero degree.

Once the handicapped person is adopted and carried by the buoyancy of others, it will become clear whether, so to speak, he introjects himself – whether he nestles in the other's buoyancy – and whether the buoyancy has sufficient bearing power to become a project.

Essential to this process is the ethical condition that the other person's buoyancy originates in his own lack and not in the handicapped person's lack. In other words, that different kinds of mirror relations are undone, that the mirror is broken, allowing two different people to talk to one another in private with a broken voice. Only then do the portraits disappear and a face-to-face encounter is possible.

I should like to conclude by quoting from the final passage of Kenzaburo Oë's *A Personal Matter* when Bird, through the acceptance of his handicapped baby and therefore through the acceptance of his own handicap, is reborn himself, as it were. Bird thus becomes 'Rebirth'.

He wanted to try reflecting his face in the baby's pupils. The mirror of the baby's eyes was a deep, lucid grey and it did begin to reflect an image, but one so excessively fine that Bird couldn't confirm his new face.[21]

NOTES

1. Oë, K. (1994) *A Personal Matter*, London, Picador, pp.67–8.
2. Freud, S. (1920) 'The Question of Lay Analysis', in James Strachey, ed., *The Standard Edition of the Complete Psychological Works of Sigmund Freud*, 24 vols, London, Hogarth, 1953–73,

vol. 20, pp.179–250. In this context, it is all the more mean-ingful that Freud used but once the word *'Schwachsinn'* when illucidating in 'The Future of an Illusion' the problem of *Denkschwache* and *Denkverbote* in women: the dark continent, notably the woman, cursed with physiological weak-minded-ness, after a term coined by Moeblus. Apart from that, this word may be found in a couple of texts in the *Nachtragsband, Texte aus den Jahren 1885–1938*; more specifically in *Theoretisches (J. Breuer) (1895) Vier Dokumente über den Fall 'Nina R'.* in which he deals with Janet's notion of *'insuffisance psychologique'* in relation to the origin of hysteria.

3. I refer here to the book of the same name by E. Heinemann (1990) *Mama Africa, Das Trauma der Versklavung*, Frankfurt, Nexus Verlag.

4. Oë, *A Personal Matter*, p.135.

5. The process of increasing fusion is here linked with the notion of *'Entmischung'* as developed by L. Szondi in 'Die Triebent-mischten' where he refers to the same notion in Freud's 'New Introductory Lectures on Psychoanalysis', *S.E.* 22, pp.3–182.

6. Anzieu, D. (1973) 'La Bisexualité dans l'autoanalyse de Freud', *Nouvelle Revue de Psychanalyse*, 7: 179–91.

7. For both the historical and cultural-anthropological theme, see Vandenbroeck, P. (1987) *On Savages and Jesters, Farmers and Beggers. The Image of the Other One, an Exposition about the Self*, Exhibition catalogue, Antwerp, Royal Museum of Fine Arts; Corbin, R. (1989) *Savagery and Civilization. The European Imagination in Africa*, Baarn, Ambo.

8. In this context, it might be useful to draw attention to the Ancient Romans' habit of calling a person who, on the level of intelligence, did not have a stick to lean on, an *imbecillus*: liter-ally, someone who did not have a *bacillum* (a stick, rod).

9. Freud, S. (1901) 'The Psychopathology of Everyday Life', *S.E.* 8. As if this thought arose within some kind of 'normalistic thinking' even before the term existed. Moreover, Freud indi-cates that in this slip of the tongue he describes, the psycholog-ical disorder was replaced with a physical one.

10. I refer here to Lacan's theme of the 'division of the subject'.

11. Translator's note: English neologism invented by Lacan.

12. For an extensive analysis of this phenomenon, see the work of P. Legendre; more specifically *L'amour du cenescur* (1974), Seuil, Paris; *Les enfants du texte* (1992), and *L'inestimable objet de la transmission. Etude sur le principe généalogique en Occident* (1985), both published by Editions Fayard, Paris.

13. Ferenczi calls education 'an intropression of the educator's *Uber-Ich'*.
14. Freud, S. (1914), 'On Narcissism. An Introduction', *S.E.* 14, pp.67–102.
15. See note 8 above.
16. J. Quentel (1993), *L'Enfant, problème de génèse et d'histoire*, Bruxelles, Editions De Boeck.
17. I refer here to the first volume with the same title of Freud's 'Some Character Types met with in Psycho-Analytic Work', *S.E.* 14, pp.310–33
18. I am quoting from Kangoeroe VZW (1996)*Thin Air, Red Earth. Kangaroo Parents write about their young handicapped children*, Gent, Kangoeroe VZW.
19. De Neuter, P. (1994) 'Ni *ange*, ni bête ou: la nécessaire intrication des trois régistres du corps humain', in B. Feltz and D. Lambert (eds), *Entre le corps et l' ésprit*, Bruxelles, Mardaga, pp.247–67.
20. Schiller, F. (1795) 'Die Ästhetische Erziehung des Menschen' ['Letters on the Aesthetic Education of Man'], *Werke*, brief 26, Zweite Band, Sodler Ausgabe die Tempel-Klassiker.
21. Oë, *A Personal Matter*, p.165.

5 Psychotherapy in a Village for People with Learning Disability

PAUL BERRY

Dual Diagnosis

It is now accepted that between 30 per cent and 40 per cent of people with learning difficulties (that is, who are mentally handicapped) are also mentally ill (see, for example, Menolascino 1990). It is also becoming clear that this group do not easily fit into the mainstream of 'normal' society; they make great demands on parents and staff, and generally require long-term intensive care from professionals in several disciplines including medicine, education, psychology, speech therapy and physiotherapy. This group of clients presents perhaps the greatest challenge to service providers today.

The treatment of these clients is slowly being formalised, and the pioneering work of those who have identified the dually diagnosed as a special target group is now being documented. My role today is to report on a specific programme of care and therapy for this group which has been developed in North Germany by a team of psychiatrists, psychologists and other therapists from several disciplines.

For over fifteen years, Dr Christian Gaedt and a team of therapists have worked carefully with this group of residents in Neuerkerode, North Germany, and have developed a system for the identification and treatment of these residents. There are approximately 840 residents in Neuerkerode and about 320 are currently registered with the Department of Psychology and Psychiatry as presenting with symptoms of mental illness.

In order to understand the treatment of these special residents, it is important to understand how Neuerkerode village works as an '*Ort zum Leben*' (a place to live) for mentally handicapped individuals. At the cornerstone of all the services in Neuerkerode is the concept of '*strukturelle Betreuung*', perhaps best translated as 'social structuring'. Basically, this refers to the careful social structuring which mentally handicapped people require to achieve their autonomy and independence. This structured approach brings together the residential care staff who carry out the day-to-day services that the mentally handicapped residents require – those involved in operating the sheltered workshops, the doctors who maintain a special general practice for primary medical care, and the therapy departments which consist of a team comprising a psychiatrist, psychologists, occupational therapists, physiotherapists and others. It is only through careful co-operation between all of these groups, of which the therapy teams are only a part, that an appropriate set of social structures for the residents can be achieved – hence the term '*strukturelle Betreuung*'.

I will speak more of how the system in Neuerkerode operates later. First, I would like to present a synopsis of some case studies involving dually diagnosed residents because they illustrate clearly some of the problems facing all professionals working in this field. I want to begin with the diagnostic process because it is central to the challenge of providing services for the dually diagnosed.

One of the most important aspects of the work of the therapists in Neuerkerode concerns the diagnostic process, since there is a great discrepancy between the behaviours of mentally handicapped residents presenting with mental health problems and those observed in the general population. One of the most pervasive diagnostic issues is that 'behaviour problems' in general tend to be easily identified and treated through classical behavioural methods, but the deeper underlying causes may never be identified, properly diagnosed, or treated. In the end, a behavioural approach alone may lead to confusion resulting in even greater care and treatment problems for the residential staff and a continuing exacerbated mental health problem for the already disabled resident. When between 30 per cent and 40 per cent of mentally handicapped people present with mental illness problems, they have the right to, and we as therapists have the duty to provide, appropriate treatment, and this invariably demands a careful analysis of the residents' mental handicap, mental health and overall health status within a life-span framework.

Some examples of depressive behaviour in mentally handicapped people may help to understand some of the problems in the diagnostic process.

Case 1

Barbara S. is a severely mentally handicapped woman who has lived in Neuerkerode for years. She was referred to the Department of Psychology and Psychiatry as presenting with extremely self-injurious behaviour (biting herself, kicking herself, banging her head with her fist, poking her eyes and using her finger nails to make deep gouges in the skin of her arms and legs). She cannot talk but often makes groans and shrieking noises. At night she is reported to be awake, but in the day she sleeps spasmodically in a corner of the residential facility in which she lives with a blanket over her whole body. She can walk only with great difficulty and support, is deaf, and has only very limited tunnel vision. Staff had difficulty in interesting her in anything but food which she generally stuffs into her mouth.

Case 2

David B. was referred because he was especially aggressive. In the first case discussion he was described as sometimes being like a 'wild animal' and one of the residential managers made the point that, if nothing else, an hour of therapy would a least bring an hour of relief for her residential care staff, so great were their frustrations. David is a physically strong man, eighteen years old, who is also physically handicapped but can walk alone with difficulty. He is completely deaf and has a visual problem. Most of the day he has to be restrained in a specially made wooden chair. He sleeps in a comfortable bed which is built like a small house and needs to be restrained in it each night. His room is bare because he destroyed everything he could of his own and often also the property of the other residents. He tore his clothes to the point that he had no trousers left and often smears his own excrement over the walls of his room or the residence. He often needs to be restrained from destructive behaviour to both others and objects by the residential staff and, as his strength is so great, this is becoming more and more difficult.

Case 3

Karel K., also eighteen years old, is difficult to manage. She bites the staff and sometimes bangs her head against the wall so hard that the staff fear for her life. She mostly lies on the floor of the residence staring at the ceiling, but sometimes seems to enjoy listening to music or playing with blocks (knocking them together), and the residential staff try to play with her in this way as often as they can. Often, however, she pokes her fingers into her ears which results in many ear-infections, dribbles and cries. She is becoming more and more difficult to handle and seems to be 'drifting away'.

Case 4

Edgar B. makes his care givers resort to physical force because of his destructive behaviour and deliberate attacks on other people – staff and residents alike. The fights end when he is overwhelmed and lies exhausted on the floor. Then he breaks down, makes apologies to his subjugators, condemns himself and displays depressive behaviour.

These cases are examples of mentally handicapped/mentally ill residents being treated in Neuerkerode. While the above cases stress the symptomology rather than the therapeutic and diagnostic analysis, they highlight the problem of case analysis. The work of the therapists is concerned with an analysis of the case history searching for evidence of early disturbances in object-relations particularly in the mother–child interactions, and especially looking for evidence of re-enactments in the current disturbances of the resident's behaviour. In the analysis of the current status of the resident, an evaluation of the transference and counter-transference will be undertaken. In addition to a discussion of the history of the case, an analysis of the resident's current living conditions and whole psychosocial environment will be taken into account in the treatment process.

These cases are, however, by no means unique to our village and will be found in most catchment areas. They illustrate not only the extent of the problems faced by residential care staff but reflect the need for a careful 'social structuring' ('*strukturelle Betreuung*'), of which the therapy department is but one component and involves co-operation from many different professional staff in a therapeutic setting. These cases also indicate some of the problems in the diagnostic process. The problems of these residents are deep-seated, cannot be treated superficially and will probably require long-term care.

It is the experience of the psychologists involved over many years in the treatment of such residents that the following general points can be made.

1. Sometimes the *same* behaviour of the resident has a quite different meaning (for example, head-banging may mean 'I hate myself' or 'I hate you').

2. The *more* handicapped the resident, the *more difficult* it is to understand the meaning of the behaviour (for example, severely handicapped people tell us all kinds of things about their world, but we need to be vigilant in identifying the meaning of their signal).

3. The *transference of the reactions of the staff* can have a most influential impact upon the resident (for example, staff may react with pity to head-banging or with anger – the effect of the counter-transference will have a very different effect upon the resident).

MENTAL HANDICAP AND DEPRESSION

Since Gaedt (1990) has written widely on depression in the mentally handicapped, and as this is a frequent condition found in this group, it may be helpful to consider this work now in some detail. Gaedt identifies three groups of mentally handicapped individuals presenting with different kinds of symptoms resulting in a diagnosis of depression. The three classifications are: self-unstables, self-destroyers and quiet depressives.

Gaedt begins by stating that there are a very substantial number of clinical manifestations which relate to the diagnosis of depression, but in the mentally handicapped these symptoms, or often clusters of symptoms, cannot be found in the classical psychiatric textbooks. This, adds Gaedt, is due to the immature defence mechanisms and other psychosomatic variables affecting the behaviour in this group. Indeed, Sand (1993), also a psychologist working in Neuerkerode for many years in this field, states that the predominant disturbances in development are associated *with weak ego-functions and early object-relations disturbances.* Unless we begin to think in these terms we will be unable to diagnose mental illness in the mentally handicapped, and appropriate treatment will be denied.

Gaedt points out that the therapist needs a good understanding of the processes which are intertwined with both the developmental level and the life-history of the person. *Since the therapist cannot at the moment rely on the classical text book for an interpretation, this makes the process all the more difficult.*

Gaedt, referring to Sandler and Joffe (1980), states that a depressive affect results when a person feels helplessly threatened by a situation characterised by separation and loss. The trigger is the feeling of helplessness and vulnerability to uncontrollable forces. In the mentally handicapped the threshold is lower and the person feels unworthy of affection and an inability to change the situation. Depressive reactions are also due to the struggles for separation and the search for autonomy. Such phase-specific developmental stages have been described in normal early child development by Mahler (1968) and her colleagues.

In this stage the child leaves the security and protection of the mother and gives up the fantasy of her omnipotence. These are prerequisites for adjusted development. So many mentally handicapped people have problems due to disturbances in these early important stages of development that, in adulthood, when they present with complex symptoms, the therapist is forced to go back in time and discover how the resident coped with these very early experiences. Of course, many residents are non-verbal or have little verbal ability, and this makes a careful reading of the case history essential.

In this connection, I am especially grateful to the work of Valerie Sinason whose book *Mental Handicap and the Human Condition* (1992) is essential reading. Sinason, in her chapter 'Finding Meaning without Words: self-injury and profound handicap', is one of the first to have undertaken long-term analytic therapy in this group, and in particular with a profoundly handicapped woman (Maureen), and illustrates clearly how powerful a therapeutic tool this may be. It is Sinason who points out again and again how important the early months of life are for the severely mentally handicapped and how the woman, Maureen, had regular massive outbursts of self-injury – to the extent that they were life-threatening – when she experienced the loss of a special residential key worker. All of this could relate to the experiences she had experienced as a small baby, and concerns separation anxiety and the feeling of being unsafe. I refer again to Sand's comment that most of the problems here are related to weak ego-functions and poor object-relations.

In the interpretation of behaviour in this group Sinason says: 'When I am unsure (of what you mean) I comment: "I wonder if you are feeling ... when you do that. Maybe it is hard for you to know that I do not know why you are doing that. Perhaps you imagine I can guess properly. Well, sometimes I do think I know and sometimes I might guess and then I could be right or wrong."' Would that we could all reflect with our mentally handicapped/mentally ill residents in this way!

I want now to return to Gaedt and the three classifications of depression in the mentally handicapped.

Very frequently the self-unstable has suffered from disappointing events and tries to keep these events from rising into conscious awareness. For example, they may become restless and resort to screaming when confronted with a visit from the parents. They may even appear to be distressed by the impending event. In extreme cases they may rip clothes or cover themselves with their excrement. Often the person retreats into a fantasy world as a defence mechanism (Sandler and Joffe 1980) accompanied by rocking or thumb sucking. Also there may be compulsive rituals, 'silly' behaviour (often found in stressful situations), aggression and auto-aggression. The person is reliving his/her feelings of helplessness and powerlessness; these people often feel unworthy of love.

The self-destroyers practise self-devaluation and an unstable regulation of self-esteem. Self-devaluation develops into an inner self-destruction. The aggressive behaviour (as in the case of Maureen above) is often associated with a change in personnel. The auto-aggression is often eye-gouging or hard head-banging against a wall. The mentally handicapped self-destroyer cannot cope with disappointments and may eventually withdraw from the external world. At this point the disappointing 'bad' object is internalised and the conflict transferred to the inner self.

The quiet-depressives often want to stay in bed all day; often they do not refuse to eat but they must be fed. Many do not speak although previously they were reported to have some spoken language. They may be incontinent, but care staff often feel that they are able to use the toilet. These quiet-depressives, unlike the self-destroyers and the self-unstables – who tend to be very visible and present great problems to care and therapy staff – tend to be unnoticed and they 'live in the shadows'. They often have typical symptoms of depression – an empty gaze, a facial expression of resignation, slowed-down movements and little spontaneous activity. Attempts to 'make contact' with them are difficult and often the care staff feel rejected. Gaedt suggests that this state corresponds to psycho-physiological deprivation. These people have 'given up' and have decided to organise their lives to burn on a low flame.

Structured Therapy Services for Mental Handicap and Mental Illness in Neuerkerode

It is clear that the cases mentioned above and their treatment is no easy matter. It requires a combination of approaches from therapists and care staff. In Neuerkerode psychotherapy plays a major part in 'strukturelle Betreuung' ('social structuring'). How is a resident referred? What services are offered? How are the results evaluated?

Gaedt has recently spoken (Gaedt 1995) of the principles underlying the treatment/therapy process which has been developed over the past fifteen years. I shall refer extensively to this paper. In it he identifies eight specific aspects which underlie the diagnostic-therapeutic process and the structured principles which lay down the ways in which the Department of Psychology and Psychiatry and the educationally based services of the staff in the residential units co-operate in the treatment programme. I will now present these eight points.

- On the one hand, the educationally based services in Neuerkerode operate independently of the therapeutic aspect. On the other hand, both of these areas are closely linked. This interdependence is necessary for successful co-operation.
- The residential staff, operating under pedagogical/educational principles, decide which measures should be taken in the case of a behaviourally disruptive staff member. In particular, they decide if and when therapy services become involved. They are solely

responsible for this decision. At this point, the staff in the residence fill out a referral form which is the basis for the next stage.

- If the decision to call in the therapy department is made, a time-consuming but absolutely essential first case conference is held. The case conference (*das Erstgesprach*) is attended by two psychologists and frequently the psychiatrist, and takes place in the residential group in which the client lives. At this point it needs to be stressed that the overall living conditions in which the client finds him or herself are taken into account. It is possible in such a case discussion to identify aspects of daily life which have caused the problem and which can be modified by the pedagogical/care staff. In any case, in this way a realistic impression of the client's personality and symptomology is obtained. The background information is then used to establish and categorise the observed disruptive behaviour. It can be seen from the earlier case studies how important it is to carefully consider this initial data, which often leads to a much deeper analysis of the case.

- The therapists (psychologists and medical staff) decide independently as to the diagnosis and the measures to be taken. This takes place in the therapy conference held each week. A report is given by the psychologists and psychiatrist who attended the earlier case conference in the residential group. Concerning these issues – of diagnosis and treatment – the psychologist has the jurisdiction. However, even though the therapist has the major responsibility in the diagnosis and other questions, the relationship between the educational and the therapeutic aspects is an equal one. The educational/residential staff play a very major role in this framework of co-operation. They can reject the proposed treatment at any time (as, of course, can the resident him/herself). This position guarantees that there is a consensus between all those concerned in the therapy process.

- In the therapy process, the therapeutic and educational aspects are combined. The authority and views of the educational/pedagogical staff must be respected. At this point, however, it is not the only consideration but rather a complement to the therapeutic thinking and strategies.

- The educational and therapeutic aspects cannot always be strictly separated. They complement each other and work side by side. Hence the therapy process must always begin and end taking fully into account the daily life and life-style of the resident.

- Psychological knowledge is absolutely indispensable and must be firmly embodied in the therapy service. This is not simply limited to the necessity of using appropriate medication and its monitoring (a specially devised symptom questionnaire is used to monitor the effects of medication; this is always filled out, often after much discussion, in the residential unit with the educational staff). The psychiatrist remains the essential link between the medical and psychiatric facilities in Neuerkerode.

- The therapeutic care of the mentally ill and mentally handicapped must include the possibility of both long- and short-term treatment as well as the possibility of care outside of the residential group in which the client lives. This means that out-patient treatment in a twenty-four-hour facility must be available. In this special case the educational and therapeutic services must be preserved and in order to ensure this the qualifications of all staff are important (and this includes regular in-service activities (*Fortbildung*)). The careful structuring of the daily life of the client within the educational/therapeutic framework is the objective of the residential and clinical staff.

It should be noted that there are other aspects of the structure of the therapy process in Neuerkerode. These include occupational, speech and physiotherapy. There is also a special 'workshop' which caters especially for the mentally handicapped/mentally ill residents. All of these services need to be carefully organised to provide optimal and comprehensive services for the individual resident.

The ways that mentally handicapped residents in Neuerkerode are served by the residential and therapy staff, apart from one-to-one therapy or advice/case discussion in the residential group itself, are also important.

First, there is a 'secure unit' – the Beo (*Beobachtung Gruppe* – observation group). This unit serves approximately ten very disturbed residents who require intensive therapy, twenty-four hours a day; is staffed by specially qualified personnel and is led by a full-time psychologist. The residents in this group take part in village life, the Dorf Krug (Pub), the Kiosk (cafe), the shop in the supermarket, attend the weekly 'disco', and so on.

Then there is a '*Tag und Nacht Klinik*' (twenty-four-hour intensive care unit for emergency cases). This unit serves about four to five residents and is basically an intensive psychiatric/therapy unit. Residents usually stay for about four to five weeks in this unit. There is also a local psychiatric hospital which has a wing serving mentally handicapped people. While this is seldom used by the residents of Neuerkerode, it is a facility outside the village which can provide special services if they are unavailable on site.

In the '*Therapie Haus*', there are three staff members who undertake occupational therapy with mentally handicapped/mentally ill residents. There is also a speech therapist position.

There is a special workshop for the dually diagnosed attended by approximately twenty residents. Here an approach which aims to rehabilitate these clients to a sheltered workshop takes into account their special difficulties associated with their mental illness.

Michels (1993) has been involved in regional planning, and has concentrated on the dually diagnosed. This work is important in the planning and development of a comprehensive multifaceted service which may often be provided by several agencies (private and government) working co-operatively.

It should be stressed, however, that the mentally handicapped/ mentally ill are mostly provided with services in their own residential group and within a multidisciplinary system which has been described above. It should also be said that the term 'strukturelle Betreuung' ('social structuring') in Neuerkerode is achieved because it is a village – with citizens and facilities which serve those citizens. While it is relatively large in size, it is not an 'institution' (it never was) and is 125 years old – and thus has not only facilities, services, and a multitude of buildings in varying architectural styles, but also traditions (just like most villages). It is perhaps easier in such a setting to provide a lifestyle of quality for its residents/citizens which can cater for their varying and often demanding needs. Alone, in the community, without massive support and management, the dually diagnosed may well either be lost or sink into a deteriorated mental state from which they cannot recover. The mentally handicapped/mentally ill do not seem to fit easily into the mainstream of society. This may be uncomfortable for us to accept at the present time when European social policy moves not only towards 'mainstream normalisation' as the highly preferred kind of service provision, but also towards the privatisation of services. Nevertheless, there is some hope that 'places to live outside the mainstream' have an important role to play in service provision for at least a section of the mentally handicapped population.

CASE STUDY AND CONCLUSIONS

To conclude, I would like to refer to the case mentioned earlier of Karel K. (case 3). Karel had been referred to the Department of Psychology and Psychiatry some years previously. She had had several periods of extremely disturbing behaviour. In the meeting reviewing the case, the two psychologists referred extensively to the case records. There was an indication that the use of a neurolepticum (Neurocil) had had a positive effect although this had been withdrawn after a period of relative stability. Also, in the past Karel had not had individual psychotherapy (but she had had occupational therapy with good results).

In this meeting the educational care staff had expressed doubts about the use of medication even though the history of the case indicated its beneficial results; one of the reasons was that they feared a personality change in the resident and wished to try other methods first. They were quite positive about the use of psychotherapy.

After several long discussions it was decided to begin psychotherapy with Karel – three times a week. No medication was recommended at this point. Other measures were also jointly undertaken – for example, a rating scale was filled out three times a day for several months since there was the possibility that the periods of extreme auto-aggression and aggression were associated with the onset and duration of her menstrual periods which may have caused some extra pain and fearfulness in Karel.

The therapy began and slowly a relationship was beginning build up between Karel and her therapist. However, both in therapy and in the residential setting and special school there was still evidence of the extreme negative behaviour patterns which seemed to suggest that Karel was sometimes a quiet-depressive (withdrawing, lying on the floor with her fingers in her ears soaked in her own saliva) and a self-destroyer (banging her head against the wall, hitting her head with her fist and striking the residential care staff). While the onset of therapy provided an indication that this extreme behaviour was decreasing, it was still present in some form in the daily life of Karel.

One day, some two months after therapy had begun, Karel bit the breast of one of her special care staff and the staff member had to take some time off work. At this point the care staff requested a further meeting with the psychologist and requested a review of the medication situation.

It was decided at this meeting to recommend the use of Neurocil in conjunction with the therapy. This brought about a substantial and beneficial change in Karel. She began to be more (positively) active at school (drawing soon after the medication a bright picture of the sun in red and orange colours, which she had not done before), was more stable in the residence and more outgoing in therapy. Her facial expression was brighter. At the time of writing, therapy continues three times a week, there has been no change in medication and Karel is reported to be much more stable. Even so, she sometimes reverts to aggression and auto-aggression. She probably will always express symptoms of depression, but at least at the moment they are less frequent and non life-threatening.

This case seeks to clarify Gaedt's points which were mentioned earlier: that co-operation and dialogue between educational/residential and therapy staff can have a stabilising and beneficial effect, within a therapeutic setting, of the daily life of a severely mentally handicapped/mentally ill resident. Thus the quality of life is enriched and greater autonomy in the individual established.

REFERENCES

Gaedt, C. (1990) 'Selbstbewertung und depressive inszenierungen bei Menschen mit geistiger Behinderung', *Neuerkeroder Beiträge 6*, Neuerkerode.

Gaedt, C. (1995) 'Psychotherapeutic Approaches in the Treatment of Mental Illness and Behavioural Disorders in the Mentally Retarded: the Significance of a Psychoanalytic Perspective', *Journal of Intellectual Disability Research*, 39, 3: 233–9.

Mahler, M. (1968) *On Human Symbiosis and the Vicissitudes of Individuation*, New York, International Universities Press.

Menolascino, F. (1990) 'Mental Retardation and the Risk, Nature and Types of Mental Illness', in A. Dosen and F. Menolascino (Hrsg.), *Depression in Children and Adults*, Leiden, Logan.

Michels, M. (1993) 'Erhebung zum Bedarf diagnostischer und therapeutischer Angebote in der Region Braunschweig-Wolfenbüttel-Helmstedt', in C. Gaedt, S. Bothe and M. Michels, *Psychisch krank und geistig behindert*, Dortmund, Verlag Modernes Lernen.

Sand, A. (1993) 'Diagnostisch-therapeutische Dienste für geistig behinderte Menschen mit einer psychischen Störung', in C. Gaedt, S. Bothe and M. Michels, *Psychisch krank und geistig behindert*, Dortmund, Verlag Modernes Lernen.

Sandler, J. and Joffe, W. (1980) 'On depression in childhood', Psyche, 5: 413–9.

Sinason, V. (1992) *Mental Handicap and the Human Condition*, London, Free Association Books.

6 Father and Son

COLETTE ASSOULY-PIQUET

When he read somewhere that the male celatius, a deep-sea fish common to Danish waters, lived its life attached like a wart to the larger body of the female, he dreamed that he was the female fish suspended deep in the sea with his son embedded in his body like the smaller male, a dream so sweet that waking up was cruel.[1]

In these few lines of his novel *Teach us how to Outgrow our Madness*, Kenzaburo Oë evokes the sexual fantasy which underlies the relationship of a father with his mentally handicapped son; a relationship which the father describes elsewhere as an oppressive symptom in expressions such as: 'it's a burden', 'a yoke', or 'fetters'. The fabric of the novel comprises several stories describing the birth and daily life of the handicapped child.

We know that Kenzaburo Oë is himself the father of a mentally handicapped child. In his work, where autobiography and fiction are intimately entwined, he speaks about this painful experience of paternity. The theme of his son's birth is approached from many different angles, so much so that it is difficult to do justice to all the variations when isolating one story from the work as a whole.

It is a strange and very remarkable story whose spiral construction requires the reader, if he (or she) hopes to understand and fully appreciate its subtlety, to backtrack often and even to re-read it two or three times, particularly as each word in the narrative is important, all the signifiers together forming an extremely complex network.

The novel begins with a very dense and enigmatic paragraph:

In the winter of 196–, an outlandishly fat man came close to being thrown to a polar bear bathing in a filthy pool below him and had the experience of very nearly going mad. As a result, the fat man was released from the fetters of an old obsession, but the minute he found himself free a miserable loneliness rose in him and withered his already slender spirit. Thereupon, he resolved for no

logical reason (he was given to fits of sudden agitation) to cast off
still another heavy restraint ...[2]

At the heart of the story there is a scene at the zoo where the main
character, who is only ever referred to as 'the fat man' (that is, by his
symptom), is threatened with being thrown into the polar bear's pool
by a gang of hoodlums. This scene is only recounted three-quarters
of the way through the story but is the object, both before and after
its description, of a very large number of allusions which all lead back
to the same point. 'The harrowing experience' at the zoo is in fact
central to the story, since it will have decisive subjective consequences, bringing about a real shaking off of the symptom: 'the fat
man' admits that he has been released from an 'obsession' and has
acquired a 'cruel freedom' in relation to the handicapped son to
whom he was abnormally attached.

This leads him in turn to distance himself from his own father,
from his father's alleged 'madness', self-confinement in the 'storehouse', and death. The zoo scene occurs in the context of two tele-
phone conversations between the man and his mother which might
be regarded as two long monologues since the mother at first withdraws into hostile and obstinate silence faced with her son's insistent
questions about his father's reclusion. She only replies later on in the
form of public announcements which are like battle engagements
against her son who harasses her. These two enigmatic announcements, each comprising a short text and a quotation, seem intended
to safeguard the secret at all costs, giving the impression that the
father's reclusion was the result of a disturbed mind, but they are also
filled with allusions which only the son can understand. By
connecting these writings and the memories that come back to him,
he is finally able to lift the veil behind which his mother kept his
father's story hidden: he discovers, for example, that his father had
cowardly betrayed his friends during the war. He then compares the
shock provoked by his mother's letter and the shock he received in
the form of his son Mori. Following the mother's second announcement and the considerable personal effect it had on him , the story
ends with the uncertain way in which this man, who had shaken off
both the burdens from which he had been unable to free himself up
to then, painfully experiences a double liberation.

From the very first paragraph, quoted earlier, many issues are
raised which are subtly linked throughout the story, forming a web
around this man's quest to understand his life-story, and, as the title
suggests, to understand his own madness as well as his father's.

It is a quest which tells of a personal journey in the sense of a liberation, one could even say a *rebirth*, since as a result of these events

the character experiences himself differently; a quest which carries with it a remarkable conception of the gestation and birth of a child (his own child, but also himself) in which sexuality, madness and death are inextricably entwined.

It is the important moments of the father's personal experience that I want to explore in this text.[3]

THE TRAUMA OF THE BIRTH ANNOUNCEMENT

The announcement of the birth of the handicapped child is experienced by the father as a trauma, a real catastrophe, and in other writings of Kenzaburo Oë, even as a cataclysm comparable to Hiroshima: we know that the author was anxious to publish *A Personal Matter*[4] his first novel in which he tells of the birth of his handicapped child, and *Hiroshima Notes*[5] in the same year.

Even so, we need to understand the nature of this traumatic event described as an explosion causing considerable destruction. In *Teach us how to Outgrow our Madness*, the author says little about it except for these few words: 'Later, looking back, he had the feeling he had been counting on the birth of his child as a first step toward a new life for himself which would be out of the shadow of his dead father.'

But these words are certainly very significant. 'The fat man' makes a connection between the birth of the abnormal child and his own father's 'madness'. What he denounces is the secret obstinately kept by his mother, her lies or her silence and her absolute control over what was known of his father's past:

> his mother soon would age and die without having disclosed the explanation she had kept secret all these years, not only for his father's self-confinement and death but the freakish something which underlay it and must also account for his own instability and for the existence of his idiot son, an existence which, in as much as it presented itself in a palpable form, he assumed he could never detach from himself.[6]

From then on, what he risks is being nailed by his mother to the signifiers of his father's 'alleged' madness and doing the same to his son. Is this son not an idiot – the proof, retrospectively, of his father's madness?

THE FAILURE OF PATERNITY

Everything happens, then, as if the paternal genealogy had fallen to pieces as a result of this birth. The mother's secret, combined with a suspicion of something unseemly, leads the reader to speculate about the father's failure, a failure of paternity. The mother only referred to this reclusive father by the scornful expression 'the other' no doubt reflecting the father's self-confinement, his silence, his dark glasses, his back turned in his barber's chair, his secret, his madness, or again, his illness. But also casting him out into an unspecified place eliminating him from her world like a piece of scum. There are numerous signifiers in the novel linked to this idea of something unseemly, a piece of *scum*: the dirty water, the dirty yellow bear, the stench at the back of the zoo, the rotten sardines, the child's yellow teeth which are never brushed, the allusions to toilets, the man thrown into the pool like a piece of shit.

Lacan's invention of *the object a*[7] comes to mind here. In the novel, this *object a* is no doubt the anal object but, above all, it is the look.[8] There are many signifiers which draw attention to this: the secret that must be kept hidden, blindness, the dark storehouse, dark glasses, the eye examination, the child's eyeball, the mirror ... . Completely identified with this look, the father – a shameful object who withdraws from looks by retreating to the storehouse – can no longer occupy the place of father and grandfather. By its birth, the handicapped child recreates this function of being a piece of scum, a tarnished object, a failure, something shameful, as this striking scene shows where, after the announcement of the handicapped child's birth, the man 'took the form into the toilets, sat down in one of the cubicles and began to giggle uncontrollably'.

After that, how was this being, this waste object who cannot have child status, to be given a name? Faced with this intractable dilemma, his father resorts to a foreign language and chooses a name which is not really a name:

> At the time the operation was in progress, his baby was in the process of being required to decide whether he would die or be an idiot, one or the other. Could such an existence be given a name? ... recalling from the Latin vocabulary he had learnt at college a simple word which should have related both to death and idiocy, wrote down the character for forest and named his son Mori.[9]

From that point on, the child is placed under signifiers which refer to his grandfather's madness and death, completely identified, like him, with the *unnameable*.

THE FATHER'S DEATH WISH

After a traumatic event the father sometimes has the desire to get rid of the problem, to do away with the cause of it, the handicap, or the child itself.

The father's death wish regarding the abnormal child is not always conscious or expressed. In this novel, it is not. However, it should be noted that in Kenzaburo Oë's work, the variations on the theme of the birth of a handicapped child are very significant as they are mainly concerned with the father's death wish towards the handicapped child: sometimes this death wish is clearly expressed (*A Personal Matter*), sometimes it is accompanied by an attempted murder which the father renounces at the last moment, sometimes the attempt results in a murder and the actual death of the child ('Agwee the Skymonster'[10]), and sometimes, as in the novel we are dealing with here, the death wish is not expressed explicitly.

This death wish, which is often expressed by parents (or others) through words such as 'get rid of it at birth, kill it', underlines to what extent the child is identified with a waste product which needs to be got rid of. It is not a matter then of killing a child but of getting rid of a being who cannot have child status. The toilet episode is indeed there to suggest that the father who is painfully hurt is also concerned with elimination, although this is only hinted at discreetly.

But this is not the chosen course of action: 'the fat man' himself – who is described as looking like a skeleton at the time of the child's birth – is certainly also identified with his scum-father to envisage getting rid of the problem like that. The child is adopted, accepted, and the first indication of this is that the child is given the surname Eeyore 'borrowing the name of the misanthropic donkey in Winnie-the-Pooh'. His father can no longer call him Mori without being reminded of the toilet scene and his awful fit of laughter. From now on, Eeyore is a cartoon character identified with a little pet, albeit somewhat melancholy, who can once again inhabit the world of little ones.

THE FANTASY OF RESHAPING

The handicapped child's acceptance and adoption are only possible if the father gets involved for a certain length of time when the child is in a way 'carried' a second time. The extraordinary bond which unites the father and son in this novel can be interpreted at the level of this fantasised 'second pregnancy'. It is as if the child who is considered incomplete should be reshaped, repaired, started again by the father who, from then on, substitutes for the mother in a contact of bodies which is well illustrated by the metaphor of clasped hands:

> until the decisive day when he was nearly thrown to a polar bear, the fat man had never failed to sleep with one arm extended toward his son's crib, which he had installed at the head of his bed.

In fact, his wife had quit his bed and secluded herself in another part of the house not so much because of strife between them as a desire of her own not to interfere with this intimacy between father and son. It had always been the fat man's intention that he was acting on a wholesome parental impulse – if his son should awaken in the middle of the night he would always be able to touch his father's fleshy hand in the darkness above his head.[11]

It is known that handicapped children often induce their parents to be over-protective[12] as if they needed to compensate for deficiencies by making extra efforts, by attempts at reparation which often contradict the inescapable reality of the handicap. In the imaginary realm, such overprotection is a bodily envelope which seeks to envelop the child and even to form a second layer in order to erase the handicap. *Underlying the need for this envelope is the fantasy of a foetus or of an unfinished baby, not completed, which needs reshaping or remaking.* But is it not the parents who are also trying to look after themselves, repair themselves, handicapped, too, by the hurt of the birth? 'Wasn't it possible that he had slept with his arm outstretched so that the hand with which he groped in the darkness when uneasy dreams threatened him awake at night might encounter at once the comforting warmth of his son's hand?' Elsewhere the father speaks of 'the child on his shoulders … the warm and heavy presence on his shoulders which sometimes felt to his confusion more like his guardian spirit than his ward'.

THE FATHER–SON DYAD

Through this attempt at mutual repairing a strange dyad between father and son forms as if they were directly plugged into each other.[13] This extraordinary couple that they form is described in the various episodes of their daily life:

- During Eeyore's operation following his birth, his father is asked to give some blood and does so in such abundance that it looks as if he is trying to establish a kind of 'transfusional' communication with his child as if they were from then on to be linked by an umbilical cord.
- The daily meal at the Chinese restaurant consists for both of them of a large bowl of pork noodles in broth which is to a large extent responsible for their obesity. This shared meal is accompanied by an astonishing mirror relationship recounted as follows: 'Eeyore, the pork noodles and the Pepsi-cola were good?' And when his son answered, 'Eeyore, the pork noodles

and Pepsi-cola were good!', he would judge that complete communication had been achieved between them and would feel happy.

• Following the episode where Eeyore's foot is scalded, an astounding relationship between the father and son develops as if they had become communicating vessels of a sort:

> the fat man began through clenched teeth to express cries of pain himself which so resembled his son's screams that they merged with them indistinguishably. His leg had actually begun to throb (he believed!) with the pain of a burn ... From that day on, insofar as the fat man was aware, whatever pain his son was feeling communicated to him through their clasped hands and never failed to produce in his own body a tremor of pain in unison.[14]

A CLOSED WORLD

This father–son couple is described by the author as a closed world, a roundness without imperfection, a completeness without differentiation, in other words *without castration*, of which the father's obesity, like his son's is the symptom, and the closely-knit couple of celatius fish mentioned at the beginning of this chapter, the most remarkable image. Another image which punctuates the novel is the earthly sphere-egg-eye:

> Eeyore's eye was laid bare by a slender instrument which the doctor inserted under his eyelid. It was truly a large sphere, egg-white in colour and what it felt like to the fat man was the earth itself, the entire world of man ... with this eye the fat man identified all of himself.[15]

How is this to be understood? The child's handicap is no longer experienced as a lack, a deficiency, an incompleteness: it is denied and turned into its opposite. The child becomes the little male, a precious object carried by an enormous female-father. Serving to block the father's anxiety, he is placed in the position of a *fetish phallus-object*. Behind the erotic image of this couple united like male and female celatius, forming a perfect whole, the figure of what cannot be castrated emerges, where sexuality, madness and death are intertwined.[16]

The father–son couple cannot be castrated but are not invulnerable for the world around them threatens and endangers them repeatedly. When others are not simply mixing with them or feeding them, they become real persecutors, like wild beasts in the zoo. For example, the policemen who want to enforce the regulations, the doctor who treats the scalded foot, the nursing staff and the ophthalmologist during Eeyore's eye examination and finally the hoodlums who attack the fat man at the zoo. Admittedly, what is in danger is not simply the father or the son, it is the closely-knit couple that they form, the erotic link which unites them. Thus, during Eeyore's eye examination, the fright felt by the fat man when faced with the gulf which threatens to open up between them, shows how their union is in trouble.

A jagged fissure opened up between himself and his son. And the fat man forced the first finger of his right hand between Eeyore's yellow, gnashing teeth (not until after his experience above the polar bear's pool would he recognize that he had done this because he was afraid of that fissure, afraid that if he saw to the bottom of it he would have to confront what certainly would have revealed itself there in its true form, the self-deception impregnating his conscious formulation Eeyore = the fat man).[17]

After that, it is not surprising that this 'pregnancy', experienced both as a pleasure and as an intolerable weight, like something *rather too much than not enough,* became a real symptom.[18]

AN INTERMINABLE GESTATION

Their is a risk that the unfinished, incomplete child-foetus will be interminable, that is, borne throughout life without the father ever being able to give birth to it, 'to evacuate it'. If a second birth of the child is to be possible, an act is required, described in the novel as a semblance of acting out, provoked by a violent attack by external persecutors.

Let us return to the crucial scene at the zoo. The fat man inadvertently wandered with his son into an area behind the polar bear's enclosure where he suddenly found himself encircled by a group of hoodlums whom they had disturbed while they were up to something most probably illicit. Taking the fat man for a policeman, the hoodlums started interrogating him aggressively, kicking and punching him, finally hoisting him into the air to swing him back and forth above the polar bear's pool. Having no alternative but death or madness for himself as well as his son, he allowed himself to fall:

As he tumbled, screaming, screaming into the darkness, he saw his own eye, an eye laid bare, the pupil which filled its brown, blurred centre expressing fear and pain only: an animal eye ... he was becoming a single colossal eye being lofted into the air, the egg-white sphere was the entirety of the world he had lived ... No longer was he even the fat man. He was an egg-white eye, a one-hundred-and-seventy-pound, enormous eye ...[19]

It is the fat man himself who is literally ejected from the closed world of the dyad, thrown like a huge turd into the fetid stench of the pool, totally reduced to a bit of waste and henceforth identified with his father. Does this not amount to saying, then, that the mother who rejected the father by designating him as 'the other' is the foremost of the persecutors?

However, the story would end there if the fat man had really been thrown into the bear's pool. In fact, a large stone is thrown in instead of him and he simply gets splashed by the fetid water. Wandering for hours, beside himself and delirious, he is later found by the zoo-keepers in the 'public toilets'.

Nevertheless, he comes through this ordeal changed, for he discovers that his handicapped son, who had been found by the police, was having supper with them as if nothing whatsoever had happened, thanking them with his perpetual refrain: 'Eeyore! The pork noodles in broth and the Pepsi-cola were good?' In this way, the dyad fell to pieces leaving the man distraught, facing his lost illusions and his new-found 'cruel freedom'.

What does this semblance of acting out mean? The act is only mimed; a stone was thrown instead of the man. Through this substitution the aggressors' murderous deed becomes a kind of sacrificial ordeal. And what is sacrificed is the father's blindness in an inter-minable gestation of an interminable child.

We have often met exhausted parents on the edge of despair wishing for their child's death or their own, as if a real death was a door through which one has to pass in extreme situations of loss if a space for desire is to emerge. Sometimes an attempted murder is committed *in reality*: and it happens – although not always – that the murderous gesture is *forestalled* by a word, a murmur, a look or an appeal to the Other. This *forestalled act* takes on the significance of a sacrificial act, leading to a subjective change which is worked through in valuable ways such as literary creativity, founding institutions or other achievements.[20]

Abraham's sacrifice (Genesis 22) is a case in point of such fore-stalled acting out. Just when the knife is about to strike Isaac, Abraham's hand is held back by the word of God and a ram is sacri-ficed instead of his son. By going through what has to be seen as an ordeal, Abraham risks losing what is most precious to him, 'his son, his only son, whom he loves'. He leaves things up to ... whom? In the biblical text it is said: 'To the unknowable One who will see for him.' We can say then: to what he cannot see himself but what the Other can see, *without him knowing*; to what will surprise him and turn his murderous gesture into a symbolic sacrifice.[21]

When the fat man abandons himself in desperation to his attackers, he gives himself up to the unknown which overwhelms him from all sides; he leaves things up to the Other who makes the acting-out masquerade into a real ordeal, the subjective effect of which is indisputable.

THE BIRTH OF DIFFERENCE

The end of this period of gestation is followed by another birth, just as painful, of the man himself as a son snatched from his own father's madness. The first ordeal leaves him distraught, in a miserable state, enveloped by the stench of rotten sardine scales which stick to his skin and completely identified with the scum that his father had become, stuck in his madness just as his son had been stuck in his own: 'his hot hand was clutched in the hand of a hippopotamus of a man sitting with his back to him in a barber's chair in a dark storehouse'. Which is why, after being violently dragged away from his son, he tries to tear himself away from the shadow of his dead father and decides to declare war on his real persecutor, his mother, so as to discover at last the secret which obscured his father's past and which affected him so much. So, the father, whom his mother called 'the other', becomes for him 'the Other, the Man'. He recalls a poem by an English poet where the word 'man' was written with a capital 'M': 'The voice of Man: O teach us to outgrow our madness.'

'If that voice – "O, teach us how to overcome our madness" – is the voice of the Man then "our madness" means the Man's and mine', the fat man told himself.[22]

His victory over his mother, the return of the documents that she had concealed, the denunciation of her lies and the final discovery of his father's betrayal were to have as great a subjective effect on him as the zoo episode. He burns all the documents he had written and gives up all idea of writing his father's biography. He even goes on a slimming course. Could it be said that at the end of this journey, something in him has finally freed itself?

And one bright spring morning he had come out of the sauna and was taking his shower when he discovered a swarthy stranger who was nonetheless of tremendous concern to him standing right in front of his eyes. Perhaps his confusion had to do with the steam fogging the mirror – there was no question that he was looking at himself.[23]

He discovers that he is different, different from himself and his father,[24] veiled by the steam which is there both to hide and to designate the incompleteness in his reflected image resulting from the phallic lack.[25] From then on, he is left to his solitude and distress in a confrontation with his own madness, having 'neither a father nor a son with whom to share the madness closing in on him. He simply had the freedom to confront it alone.'

So he begins writing crazy notes and letters to 'the Other' which repeat over and over the prayer 'teach us ...'. Then 'and as if he intended these notes to be discovered after his death, he locked them in a drawer and never showed them to anyone'.

Everything takes place as if the moment the secret is discovered, it is once again shut away in a draw, out of sight. Not quite, however, since we as readers share the secret with the author. The simple word 'testament' is evocative of the fact that the novel could only be written if the author, as distinct from the character, had opened the drawer just as an executor does after the death of someone who has entrusted him with his estate. Is this not a way of saying that the character, the author's double, is indeed dead from now on, making place for a new man thanks to the act of writing. Perhaps it is also saying that the reader is placed in the position of the witness, of the Other to whom this story is addressed. Of the Other who is invoked in this prayer 'part of his body and his spirit', in this very beautiful prayer which was the inspiration for the title of the novel: 'The voice of Man: O teach us to overcome our madness.'

NOTES

1. Oë, K. (1989) 'Teach us how to Outgrow our Madness', in *Teach us how to Outgrow our Madness*, London, Serpent's Tail.
2. Ibid.
3. I am especially interested as we recounted a very similar journey in *Regards sur le handicap*. Assouly-Piquet, C. and Berthier Vittoz, F. (1994) *Regards sur le handicap*, Paris, Hommes et Perspective-Desclée de Brouwer.
4. Oë, K. (1995) *A Personal Matter*, London, Picador.
5. Oë, K. (1995) *Hiroshima Notes*, New York, Grove Press.
6. Oë, 'Teach us how to Outgrow our Madness'.
7. Lacan, J.' Le séminaire, L'angoisse' (unpublished).

8. Lacan, J. (1998) Seminar Book 11: The Four Fundamental Concepts of Psychoanalysis, New York, W.W. Norton.
9. Oë, 'Teach us how to Outgrow our Madness'.
10. Oë, K. (1989) 'Agwee, the Skymonster', in *Teach us how to Outgrow our Madness*, London, Serpent's Tail.
11. Ibid.
12. Cf. Assouly-Piquet and Vittoz, *Regards sur le handicap*. The severely handicapped or seriously ill child provokes such fantasies. The parents are then involved in an endless and depressing process because they are not able to give up this interminable position with 'an interminable child'.
13. Cf. ibid.: 'Le "monstre hybride"'.
14. Oë, 'Teach us how to Outgrow our Madness'.
15. Ibid.
16. Cf. Assouly-Piquet and Vittoz, *Regards sur le handicap*: 'L'enfant merveilleux'. Often placed in the position of an *enfant-phallus éternel et démesuré*, the handicapped child draws those around him into relationships which test limits and boundaries.
17. Oë, 'Teach us how to Outgrow our Madness'.
18. Freud, S. (1926) 'Inhibitions, Symptoms and Anxiety', in James Strachey, ed., *The Standard Edition of the Complete Psychological Works of Sigmund Freud*, 24 vols, London, Hogarth, 1953–73, vol. 20, pp.77–175.
19. Oë, 'Teach us how to Outgrow our Madness'.
20. Cf. Assouly-Piquet and Vittoz, *Regards sur le handicap*: 'Folie d'amour, l'example de L'Ababa'.
21. Cf. ibid.: 'L'enfant retrouvé'.
22. Oë, 'Teach us how to Outgrow our Madness'.
23. Ibid.
24. Freud, S. (1919)' The Uncanny', *S.E.* 17, pp.217–74.
25. Lacan, *Le séminaire, L'angoisse*.

7 The 'Organisation' of Mental Retardation

DIETMUT NIEDECKEN

Psychoanalysis has always striven to reconstruct damaged human subjectivity. However, with a few exceptions, mentally retarded people have long been excluded from this enterprise, a fact which has not yet been acknowledged by mainstream psychoanalysis. This happened – and still happens – as a matter of course, as if such a state of affairs required no justification and could not be questioned. Ever since precise diagnostic methods were developed to establish the existence of abnormal physical conditions, there seems to have been no further need to enquire whether mental handicap might be understood as resulting from social and psychological developmental difficulties. It has been taken for granted that mental handicap is a deficient state in which psychodynamics play but a minor role and where development is irrevocably determined by organic conditions. Reflecting on the psychodynamics and socialisation of mental handicap has seemed more or less pointless. Consequently, most psychoanalysts believe that mentally handicapped people cannot be understood and treated psychoanalytically and that psychoanalytic theory cannot contribute to an understanding of their specific mental states.

In my book *Namenlos* (1989), I attempted to understand mental retardation in psychoanalytic terms. I followed Maud Mannoni (1972) in her approach to the subject and based my views both on Lorenzer's (1972) systematisation of psychoanalysis as a theory of social interaction, and on Mario Erdheim's theory (1982) of the social generation of unconsciousness. In my view, mental retardation should be regarded as a kind of social institution constituted by three organisational stages: diagnosis, social phantasms about 'being handicapped', and methods of rehabilitation which are based on those phantasms without reflection. My approach differs from others such as those of Gaedt (1990) and Sinason (1992), insofar as I do not differentiate between a primary handicap and a secondary handicap which overlays the former due to social discrimination. Although I do not follow Mannoni in her Lacanian orientation, I agree with her view that mental handicap is developed from the very outset of the process of socialisation in which the death wishes of care givers triggered by diagnostic information or some unusual, 'uncanny' (in the sense of Freud's *unheimlich* (1919a) perception of the infant are the driving forces of this development.

On an individual level, mental retardation may be described as an impairment of the capacity to symbolise which is systematically developed in interaction with these 'organisers'. Mental handicap becomes almost irreversibly 'organised" in a manner similar to that which Balint (1964) described as 'organising illnesses' in the interaction between a patient and his or her consultant. This 'organisation' means that autonomous imaginative capacity and symbolic interaction is inhibited or destroyed. As a consequence of this deficiency of symbolic capacity, the mentally retarded ego is condemned to silence – a silence which has its counterpart in the silence of mainstream psychoanalysis on the subject. I therefore am inclined to understand the latter as an expression of collective counter-transference responsible for unconscious death wishes.

The ideas which I am going to present now are but speculative enquiries. In order to explore them further it would be necessary to make investigations in several fields. These ideas are intended to serve as pointers for further discussion and not as a ready-made theoretical concept.

We cannot know anything factual about human nature without taking into account that all observable facts are social facts, products of an interaction of biological human nature with the social context in which it unfolds. Thus, we also have to see mental handicap as a result of interaction. This interaction is influenced by unusual biological conditions as well as by the specifically changed attitude of the social surroundings which derive from such conditions. What we call the symptoms of the mentally handicapped condition are always produced phenomena, 'facts' in the original sense, and never just nature. Mentally handicapped nature is socialised, as is all human nature, and can only be understood if this socialisation process is taken into account.

MENTAL HANDICAP AND REPETITION COMPULSION

In this chapter, I want to investigate the well-known phenomenon that the lives of mentally retarded people are ruled by stereotyped behaviour and repetitions to a much larger extent than those of non-retarded people. As a result of such compulsive repetition, mentally retarded people usually meet with misunderstanding, disrespect and ridicule which add to the general attitude of prejudice. My claim is that the common root of these repetitions and stereotypes is what Freud called repetition compulsion (1919b) – repetition compulsion in its most archaic form, to be sure. In presenting two cases, I shall try to show how such stereotyped behaviour may be developed during the socialisation process of mental handicap.

The first of my examples is not drawn from my own personal experience. The stereotyped behaviour in it is constructed as a scene and acted in conjunction with the social environment. This allows me to approach it psychoanalytically despite the limited information at my disposal.

Mr K. is a good-looking man who at first sight does not appear handicapped. There is little information about his childhood. He was left by his mother and brought up in various homes and institutions. He is known by those close to him as somebody who regularly gets himself into impossible situations. As he does not appear handicapped, he awakens hopes and illusory ideas about his competence and independence especially in his employers. He then attempts to live up to these expectations, trying to conceal all signs of failure. To sustain his employers' hopes, he has to use lies and pretensions. Quite regularly, these situations result in a complete breakdown in which he is unmasked and ridiculed as a confidence trickster. He is then not only dropped abruptly by his disillusioned and disappointed employer, but also severely reprimanded and humiliated.

There are phenomena which are even less accessible than such patterns of compulsive behavioural repetition: those which we usually call stereotyped behaviour in severely retarded people. These stereotyped patterns are no longer scenic in character. In order to find meaning, even in such bizarre phenomena, we have first to try and situate them within an interactional context. There is no possibility of developing a model of understanding from outside the situation and thereafter trying to prove its heuristic value as an interpretation in the therapeutic interaction as we are usually able to do in psychoanalysis. The only clue to a possible understanding of such patterns lies in the counter-transference they provoke. It seems that in such cases something needs to be completed through the self-observing presence of an empathic object before the interaction can be recognised as such. I shall now relate an example from my own experience.

Hans, a young man who cannot speak and has little understanding of language, has developed a symptom which makes everyone shrink away from him in disgust. He ruminates for long hours every day and sometimes regurgitates and spits over the person who has to take care of him. He provokes this regurgitation and occasional vomiting by pressing his thighs into his stomach in the crouching position. Often his care givers try to make him stretch and relax but to no avail. Not until I got to know Hans well, did I come to some understanding of the situation. While the case was reported to me, I listened with growing disgust, if not panic. I have always tried to avoid people with such symptoms but this time I could no longer do so. Just after I had been told about Hans, he entered the room and, as if he knew that I had been asked to help his care givers understand him better, immediately got onto the sofa in a crouching position and began to ruminate. I felt massive ambivalence: on the one hand, everything in me wanted to flee; on the other hand, I wanted to see the task that I had been given through and demonstrate psychoanalytic understanding even under extreme conditions. In this ambivalent state, I tried to make contact with Hans, which promptly misfired: I moved towards him too quickly and addressed him by his name. He got up abruptly and left the room. I had obviously frightened him.

These examples have been chosen at random and could easily be replaced by others. They seem hardly accessible to our usual psychoanalytic understanding. Usually, we try to understand the meaning of symptoms in communicating with the healthy ego-parts of our patients. This is the basis of the working alliance. The patients themselves experience their symptoms as foreign to them and are able to look at them from a distance. This kind of self-awareness is impossible for Hans and Mr K. can hardly be expected to exercise it to the extent needed in the usual psychoanalytic setting. Their lives seem more or less completely governed by their symptoms. If it is repetition compulsion with which we are concerned here, then it seems to be so powerful that their is little room left for anything else to play a role in their lives.

INTROJECTION AND MENTAL HANDICAP

Let me now make a few theoretical points before trying to offer an interpretation of the examples given.

According to Lorenzer (1972), all human experience and behaviour is based upon a complex of interaction forms. Such interaction forms develop from the outset of the process of childhood socialisation inasmuch as the natural physical needs of the child and the repetoire of psycho social actions performed by caregiving persons must come together to form a congruent pattern in which both physical needs and social possibilities are brought into in a mutual gestural exchange. Interaction forms are internalised and introjected as experiential possibilities and, if the process is successful, they become a symbolisable element of human experience and functioning.

The complex process of the development of interaction forms and introject-complexes – I am now departing from Lorenzer's terminology and am referring to Harold Lincke (1971a, 1971b) and Winnicott – will only be successful when there is 'good enough' mothering. According to Lincke, an introject capable of being symbolised will only develop if the person caring for the child is successful in creating the illusion that the world is exactly as the innate biological-instinctive pattern leads the child to expect. This occurs through his or her practice of responding adequately to the child's physical needs, recognising and picking up the child's intentions from his or her gestures. If the mediation between biological structure and social practice is successful, a feeling of coherence, meaningfulness and security in the world will result as an expression of the subjective structure of the complex of introjected interaction forms. This feeling of meaningfulness, of coherence, is as indispensable as the biological roots from which it evolves.

My thoughts on the 'organisation' of mental handicap which will be developed in the course of this chapter are mainly based upon Lincke's studies on introject formation and the development of the experience of coherence and security in the world. Lincke (1971a) notes a critical situation which must inevitably arise time and again during development due to the specifically human situation of physiologically premature birth. This situation is that biologically based inner impulses occur according to a fixed schedule which is far ahead of motor development, so that the young individual is not yet in a position to translate these impulses into real life actions in an appropriate way. Hence, a dangerous contradiction arises between the impulse and its potential for realisation. Lincke mentions, for example, an early contradictory impulse between tearing the prey apart and the concomitant social situation where the only available prey would be the mother upon whom the child is totally dependent for all his or her vital functions at this stage. This model of an oral conflict situation resulting from the disharmony of human development assumes that, as the impulse to bite occurs, a biologically based natural inhibition mechanism is activated, namely the inhibition to bite members of the same species. A successful outcome of socialisation makes it necessary that through the mediation of caring interaction, the actual realisation of the impulse is inhibited thus becoming an intrapsychic possibility for a potential symbolic interaction pattern, an introject. In such introjects instinctive impulses are united with inhibitory mechanisms. constituting the elements of the developing capacity for imagination independent of situations. This is how human drive structure is formed through introjection and becomes the content of human thought, fantasy and imagination.

In accordance with this model of introject formation, but going beyond the generally unavoidable developmental crises, I propose that the crisis situations which arise during the socialisation of infants and young children who become mentally handicapped are much more difficult to manage. Furthermore, the outcome of these crises do not create the prerequisites for human imagination and thinking; on the contrary, they seem more likely to impair them lastingly.

If for any reason during early interaction, the infant's activities, his (or her) spontaneous gestures, endanger his life by triggering death wishes in the early care givers, the innate biological mechanisms for responding to life-threatening situations – physiological anxiety responses (Stern 1972) – will be aroused. This will immobilise the infant where the realisation of his intentions is concerned, an experience which may lead to a channelling of the development of the autonomous imaginative faculty in a more or less drastic, hampering way. The result of such a process would be an 'organisation' in the sense of a merging of physiological anxiety responses with intentional gestures through which the introjects would forfeit at least part of their stimulus autonomy and the interaction forms would remain bound to organic-reflexive responses. Such interaction forms would essentially remain unsymbolised and, under unfavourable conditions, would remain permanently unavailable for symbolisation. Mentally handicapped development would then be seen as a retrobinding of experience to the organic sphere under unfavourable conditions, as the only opportunity for mediation which the individual can find in his or her environment under the circumstances.

The outcome of this mediation process would, on the one hand, very probably be a progressive, that is, healthy one, because it ensures the survival of the individual faced with a given threat. On the other hand, the 'organisation', that is, the fact that vital life impulses must remain at least partially withdrawn from the sphere of autonomous imaginative faculty, would hamper the individual's social and motor development towards autonomy, at least to some extent.

From ethology, we are familiar with flight instincts and death-feigning reflexes as reactions to situations of acute threat. In what follows, I shall refer to the proposed instinctive response patterns of infants facing acute threat by their prototypes in the animal world – although I do not claim that this is correct from an empirical-biological standpoint – because the idea of the death-feigning reflex or flight instinct is more appropriate than the concept of physiological anxiety responses to make us aware of the affective catastrophe which I regard as the central driving force in the socialisation of mental handicaps. The objective here is merely to present a model for understanding which presupposes an 'organised' biological component of this pattern type. Thus, in the case of mentally retarded development, death-feigning and flight impulses could be triggered simultaneously with instinctive search motions, intentional gestures aiming to satisfy basic life needs or – in the most severe cases – simultaneously with vegetative impulses. Such a process would have to appear as organic damage since mental space, the internalised 'potential space' (Winnicott 1960) in which a disorder could manifest itself as a mental one, has not yet been established. Vegetative impulses and early intentional gestures which have merged with a death-feigning reflex in such a way could be internalised and become situation independent in the course of introject formation. However, together with the impulse, the death-feigning reflex would also become situation independent and generalised, and – due to its nature as a reflex – would always remain bound to reflex-triggering internal stimuli. The main difference with undisturbed introject formation is the fact that vegetative or intentional impulses welded together with such reflexes as introjects would become situation independent but at the same time would remain tied to regularly recurring inner stimuli that have become reflex cues. Such a socialised impulse which has been welded together with a reflex would always remain bound to organic functioning in a reflex-like way, its symbolic separation from where it is knitted together with the reflex would necessarily remain incomplete and thus all participation in social life would involve the dynamics of the reflex.

ANALYSIS OF THE FIRST CASE

Following these introductory remarks, let us now look at the case of Mr K. Due to the fact that I know nothing about Mr K.'s early years I have to rely solely upon the scene which he repeated over and over again in order to reconstruct his early experiences. In Mr K.'s enactment we find the most traumatic affective experience to be the disintegration of illusion and the ensuing feelings of shame, exposure, humiliation, unbearable loneliness and helplessness: a lone individual suddenly standing naked before the eyes of the whole world. On the other hand, there is the awful disillusionment of the counterparts who have now to recognise that they have supported a phantom. In the reconstructed model, the scene can be interpreted in the following way: the look of disappointment following a long period of concealment can be deciphered as the first look after being born which initiated and determined the first interaction between mother and child. This was dominated by such an affect of shame. At this point, I wish to draw attention to the fact that here, as well as elsewhere, I do not assume any personal fault on the part of the mother in question. Rather, it is the conditions which hinder normal maternal capability and which force the mother to fill the resulting emptiness with phantasms – phantasms which culture puts at our disposal for such extreme situations and which serve as a kind of anchor making it possible to avert an otherwise fatal threat to the mother–child relationship (Niedecken 1989, p.108ff.).

We can assume that the first interaction between infant and mother after birth is reproduced in the situation enacted by Mr K. The mother in this scene was not able to see her newly born child as a magnificent product of an act of love. The reason for this could have been a certain uncanny or confusing perception of the infant or perhaps also a generally traumatic and frightening situation revolving around the birth itself. Fear and confusion may have led her to experience this child more as physical evidence of her disgrace and her being at the mercy of someone else. It is as if looking upon her new-born child, she reconstructed the act of procreation as being an extremely humiliating experience of being raped, of being completely at the mercy of another person, and as if this new-born baby – the product of this act – was unbearable evidence, and a manifestation of her own helplessness and disgrace. Perhaps this mother experienced pregnancy as a manifestation of her personal integrity and omnipotence which was shattered in a traumatic way at birth. Thus, the first interactions, that is, each simple act of putting on nappies, holding the infant or breast feeding would be influenced by the fact that in her child the mother sees the embodiment of her own helplessness and humiliation. In the face of this disillusionment and the renewed vividness of the atrocity, disgrace and unbearable passiveness, the only possible reaction for the mother, as I see it, is to become numb inside. This numbness encompasses two aspects. First, she becomes numb just as she became numb in the first instance. Second, since she is now in an active position, the humiliating presence of the child must trigger the inner impulse to destroy the manifestation of her shame, and she goes numb in order not to become aware of this impulse to kill.

In the scene, we re-encounter this impulse in the form of the counter-transference of those individuals who fell for Mr K.'s ploys. In the enacted scene we discover the mother becoming petrified with fright in the form of the persistent refusal of the counterparts to admit that Mr K. is not how they imagined him to be in their grandiose efforts to assist him. This fearful immobilisation of the mother in the first instance, encompassing a murderous fantasy, must trigger a death-feigning reflex in the child, which at the same time – and this makes the physical reflex twice as powerful – is a mimetic banishing adaptation to the mother's fear. The child can only embody or ward off the mother's fears in a completely passive role insofar as the child facilitates cathexis through the mother's projective identification.

At first, the scene is dominated by the mother's incapacitation due to her fear which is reflected in the death-feigning reflex of the child. Through this reaction, the child mimetically takes on mother's inner picture of horror; in other words, it takes on her projective identification. This causes a certain feeling of relief in the mother as a result of successful projective defence. Now the mother partially regains her ability to act. This triggers the flight instinct and both mother and child make use of the fading numbness to initiate hectic activity directed at warding off perception of the horror which has occurred by making it look as if nothing had ever happened, as if the horror had never occurred, as if grandiose integrity had never been endangered.

Thus, the first impulse of the child is alloyed with a death-feigning reflex. The second impulse, the feeling of life stirring beneath the surface, the search behaviour which has not been completely immobilised, can only occur now on the basis of the suspension of the infant's ability for interaction. And this is where the impulse to flight must be organised with both sides agreeing once more on an ideal description of the picture that is not grounded in any affective experiences. The lost grandiosity, the 'sparkle in mother's eyes' must be faked. What actually should have been elevated to gestural-symbolic potency, the intentional symbolic movements of the infant, is withdrawn into the somatic non-symbolisable sphere through alloyment with physical reflexes. If the organisation of the impulse to flight now restores some scope of action to the mother–child relationship, introject formation can progress. However, by means of this introject, the death-feigning reflex and impulse to flight will remain a quasi-organic necessity in all Mr K.'s intentional social interactions in the future, or at least as long as early fusions have not been dissolved by understanding.

What exactly is the 'sparkle in mother's eyes' which has to be faked by the child K. and his mother in such a self-destructive way and which later on Mr K. has to fake with his various care givers and therapists? It is recognition, maternal-mimetic attunement: the child is 'OK', it is biologically and socially 'right', it fits with her idea of it. The mother reflects to the child that she can pick up and understand his or her gestures as an expression of intentional participation in the interaction between them. From Winnicott (1960) we learn that 'the true self becomes a living reality only if the mother is repeatedly successful in responding to the spontaneous gesture ... of the infant'. By building a bridge via scenical interaction, the illusion of 'being part of nature' is successful; Balint described this as a harmonious cross-blending or as primary love. In my own words, I might describe it as the feeling that the 'child is OK' or 'I fit in with this world'. Experiencing the resolution of innate structural needs for being recognised and recognising as well as for potential symbolic space is, so to speak, uplifting. The child K. was unable to create the 'illusion', that is, a subjective feeling of being all right with his mother. Since this is obviously indispensable, Mr K. has to fake these feelings of being all right and uplifted with his social environment, too.

ANALYSIS OF THE SECOND CASE

The scenario described above differs from Hans' in exactly this aspect: the individual with stereotyped behaviour no longer has a say in the formation of phantasms about symptomatic stereotyped behaviour. This happens over the individual's head; for example, through the assumption of Hans' care givers that he is so far removed from the world of normal human feelings that rumination must be 'fun' for him. In 'stereotyped behaviour' such as self-mutilation and symptoms of hospitalisation, what once must have been a search gesture is no longer even embedded in a scene. Rather, the gestural component of the offer to interact apparently no longer meets with a meaningful response and so the search for an interaction counterpart is directed towards one's own body. This creates an obstacle to scenic understanding, dooming every attempt at understanding to failure from the outset. This impossibility does not result from a lack of information or empathy but is symptomatic of the almost complete exclusion of persons such as Hans from the symbol mediation of human interaction.

In my contact with Hans, the only chance I saw for understanding was by attempting to form a relationship with him in which the symptom would be integrated. So the first step was to establish a symbolic space which could be the basis for an understanding. Obviously, such a construction of symbolic space from almost total destruction demands certain prerequisites; at least a firm hold on theory which can offer a containing function and substitute for the hold lacking in the subject, who is held captive in his stereotypes as far as language and scenic structure are concerned.

My first, unsuccessful encounter with Hans affords only a vague idea of what the meaning of his behaviour might be. The feeling of disgust emerging within myself and identificatory retching reflexes produced feelings of panic. By treating Hans too brashly, I drove him away. Here, one might think of an abortion fantasy, the desire to get rid of the feeling of an alien element rising up threateningly within oneself with vigorous movements. Certainly this interpretation is vague since the scene provides only sparse information. A deeper understanding is only possible from an analysis of a further encounter which I had with Hans after overcoming my feelings of disgust, and which had a positive outcome.

Hans had retired to his room and I found him there crouching on his bed, ruminating continuously. Alone with him in his room, I withdrew into a corner to be as far away from him as possible and first tried to control my feelings of repulsion by breathing deeply in and out. I concentrated on this until my panic subsided and I felt calmer. I also began talking to myself – first, because it helped me to keep calm, and, second, to try and make sense of this unbearable situation in which I found myself locked up in a room with someone I dreaded. I verbalised what I felt: the uncanniness of the situation, my panic, then the gradual lessening of my feelings of nausea through regular breathing; the feeling that through the nausea and disgust, Hans existed; the idea that whatever Hans was and felt I should also experience in my own body; namely, nausea as a kind of inner pressure inside me which sought relief through burping. As I became aware of this projective identificatory process I began to talk about the need for relief, not only for me but also for Hans: I had the impression that he had never known what a relief it could be to burp. (Since I had to assume that Hans' grasp of everyday language was very limited, I did not try to put this in simple 'handicapped-appropriate' words but spoke to him instead as I would with an infant who has ears for the emotional content of the spoken word which he can understand very well in his own way long before the meaning of words becomes important to him (cf. Eliacheff, 1993).) When I had said this, the situation changed radically: I was no longer dominated by disgust; I still felt it but had gained some distance from it in that I now found it meaningful. Achieving greater calmness enabled me to attempt to make an initial contact with Hans: I repeatedly threw a ball to him and then went over to pick it up. This time my approaching him did not drive him away. Instead he allowed it to happen, risked glancing at the ball, and tried to take hold of it. Then he glanced at me out of the corner of his eyes, finally took the ball and let go of it again when I made a gesture for him to do so. As soon as he could release the ball – which I interpreted as the burping and spitting of an infant needing to expel the excess inside him (just as I had been 'too much' for him in our first unsuccessful meeting) – the situation also changed for Hans. He lay down and carefully pulled his blanket over his whole body including his head. His posture was almost the same as it was at the beginning: hands and legs drawn into the body with shoulders rounded – the embryonic position. However, there was one important difference: his head was no longer drawn in and he was now generally relaxed. He stopped ruminating and I heard him breathing deeply and regularly. I sat down next to him, breathing together with him and all the while talking to him about this. He responded by scratching his bed and so I did likewise. A dialogue of great intensity and beauty developed from this scratching and breathing. I gently touched his feet and then his back which was covered by the blanket. I started to feel like a pregnant woman caressing her child tucked away safely in her belly while communicating with it in a vegetative way. I no longer experienced Hans through feelings of disgust and nausea in myself but as a tender object relationship which could be cathected. Our dialogue lasted for some time; finally Hans poked his head out from beneath the blanket and inspected the room with a look of quiet curiosity as if he were looking at it for the very first time.

From my affective involvement, this encounter with Hans can easily be interpreted as a pregnancy scenario, and not only because I eventually fantasised I was pregnant myself. Regurgitation, pressure on the stomach, the desire to breathe deeply, are all vegetative expressions of a pregnancy and birth scene. Hans' eventual emergence from under his bed cover and his calm but attentive look also resembled a birth scene. Thus, one is tempted to look for the first breakdown in the interaction between Hans and his mother during pregnancy, and to regard it as the prototype for the failure of my first attempt to approach him. In the first scene, I tried to ward off the inner pressure filling me with panic by removing Hans from my perception by 'aborting' him. In the original scene I have reconstructed this might have been the pregnant woman's feeling – that the foetus growing inside her was a foreign body creating panic and nausea, threatening her physical and mental integrity and that she must destroy it by vomiting or, more actively, by making strenuous movements which would lead to a miscarriage.

However, the fact that Hans was able to create a regressive scene relatively quickly making it possible for both of us to achieve contact, suggests a different interpretation. This interpretation would be that he fell back on an interaction form that had been successful during pregnancy but for some reason either came to an end after birth or acquired a destructive context at a later point in time. Perhaps it was an encounter accompanied by feelings of uncanniness and insecurity during or after birth which first caused the mother to retrospectively cathect a normal feeling of ambivalence towards pregnancy with feelings of panic and disgust, feelings which I had for Hans when we first met. The counter-projection could have led the mother to react with panic and repulsion to the normal burping and spitting of her infant, insofar as it had become an expression of a killing fantasy through the process of identification. This in turn caused the vital expressions of letting go, releasing and spitting out to become associated with the death-feigning reflex in the infant. This merging of impulse and anxiety response now had even more drastic consequences; namely, an almost complete destruction of symbolic capacity, as in the case of Mr K. In Mr K.'s case, the death-feigning reflex was alloyed with an intentional gesture; in other words, an active impulse which was not completely indispensable as such, since the satisfaction of physical needs was not fundamentally called into question because the impulse became immobilised in the death-feigning reflex. In Hans' case, a vitally indispensable vegetative expression, burping and vomiting, formed an indissoluble bond with the death-feigning reflex. Thus, the vegetative impulse had to find expression in the symptom of rumination in which the irreconcilable contradiction between life needs and mortal threat is maintained for ever. The indispensability of vegetative expression becomes apparent in the perpetual repetition of rumination, whereas death-feigning is realised by the symptom substituting almost totally for active participation in life and (symbolic) interaction.

REFERENCES

Balint, M. (1964) *The Doctor, his Patient and the Illness*, New York, International Universities Press.

Eliacheff, C. (1993) *A corps et à cris. Etre psychanalyste avec les tout-petits*, Paris, Odile Jacob.

Erdheim, M. (1982) *Die gesellschaftliche Produktion von Unbewusstheit, Eine Einführung in den ethnopsychoanalytischen Prozess*, Frankfurt, Suhrhamp.

Freud, S. (1919a) 'The Uncanny', in James Strachey, ed., *The Standard Edition of the Complete Psychological Works of Sigmund Freud*, 24 vols, London, Hogarth, 1953–73, vol. 17, pp.217–74.

Freud, S. (1919b) 'Beyond the Pleasure Principle', *S.E.* 18, pp.3–64.

Gaedt, C. (1990) *Selbstentwertung – depressive Inszenierungen bei Menschen mit geistige Behinderung*, Neuerkerode.

Lincke, H. (1971a) 'Der Ursprung des Ichs', in *Psyche* 25: 1–30.

Lincke, H. (1971b) 'Es-Autonomie und Ich-Entwicklung', in *Psyche* 25: 801–30.

Lorenzer, A. (1972) *Zur Begründung einer materialistischen Sozialisationstheorie*, Frankfurt, Fischer Verlag.

Mannoni, M. (1972) *The Backward Child and his Mother*, trans. A.M. Sheridan Smith, New York, Pantheon.

Niedecken, D. (1989) *Namenlos, Geistig Behinderte verstehen*, München, Piper Verlag (1994 Lizenzausgabe dtv unter 'Geistig Behinderte verstehen').

Sinason, V. (1992) *Mental Handicap and the Human Condition*, London, Tavistock.

Stern, M. (1972) 'Trauma, Todesangst und Furcht vor dem Tod', in *Psyche* 26: 901–28.

Winnicott, D.W. (1960) 'Ego Distortion in Terms of True and False Self', in *The Maturational Process and the Facilitating Environment*, London, Hogarth, 1965, pp.14–52.

8 Psychoanalysis and Mental Retardation: A Question of 'Not-Wanting-To-Know'

CLAIRE MORELLE

INTRODUCTION

The question of knowing lies at the heart of the problematic issue of mental retardation. People with mental retardation are so defined because of the difficulties they face, notably in connection with learning processes. These disabilities limit their capacities to find a place in the society around them, which in turn does not know how to accommodate them.

Mental handicap raises questions related to the epistemophilic instinct and its future as much for the mentally retarded person as for the analyst. The 'not-wanting-to know' expressed in the words 'I don't want to know anything about it' can in fact be true of both of them.

While this chapter is concerned with 'not-knowing', or even with 'not-wanting-to-know' *méconnaissance*[1] (as a form of repression), it seeks to shed light on the obscure field of mental handicap by investigating the unconscious processes which sustain a refusal to know in the mentally handicapped person. The myth of Adam and Eve will serve as our point of departure.

THE MYTH OF ADAM AND EVE

Yahweh puts Adam into the Garden of Eden and surrounds him with living creatures so that he is not alone. Adam gives each of them a name and then wants to give himself a name but he can only do it in the presence of another who is at the same time like him and different from him. Yahweh then creates Eve by taking a rib from Adam's body. 'Then the man said: "this at last is bone of my bones and flesh of my flesh; she shall be called woman because she was taken out of man"' (Genesis 2:23).[2]

There are two special trees in the Garden of Eden: 'the tree of life' and 'the tree of the knowledge of good and evil'. The latter is forbidden by Yahweh who warns Adam: '... but of the tree of the knowledge of good and evil you shall not eat for in the day that you eat of it you shall die' (Genesis 2:17). We know the fate that lay in store: beguiled by the serpent, Eve tastes the forbidden fruit and shares it with her companion in order to acquire the knowledge of good and evil which was reserved for Yahweh alone.

By transgressing, humankind loses its innocence and is henceforth responsible for its own actions. By appropriating a privilege reserved for the gods, humankind suffers the consequences: mortality. The tree of life is jealously guarded and immortality remains the reserve of the gods.

Three fundamental aspects of this myth can be underlined:

- The question of the lack which marks Adams body after a rib was taken from it. As we shall see, the mark of the lack is a fundamental fact for the handicapped person and his family.
- Questions relating to the knowledge of good and evil, that is, that humankind can be held responsible for its actions. This knowledge therefore concerns the subjective position and consequently the question of desire as the motor of action. This knowledge is not to be confused with omniscience. It can be understood from the analytic viewpoint as the access of a desiring subject to unconscious knowledge or, in other words, to the signifiers which sustain its desire.
- Finally, the question of death in the midst of life represented by the tree guarded by the gods or, more precisely, by Yahweh in the myth described above – a tree which guarantees immortality only for the gods.

These three elements will be analysed with respect to the particular problems of handicapped people and their families and illustrated with fragments from cases.

MENTAL RETARDATION AS A MARK OF A LACK IN THE BODY

A person with mental handicap is generally affected in his (or her) ability to adapt to the world around him, to deal with language and to inscribe himself in the symbolic sphere. Being mentally retarded can mean bearing a mark which may or may not be inscribed or not on the real (le réel)[3] of the body, signified by different diagnoses, like a bad omen of an evil fairy at the foot of a new-born baby's cot. The words which define the organic impairment – and therefore the real of the hurt body – can have the status of a label, a signifier detached from meaning and sometimes from representations. The perinatal diagnosis established by medical knowledge and passed on to parents can also constitute a unique signifier, a nomination without recourse, which will define the child by his handicap and involve the family in an inescapable destiny. The diagnosis of *mental deficiency* then becomes prescriptive. The child is bearer of a signifier that he cannot escape from and with which he will attempt to identify, thus ensuring subjection to the debility which has been ascribed to him. Once he has been assigned the label 'deficient', he assures himself of a position as subject by submitting to it.

'I have Down's syndrome', says Damien, evading any questions about the origin of his handicap and his development. Damien rejects the term 'handicapped' which is just for the physically handicapped. Having Down's syndrome 21 is for him a meaningless designation, a pure signifier cut off from the various meanings which the word can carry. Damien does not know either where or when he was born; he lacks primordial symbolic reference points.

Being designated by signifiers such as 'mentally deficient' or 'Down's syndrome' or 'mentally handicapped' throws a handicapped person back onto imaginary identifications constructed on the basis of ideas of mental handicap which circulate in society at large (parents, institutional surroundings, the media, and so on). The so-called *'mentally deficient person'* will attempt to strengthen these identifications on the basis of anything which can represent not-knowing.

Speaking about their handicap and their bodies is a process which proves to be difficult, if not impossible, for handicapped people whose cerebral impairment can justify their incapacity to gain access to the symbolic order. Although part of this symbolic world, they may be incapable of understanding metaphor due to a flaw in their body reality. Parents can then act as a substitute for their incapacity to deal with the symbolic order.

Marked by the lack in the real of his body, deprived of intelligence, mentally handicapped people will sometimes try to avoid symbolic castration, depending on the attitude they take towards this deprivation.

Lang describes the deficient state as a 'psychopathology of lack':[4] 'The problem of the mentally deficient person is situated around a certain intentionality concerning his position as subject and also at the level of a reconstruction based on a functional or relational lack or a lack caused by lesion.' It is then a question of the constituting desire of the subject which can only emerge when the lack is given a name, and this depends on the desire of the Other, usually the mother.

More than any other child, a handicapped child runs the risk of putting himself (or herself) in the position of a satisfying object for the mother. He will not only be an object of his own desire, an object of care, but also an indispensable object for his mother in order to efface her own hurt.[5]

A handicapped child awakens the lack in others. This lack represented in reality by a handicap can prove to be unbearable and lead the mother (usually) to adopt an attitude of extreme solicitude in an attempt to make sense of her life which has been deeply hurt. 'I want to give him everything', 'I don't want him to be in need of anything', 'I don't want him to suffer', are statements heard regularly from parents with a handicapped child which is a way of refusing to accept the impossible by sparing the child from symbolic castration.

If there is a dimension which is specific to analytic work with handicapped people, it is probably concerned with the loss of what is lacking, a lack which is expressed and evoked by its multiple consequences in daily life. Nobody can escape the fact of 'not being all' (*ne pas être tout*), but this question is more crucial for those who are marked in the real (*le réel*) of their bodies. Questions related to lack can find expression in the utterance 'I don't know', an attitude to knowing which is often adopted by handicapped people; an 'I don't know' which is often accompanied by 'I don't want to know'.

MENTAL RETARDATION AS A RESISTANCE TO KNOWING

The epistemophilic impulse

The desire for knowledge, known as the *epistemophilic instinct*, was developed by Freud in his paper 'Leonardo da Vinci and a Memory of his childhood'.[6] Freud describes the destiny of the epistemophilic impulse through the evolution of a man who was to become a genius, Leonardo da Vinci. The thirst to gain knowledge seems to have taken hold of Leonardo when he left his natal village of Vinci to follow his father to Florence at the age of fifteen. Conscious of the huge gaps in his education, he took lessons in drawing and Latin. Leonardo was the illegitimate son of a peasant, Caterina, and the local solicitor, Piero. His father married shortly after his birth in 1452 and placed his son in the care of his grandparents who also lived in Vinci.

If, as Freud thought, the epistemophilic instinct finds its origin and strength in issues related to the primal scene, we can easily imagine the sorts of questions which faced the young Leonardo: 'Who is my father? Who is my mother? What desire was I born of?'

The questions which we attribute to Leonardo to explain his immense thirst for knowledge[7] give us an inkling of two kinds of knowing: one, conscious (related to knowledge), and the other unconscious which is revealed by the former. 'Where do I come from?' calls for an answer as much concerning the reality of procreation as an answer which would attempt to determine the nature of the desire from which the little man originated (the *che voi?* which Lacan takes up in the Graph of Desire).[8]

Intelligence and mental handicap

If in the light of Lacan, debility is considered as a resistance to knowing, nobody is exempt from it. One cannot, however, ignore the specific intellectual impairment affecting certain people who are called 'mentally handicapped'.

Intelligence is generally defined in terms of the capacity to adapt. It facilitates acquisitions and creative activity. It is in the service of self-preservation and is the basis of learning processes which enable the species to survive. It is therefore linked to sexuality. Let us note that this definition is valid both for man and animals.

For Castets,[9] human intelligence is a 'progressive organisational form of the personality'. If we refer to etymology, intelligence concerns the capacity *to read between the lines (inter-legere)* which can be understood as a capacity to move from one signifier to another, to use metaphor, to create within a space defined by the imperatives of language.

An *unintelligent* child provokes his parents into making a knowledgeable being out of him and generally refuses to accept the position of a knowing being. He is given a set of signs which permit him to find his mark in daily life and to allay suspicion. Conditioned for different learning experiences, the question of his own desire is often eluded. While held under a single signifier[10] a handicapped child cannot be introduced to knowledge which concerns the interplay of signifiers and allows for a reading 'between the lines'. According to Bruno, 'The deficient person does not read between the lines of the utterance and the enunciation, but wants to find in the line of the enunciation the ultimate meaning of the utterance.'[11]

Although he is situated in the symbolic field, he cannot be an actor in it. Considered as a person with needs and not as a person of demand, his desire cannot emerge. These are extreme cases – but frequent in institutions – of mentally handicapped people who are made psychotic[12] by the attitude they take towards their handicap and the not-wanting-to-know of those around them grappling with the *étrangeté* of mental handicap.

Resistance to knowing

Very often, Sophie replies to my questions by saying 'I don't know'. This is expressed in a nervous tone which could be heard as 'Leave me alone, I don't want to know anything about it!', but it is important to pay attention to the exact words whose ordinariness can hide what the subject is saying about herself. 'I don't know' is a statement which seems to be closed, an unquestionable fact. As a response to a question it can signify for the other person that the latter possesses knowledge which escapes the former. A mentally deficient person does not 'suppose' the other knows, he places the other in the position of knowing from the outset. The other, or more precisely the Other, is not in the position of a *subject supposed* to know but is seen as a 'knowing subject'. It is probably here that the essential difficulty of treating the mentally handicapped psychoanalytically lies: '... we notice how extremely difficult it is to introduce a mentally deficient person to analytic work: how can one trust in "the other" of whom Lacan speaks, if this other believes that a being can say to himself "therefore I am"?'[13]

A mentally handicapped person can only be satisfied with a certain and absolute knowledge of the Truth. He generally puts the other, most often the mother, in the position of one who knows, with unlimited trust, and regards all speech as absolute and definitive truth.

A person with mental handicap adopts the position of one who does not know and cannot know. Clinical experience provides us with numerous examples where a patient withdraws into mutism when he is questioned in an area which calls for a personal response. Sometimes, affected by the question, he will become anxious and try to avoid it through flight, tantrum or sobbing.

Quite different is the formulation 'I don't know any more'. Even though 'I don't know any more' can mean 'leave me alone', the wording indicates that there is a lack, a lack of words. In his seminar 'Les formations de l'inconscient'[14] Lacan studies the act of forgetting names by taking Freud's famous example of forgetting proper names, in this case Signorelli. 'Forgetting a name is not simply a negation, it is a lack but a lack ... of this name ... this lack in the place where this name should fulfil this function, where it can no longer fulfil it as a new meaning is required which demands a new metaphorical creation.'

The nuance between 'I don't know', so often heard, and 'I don't know any more' is important. In the former, it does not seem to be a matter of addressing the Other in search of more meaning. The lack is fully there, with its whole weight of *jouissance*. It would be a flawless lack to be situated on the side of the real. 'I don't know any more' implies that there has been a loss, a loss of meaning which can be understood as a call to the Other, rich with signifiers, in order to receive additional meaning.

'*I don't want to*', Sophie tells me after a meeting with her mother. Then she says 'Mummy doesn't want to', when it is about her father who died a few years ago. Her mother colludes with a law of silence so that Sophie is not touched by pain any more. 'She's already unhappy enough like that ... I don't want her to suffer.' During the same session Sophie's mother again repeats that Sophie does not suffer from her handicap and that she does not notice it. The mother expresses in this way her own suffering while not allowing her daughter to have contact with hers. Negation turns into denial; so great is the mother's anxiety that her daughter cannot attain the status of subject and therefore of someone who is suffering. Sophie's mother tries to protect her daughter and thereby bars her from any possibility of knowing.

Lacan 'invalidates any definition of mental disability based on deficiency and sees instead a fundamental malaise of the subject with respect to knowing'.[15] A person with a mental disability would be characterised by 'a sustained resistance' to any move forward in the field of knowing; he 'does not allow himself to know', states Bruno.

In Sophie's case the restriction on knowing was bound up with the issue of her dead father. In psychoanalytic work with mentally retarded individuals and their families, the life–death process is generally subjected to the law of silence.

NOT-WANTING-TO KNOW ABOUT DEATH

The statement 'I don't want to know' emerges with its full weight of resistance when speaking of death is involved. The issue of death is notably present when a handicapped child is born or when an anomaly is observed during pregnancy. Abortion, said to be thera-peutic, a gift of death a few hours before the anticipated birth or a few minutes after it has been recognised that the new-born baby has a handicap, and the prolongation of life by medical means – these are examples of the interventions carried out by medical staff required to take a stance towards the life and death issues concerning the handi-capped child. His right to life is questioned in face of the pain and difficulties that the parents will encounter in the educative task ahead. His own life value and potential for happiness are questioned on the basis of criteria related to a so-called *normal* child and the various projections which incite the *strangeness* which is so *uncanny*. The parents do not escape from the contradictions and ambivalence of their own desire. As one father told me: 'When my son is sick and

I have to take him to the hospital, I have the awful thought that he might never come back. What a relief that would be! But I would also be deeply sad.' It is rare that parents can speak so freely about it. Their own death is evoked more often and their fear for their child's future, especially when they are no longer there themselves.

Beyond these conscious questions, there is good reason to examine mental disability as a symptom in its relation to death. A disabled person is generally outside time or in a time which is not disrupted, which is not punctuated by death – immortal time. An analyst cuts time, introducing a scansion by the rhythm of the sessions and their times.

When Damien comes to a session, he begins by getting out his diary, tries to find the last entry – his weekly session – and hands it to me so that I can write down our next appointment. Damien says nothing but regularly reads his name on the cover page of his diary. An almost endless repetitive behaviour which at the same time is an attempt to exist in the transference relationship so that I guarantee him a position and so that he can be a desiring subject. Damien plays at hiding or walks alongside the walls of the room while hiding his face; he avoids the look of others and says he is afraid. Damien is afraid of dying and tries to avoid new situations; he shuts himself in his room listening endlessly to the same music, retreating into rituals aimed at reducing his anxiety. Damien reveals a problematic issue which is similar to obsessional neurosis in its trail of anxieties connected with the ineluctable mortality of man and the means of defence with which he has chosen to counter this anxiety. His troubles are interpreted in terms of madness by his parents who are extremely worried about the future development of their son. Damien cannot experience moments of anxiety without being labelled as mad; furthermore, he cannot ask himself questions about his handicap because he is considered stupid.

Damien has the same first name as one of his father's brothers who died shortly before his birth in dramatic circumstances. Damien's symptoms can be understood as a call for life or as the expression of a subject despite the place of death which was offered to him at birth by the name that was given to him.

CONCLUSION

One of the vital questions for psychoanalytic work with a mentally handicapped person is related to his symbolic inscription, whatever the real impairment with which his body is marked. Psychoanalysis does not challenge the organic impairment but is interested in the body insofar as it can be given a tongue. It can do nothing with a body which is purely an organism. It is interested in the body insofar as it is given a language and a tongue. For a subject, language is the first body, 'the first body makes the second by incorporating itself there'.[16]

The meaning of handicap will be related not to a given medical knowledge but to the signifiers which name it and to the meanings which it comes to carry.

The psychoanalytic treatment of a handicapped person could be supported by the talk of parents called to speak about their child who participates in his own way and according to his possibilities. Even with a profoundly handicapped child, it seems that there is a way of obtaining a response signifying that there is an intersubjective relationship. Noticing a look which catches the eye momentarily, or the beginnings of a smile to communicate with others, can be a premise for the founding of a subjectivity which will probably remain fragile and in a parasitical relationship with the subjectivity of the other, usually the mother. Perhaps it is our (imagined) impotence to transform the mentally deficient person into an intelligent one which leads us to exclude him from treatment. However, treating a person with intellectual impairment does not imply at all that we have to try to improve his performance. We must renounce that in order to transform our impotence into impossibility and our 'not-wanting-to-know' into 'not-knowing'. The recognition of this 'not-knowing' is at the heart of the problematic issue of the so-called mentally deficient person introduced to the desire to know and to the *scilicet*.[17]

NOTES

1. Translator's note: *méconnaissance* is a central Lacanian concept closely linked to *connaissance* (knowledge).
2. *The Bible, R.S.V.* (Translator's note: The original French text is by A. Chouraquia (1985) *L'Univers de la bible*, Paris, Lidis. It reads: 'le glébeux dit: "Celle-ci, cette fois, c'est l'os de mes os, la chair de ma chair, à celle-ci il sera crié femme isha -: oui, de l'homme – Ish – celle-ci est prise."')
3. Translator's note: the Lacanian concept of the real should not be confused with reality. It stands for what cannot be symbolised and is foreclosed from analytic experience.
4. Lang, J.L. (1973) 'Esquisses d'un abord structural des états déficitaires', *Confrontations psychiatriques*, 10: 31–54.
5. It is not simply a question of the hurt which constitutes being human, but also the secondary hurt resulting from the birth of a handicapped child.
6. Freud, S. (1910) 'Leonardo da Vinci and a Memory of his Childhood', in James Strachey, ed., *The Standard Edition of the*

Complete Psychological Works of Sigmund Freud, 24 vols, London, Hogarth, 1953–73, vol. 11, pp.57–137.

7. 'Le souverain bien est le savoir et rien ne peut lui être comparé', wrote Leonardo da Vinci, taken from the cover of Alberti de Mazzeri's book, *Leonardo de Vinci*, Paris, Payot, 1984.

8. Lacan, J. (1990) *Ecrits: A Selection*, London, Routledge.

9. Castets, B. (1964) 'Principes d'une conception structurale de l'arriération mentale', in *Annales médico-psychologiques* 3: 401–26.

10. It should be noted that this single signifier loses its status as a signifier and becomes a sign from the point when it is no longer caught in concatenation.

11. Bruno, P. (1986) 'A côté de la plaque', *Ornicar?* (Paris, Seuil) 37: 38–65.

12. This idea is found in particular in the works of M. Mannoni (1972) *The Backward Child and his Mother*, trans. A.M. Sheridan Smith, New York, Pantheon; and Lacan, J. especially in *Seminar. Book 11*, New York, W.W. Norton, and Bruno, 'A côté de la plaque'.

13. Bruno, 'A côté de la plaque'.

14. Lacan, J. (1957) 'Les formations de l'inconscient', unpublished seminar, meeting of 20 November.

15. Bruno, 'A côté de la plaque'.

16. Lacan, J. (1970) 'Radiophonie', in *Scilicet* 2–3: 55–9.

17. 'Knowing is permitted'.

9 Debility: An Enquiry into Structure

JOOST DEMUYNCK

PRELIMINARY QUESTIONS

Perhaps you will be frightened by the word 'debility'. Indeed, it is only slightly better to speak of 'debility' than, for example, 'mental handicap'. Another description would be: 'the bearer of signs', a concept which I hope will become clearer in the course of my text.

When we speak about 'debility' in a psychoanalytic context, this has nothing to do with a deficiency on an intelligence scale as measured by psychology. Not that psychoanalysis has made significant advances here. The concept 'debility' remains a marginal one. The advantage is, however, that nearly everything remains to be discovered. I would like to invite you to take a few steps with me on this path of discovery. In other words, there are no truths engraved on tablets of stone, but here are some thoughts and propositions I have developed.

First, let me say a few words about the title of this chapter. Classically, psychoanalysis has distinguished between three structures: psychosis, neurosis and perversion. These are the three possible responses to a human lack, to the fact that on the unconscious level a signifier is missing to represent the female sex in language. A woman cannot be represented by the vagina or by the breast. In the unconscious, the female sex is conceived of as the negative of the man's. The phallus, as a signifier of the human lack, represents the male, but for a woman it is conceived of as a reversed glove, inside-out, as it were. Up until now psychoanalysis has accepted that there are three ways of dealing with this lack: foreclosure, denial and repression. The psychotic reacts with a foreclosure of the Name-of-the-father. As you know, this position is not necessarily held by the biological father. The Name-of-the-Father is that position which makes it clear to a child that his (or her) mother has a lack and that the child cannot fulfil for his mother. It is the father who possesses something the mother desires. Faced with this lack, the pervert will react with denial, putting his fetish in place of his mother's lack. As neurotics, we react with repression; we do not wish to know about this lack. Let me illustrate this with three clinical vignettes; each of them about a curious organ, the nose.

A neurotic person comes to a psychoanalyst's consulting room in a state with this startling question: is my nose too small? When his girlfriend broke off with him, she made a vague complaint about his appearance. He interpreted this immediately as meaning that his nose was too small. This idea of an organ that seems too small will be taken at face value in many practices, by which I mean that therapists will take the nose to be the main issue. Thus, they can compare the nose in question with a standard sized nose or send the patient to a surgeon. But to the psychoanalyst this question has a symbolic value. Associations such as protuberance come to mind and this in turn may lead to associations with another organ that could be too small in sexual intercourse. The question this man is asking himself is whether he is man enough to satisfy this other being called woman. In other words, this nose is simply a metaphor for the phallus which may be too small to fill the black hole of the female sex. This man represses this terrifying enigma which comes back to haunt him in the form of a nose which is too small.

The family of a psychotic woman visit a psychoanalyst. The woman has agreed to enter psychoanalysis. Her symptoms have become almost unbearable. All day long she feels compelled to look into mirrors or shop windows when she is out of the house. This need not be an obsessional neurosis. No, the patient is constantly verifying that her nose is still there, that a hole has not appeared in lieu of her nose and that there are no little black spots growing on her face. After a few sessions, it becomes clear to the analyst, though not to her, that her father had given her the nickname 'little nose' as a child. As you can see, the foreclosure of the Name-of-the-Father comes back as a real hole in lieu of her nose.

The third type is the pervert whom we seldom meet in our practices. Here is an example from Freud himself (1927, p.311). There was this remarkable man whose fetish was a special shine on his partners' noses. In analysis, it became obvious that shine (*'Glanz auf der Nase'*) had to be read as 'glance'. In his early childhood the man had been educated in English. So *'Glanz'* is 'glance'; he was casting a glance, poking his nose under his mother's petticoat. This fetish, the shine on the nose, is a denial of female castration. The pervert has erected a memorial in which the castration is at once recognised and denied.

I hope that these fragments give you an idea of the three fundamental psychic structures recognised in psychoanalysis. Today, I cannot say that debility is a new structure; that would be too pretentious. Before this could be postulated, a lot of questions would have to be answered.

I believe that it is possible to speak of debility in two ways: either as a phenomenon which accompanies each of the three structures, or as something quite separate. According to the first hypothesis, one would have something like pseudo-debility or a debility that hides a neurosis. Debility as a symptom of the parents. This symptom can be the expression of a family secret that has to be kept hidden, something they do not want others to know about and of which the child is the expression. In his study of Leonardo da Vinci, Freud (1910) also spoke of debility. Freud linked early childish inquisitiveness with sexual curiosity. When this curiosity is repressed, inquisitiveness shares the same destiny. The desire for knowledge becomes restricted as well as intelligence and all this leads to debility, or 'Denkschwäche' as Freud called it (1905a).

At the other end, there is psychosis. In this case, one thinks of the foreclosure of the Name-of-the-Father, with the child being trapped in the mother's phantasm. Maud Mannoni (1972), for example, takes this approach.

The second unexplored possibility is that debility is distinct from all other structures and has its own mechanism for dealing with castration.

Lacan never argued that debility was a new or fourth structure. He proved that we are all affected by debility, himself included. We are all affected by debility in as far as we do not want to know. If we are all affected, then it is interesting to examine the differences that exist. Let us begin with ourselves. We are repressing the lack. Indeed, certainly in institutions, we as educators are required or expected to know, to have an answer ready for every possible question. If we do not, we feel like failures. Really, we ought to stop acting as if we know everything. Things start to get interesting only when we try to find out what we do not want to know and what the causes are.

Furthermore, the person affected by debility is waiting for us, smiling. He is a genius. A genius in his persistent refusal of and resistance to knowledge. This could be a definition of debility. We are no longer interested in intelligence scales or quotients and their shortcomings but with the 'not-wanting-to-know' and its causes. When I say 'genius', I mean by this that debility affects the whole person. I will now try to show how the whole person is totally affected by it.

LANGUAGE

Language is the first element. This cannot be emphasised enough. The language of a person affected by debility is a sign language. This means that there is a strict relation between a word and a meaning.

The figure of speech here is a restricted metonymy; in fact, it is constituted by a concatenation of signs. Let me try to explain. As neurotics, we use the language of signifiers. We are in a network of signifiers. Language precedes us as individuals and we are submitted to it. It is typical of our language that *one* signifier on its own has no meaning. Signification is only produced through the presence of a second signifier. With each new signifier we have a new signification, for example: I find ... / this ... / terrible ... / interesting ... .

We call a metonymy the relation of one word to another word. In metonymy, the signification is postponed. The figure of speech which brings us significations is the metaphor. Poetry uses metaphors like 'heaven is crying'. One word is substituted for another. These two devices are at work in our language and can only function with a lack, just as in a game when you have to move pieces to form a word or a picture, you can only move to a space which is empty. Thus, we have humour which thrives on ambiguities. Since there is no signifier which has a fixed signification, it can have two, three or endless significations.

Here is a joke told by Freud(1905b, p.41): People could not agree on how a particular couple had become rich. For some the man had worked hard and earned a lot of money – he had laid aside a bit (*sich etwas zurückgelegt*). For others, the woman had lain back a bit (*sich zurücklegen*) and earned a lot.

A person affected by disability cannot understand this kind of joke. His humour is a sign humour. An educator who falls down the stairs or who drops a pile of plates are favourites for him. This is only possible when his language functions in another way than ours. First of all, people affected by debility understand everything literally. Metaphors do not work. Perhaps they will know the various meanings of a word which they learn but these different significations will actually be perceived as quite separate signs. A young woman will give you three meanings for the word 'rose'. However, the significations will be kept as separate signs and will never function as a metaphor, at least, not for her. I shall give you an example which I cannot easily translate into English but the meaning of which I expect you will understand. In Flemish, a rich aunt from whom one expects to inherit is called a 'sweet aunt' or a 'sugar aunt'. An educator was joking with Ria saying that her cousin was very lucky to have such a nice 'sugar aunt' as her. Ria promptly replied: 'I can't eat sugar, because it isn't good for my diet.'

DESIRE

A second element makes explicit the question whether a 'sign-bearer' has a desire. A desire longs for an object which is lost and which one expects to fulfil the desire. As beings who speak (*parlêtres*), we never reach this object again; it has gone for ever. Well, our 'sign-bearer' translates each desire into a need. A need has a specific object which can satisfy this need. The success of a holiday can be measured by the food, meals, drinks, and so on. So the symbolic lack does not exist for the 'bearer of signs'. At a certain moment in the oedipal stage and castration complex, an object becomes a sign for the mother's love. So a child goes from an imaginary lack (frustration) to a real lack (privation) and ends up with a symbolic lack (castration).

All this requires another explanation to show how our 'bearer of signs' is somewhere between frustration and privation. I should like to describe the mechanism in debility with a neologism '*mistification*'. The lack is obscured, is in the mist but is also mystified; that means that the 'sign-bearer' believes in the Other (with a capital 'O'). The total other without any lack. Instead of a desire (singular), there are needs. This may seem an extreme statement. Do mentally handicapped adults have no desire? Well, to put it somewhat differently, one must confess that there can be a desire. The only question is: To whom does this desire belong? In most cases it is the desire of their mirror-figure, the parental couple or the educator who is the object of a transference. In other words, their desire will be someone else's. As I mentioned earlier, they are geniuses in finding out what others expect from them. One can speak of a kind of mimicry here – they change their colour depending on the subsoil on which they find their food. The emphasis on the imaginary is fundamental to all considerations concerning 'debility'.

THE IMAGINARY

That there are some consequences for our clinical practice is obvious. Most educators will have had the experience of being played off against parents. The 'bearer of signs' will confirm what his parents tell him while he is with them and will assert the opposite in your presence. One can go for confrontation and invite all participants to express their point of view. While everyone is sitting around a table, our resident will behave like a lamb impervious to the discussion, and will not understand what others are telling him. He will simply have none of it.

Another example illustrates their many quarrels and fits of jealousy. While the symbolic does not function appropriately, many of their quarrels may end up in fights. The impulse to act out is never more than one step away. The other is their mirror-other, similar-other, and as soon as he presents something which the 'bearer of signs' sees as providing '*jouissance*' (a sort of total satisfaction) and a certain totality, then he wants it and has to get hold of it. If one resident is sitting next to another and both seem to be having fun, to be happy, then a third one will try to disturb this idyllic picture in order to participate in it. When you point out where he is going wrong, you will not only experience how he hides in ignorance but also how he will try to find a similar fault in you.

Mirror-effects and reflections are always there to be grasped.

THE UNCONSCIOUS

Can we speak of an unconscious for our subject? Let us remind ourselves of the definition Lacan (1973, 1990, 1991) gives us concerning the unconscious: it is structured like a language. This means that the unconscious is working with metonymy and metaphors. These two devices are clearly recognisable in dreams. Censorship in dreams uses these two devices. This is similar for a symptom. A symptom is a metaphor and always has its language support. When put into words it acquires meaning. The 'unconscious' in debility is always open; there is no repression, properly speaking. It would be more exact to speak of 'preconscious', but further research is needed. If the proposition that the unconscious is structured like a language is correct, then it is obvious in the case of debility that it is structured in the same way as signs are, in which *one* element means *one* thing. Therefore their dreams can easily be understood, just like Freud's daughter Anna dreaming of strawberries. Should we say that their wishes are simply needs?

THE COUPLE

One of the postulates of Pierre Bruno (1986) is that people affected by debility believe in couples. I want to add the signifier '*couplélation*'. This means that he believes in the existence of the sexual relationship. Every couple is a pair. He thinks about the sexes in terms of a female socket and a plug, one can connect them for ever. A man affected by debility says he has a right to a woman and will address himself to God in the person of a priest to ask him for a woman. He is angry with parents who do not want him to have children with their daughters. He believes in what Freud calls '*Ganze Sexualstrebung*'. He believes in a satisfaction which is total, devoid of any lack or problem such as one observes with animals under the form of an instinct. Human beings do not have instincts but drives, and to be more precise, partial drives (*Triebe*).

But there is another couple, the parental couple, that exists as such for him. One can ask oneself whether this couple is not primary to the other couple (man–woman). The question I want to put here, is whether we can speak of an oedipal relationship. Is the oedipal process the same as that which pertains to neurotics. And if there is one, how is it structured?

What I would like to propose very carefully, is that we cannot speak of a normal oedipal relationship. I want to present the oedipal process of the 'sign-bearer' as a relationship between the subject and a couple in which there can be distinction but not separation. My proposition is that, on the one hand, there is the parent of the opposite sex who has become the specialist concerning the handicap and, on the other hand, the parent of the same sex who is the imaginary identification figure. This means that a subject's symptoms will be the same as those of the parent of the same sex. A child whose father is obsessive will also be obsessive. A real third position such as the Name-of-the-Father is lacking. But if we are speaking of a couple, then this means that positions in this couple can be changed. For example, after one of the parents has died, you can observe that the other will take over all the positions. In this respect, it would be very interesting to examine their mourning process more closely.

Let us return to Ria. It is the mother who acts as spokesman. Her husband seems to adopt an inferior role, although it is the father who cares for his daughter at weekends and soothes her with all kinds of salves. It is he who worries about the gravity of her epileptic fits. It is the mother who serves as a figure of identification. Ria has the same haircut and diet as her, and, at home, she does the same domestic jobs.

But this defective oedipal situation signifies something more essential. When the opposite-sexed parent becomes the specialist in the handicap, then the choice of a male or female role will not be questioned. In other words, the important questions for the neurotic, such as whether 'a man is man enough', or 'what does it mean to be a woman', will not arise.

This does not mean that on an imaginary level persons affected by debility will not identify themselves with an educator who is getting married or a sister who is pregnant. These are opportunities by which they are expressing their wishes to marry or to get pregnant. But we should know that they are not divided by these questions. The question which is of foremost importance concerns their real lack: their handicap. With this they identify themselves.

REPETITION

Finally, I would like to point out that there is a lot of repetition in their speech and behaviour. In the talk of mentally handicapped people, repetition is obvious in the form of recurring refrains. These kinds of statements or even questions are not even meant to be answered. 'Are you coming on Friday? You are not coming on Friday.' 'How are you? It's cold today. My mother said: always wear a scarf.' Often they are repeating memories. Hilaire is looking for the same wooden alarm clock he had when his parents were alive. Whereas the object we have lost causes our desire, their object is very concrete.

These are some characteristics of debility. Of course, there are other aspects that I have not mentioned. More specific observations could be added regarding the mirrror stage, the nature of their drives and so on.

THE INSTITUTION

How can we handle the question of debility in an institution? Psychoanalysis, as you know, has nothing to do with tricks. But are there general guidelines for use in institutions? We know that our 'bearer of signs' wants to satisfy the desire of the Other. He wants to identify himself with it. That questions the identity of our institution. What are our goals and ideals? These ideals are not always so obvious. Is it to play the role of the all-providing mother? Can we as an institution admit to having lacks? If not, suffocating relationships will develop for those who are living and working in that institution. Another ideal could be the love of one's neighbour. This means unconsciously: 'You have to correspond to the image we think is good for you.'

As institutions we provide care, and, in many cases, total care. No escape is possible. We take care of holidays, washing, meals, death insurance, and so on. In other words, if you want to change 'needing beings' into 'desiring beings', you cannot meet all needs. Lack has to exist in an institution, beginning with one's own lack. But how can you stimulate another person to experience his desire? Well, it is of the utmost importance to be in touch with one's own desire. However, this is not easy. We, too, prefer to remain ignorant of our own desire – unless we have had analysis, of course.

A lot of people do not want to take their responsibilities and hide behind various alibis to remain ignorant of their desire. If as an educator you want to let your desire be, then perhaps it will not be that of educating itself – which is an impossible profession, as Freud said. A desire can be met in workshops and ateliers. The educator's desire is the motor and when this desire is questioned, then a person affected by debility can develop their own desire.

Another lesson is: do not put yourself constantly in the position of 'master', otherwise you run a great risk of reinforcing the debility.

Our mentally handicapped person is always more interested in a fly buzzing around than in your *exposé*. Speaking from the position of a master is to confirm debility.

There is another social relationship we call 'the analytic discourse'. It is not so much speaking, as listening to the signifiers, which escapes our residents. It is grasping those signifiers which do not fit into the context. By playing them back, there is a chance for subjectivation. It can enable a lack to emerge and facilitate access to our 'signifier language'.

Psychoanalysis is a matter of ethical choice and not of politics.

REFERENCES

Bruno, P. (1986) 'A côté de la plaque', in *Ornicar* 37, Paris, Seuil.

Freud, S. (1905a) 'Three Essays on the Theory of Sexuality', in James Strachey, ed., *The Standard Edition of the Complete Psychological Works of Sigmund Freud*, 24 vols, London, Hogarth, 1953–73, vol. 7, pp.123–243.

Freud, S. (1905b) 'Jokes and their Relation to the Unconscious', *S.E.* 8, pp.1–49.

Freud, S. (1910) 'Leonardo da Vinci and a Memory of his Childhood', *S.E.* 11, pp.57–137.

Freud, S. (1927) 'Fetishism', *S.E.* 21, pp.147–57.

Lacan, J. (1990) *Ecrits: A Selection*, London, Routledge.

Lacan, J. (1973) 'Les séminaires', Livre XXVI (unpublished).

Lacan, J. (1991) *Seminar. Book 1: Freud's Papers on Technique*, New York, Pantheon.

Mannoni, M. (1972) *The Backward Child and his Mother*, trans A.M. Sheridan Smith, New York, Pantheon.

10 James and the Construction of Identity

MARC PATTYN

INTRODUCTION

The use of diagnostic labels tends to have a function of holding. It is an attempt to deal with the unknown, unpredictable and mixed emotions aroused by the blunt confrontation with the stranger that the other is. Diagnosis brings order and structure, especially in the chaotic and vague area of psychopathological phenomena with people with learning disorders.

In the following case I try to explain diagnostic enquiries as transferential phenomena in the relationship between a deeply disturbed patient and the institutional environment.

History

Early history

James was twenty-three years old when he arrived at the Institute for Adults with Learning Disorders. His Terman-Merrill IQ was 34; nevertheless, he talked and discussed at a higher level. He is the invalid half of twins; his brother is an unemployed photographer, his father is a salesman and his mother is a housewife.

At birth he suffered from anorexia. Because he was premature and had feeding difficulties, he had to stay in an incubator for three months. When he was three, he suffered an epileptic fit.

He went to a special school, but at the age of fifteen his parents were obliged to orientate him towards a residential setting because of behavioural problems. These problems consisted mainly of difficulties in attention and concentration. In addition, he was very stubborn and often disobedient. At that time he was labelled as 'hyperkinetic', nowadays known as Attention Deficit and Hyperactivity Disorder

(ADHD). The use of clear rules and an informal style seemed to contain him. He was described as a curious, charming and adventurous boy who needed a warm but structured environment.

Now that he has been in our institution a year, we understand that James has severe psychopathological problems. In this review I will distinguish and describe five periods. Each period is coloured by a specific pathology, diagnosis and treatment.

The first period: 'the need to manage everything'

The first period began a few weeks after his arrival. He was a very nervous man, who did five things at the same time, without doing any of them well. He wandered around the institute, opening every door and moving any objects in sight. He had an exaggerated sense of responsibility. It was as if he had to solve every problem and to manage everything himself. There was a great deal of ego-inflation. His work in the garden was a complete disaster; when the monitor was absent for five minutes after leaving strict instructions, James left our garden to do all the other gardens in the street. It was as if the whole world was his. In contrast with this uninhibited behaviour, he seemed to have everything under control within his own logical frame of reference. He rationalised every failure with a 'logical' and 'consistent' explanation. If one tried to argue with him, one lost the argument at the outset.

The consultant psychiatrist regarded his phantasies of saving the world as a defence against a delusional fear of the end of the world. During therapeutic sessions depressive feelings and moods could be recognised. Besides these manic and/or depressive tendencies we formulated the hypothesis of a masked autistic core: talking without a real dialogue, handling people like objects, ignoring limits.

Both he and his parents were against therapy with neuroleptics. They had confidence only in a doctor who had formerly treated his epilepsy. We varied his daily activities. James had to sort out and order different objects. The working and living areas were now in the same building. Our approach at this stage was one of strictness without resorting to punishment.

The second period: 'passion'

The second period began after the summer. There was an escalation of problems. His feelings for a female resident, Daisy, took on an obsessive character. Although she had a steady relationship with another man, she could not refuse his advances and enjoyed them. He would follow her everywhere. He tried to solve all her problems:

'I have to look after her, because her lover-boy might abuse her.' He spoon-fed her and sang songs at her bedroom window. When she tried to resist, he became angry and aggressive. He was convinced that he knew what she needed.

Was she the missing link in his broken mirror? Was she the one who gave him back the lost feeling of wholeness? Or was it a temporary and passionate love affair, marked by a disturbed sense of reality? What did it mean when he showed Daisy a photograph of his mother when she was young, demanding that she have the same hairstyle? (In Dutch 'her' and 'hair' is the same word, 'haar'.)

I started seeing James regularly. I soon discovered that the *only* way to reach him and to establish a dialogue was by maintaining a kind of negotiating attitude. It was his word against mine ('I have to take care of her, so I can't go to work.' 'You do not have to do this.'), but I was careful not to adopt a dominating stance towards him in order to avoid a repetition of what he was doing with Daisy. At this stage we could see elements of a rather perverse structure. He admitted that he overdid things and ignored rules, but at the same time he asked us about our own opinions, wishes and emotions. 'Aren't you the same? If you thought a little bit harder, you would agree with me.'

Looking at the family structure and history, we could see, for example, how his mother cared for him, washed him, organised his activities, in the same way he cared for Daisy. The father's role was vague. He was always at work when James went home. James' twin brother also took care of him, but was very often annoyed by his 'child-like' behaviour. For example, it was hard for him to take James with him when he met his friends. For instance, James' brother's girlfriend had the same name – a variant of the name 'Daisy' – as James' monitor at work. One of the monitors had discovered that James tended to be obedient when we informed his mother of his inadequate behaviour.

At this stage we are trying to discern the meaning of his overwhelming behaviour. With this hermeneutic approach we are trying to explore the context of the family construction. We are hard put to believe that his way of existing and behaving is the consequence of a mental disability.

The third period: 'backwards'

In spite of our attempts to understand his behaviour, we were losing our grip. During the autumn he hardly went to work at all. We noticed a great deal of aggression towards Daisy, her boyfriend and those monitors who made remarks about him. He rarely ate or slept, and neglected his hygiene such as washing, shaving or changing his clothes.

Moreover, he was very much preoccupied with female themes. He wanted to know everything about being a woman. He even wore panty hose and dresses. What was even more bizarre, he ate nothing but oranges to give himself diarrhoea so that he would have to use sanitary towels. In this context I want to mention that James is one of the first three male residents in the institution.

The fourth period: psychiatry

At this point we decided to send him to a psychiatric ward for people with a mental handicap. We wanted him to be observed more closely and to have a thorough psychiatric examination.

After a four-month observation period, the psychiatrists emphasised the importance of the organic handicap. The attention disorder, lack of concentration and memory deficiency were causing the manifest chaotic behaviour. It was impossible for him to learn anything. He could not handle the consequences of his behaviour. Therefore, the therapeutic framework should be based on a kind of token system, not attempting to change his behaviour or to avoid abnormal behaviour, but creating a network that would contain him and provide those around him with a therapeutic tool.

And now?

He returned two months ago. When he goes to work and stays there, he receives a token ('ten'). He needs a certain number of tokens if he wants to leave for the weekend. When he leaves work too early, the monitor does not go after him as he used to do each time James left work and started wandering around. Now, no one goes after him, but if he is seen by anyone, he is sent back to where he belongs.

The father is confirmed in his role as a father in two ways. First, he always receives the book of tokens and has to sign it. Second, James goes home only when both parents are present. He has a personal tutor who functions as a 'policeman': he supervises James' movements in the institute and serves as the link with the work unit as well as the parents.

James has moved to another living unit and his relationship with Daisy is strictly forbidden. We avoid discussions with him. We set limits and there is no possibility of arguing about them. His verbal capacities are more developed than those of the other people in the new unit. So he does not have to prove himself and he can take care of the others who are more dependent. This system seems to be working for the moment. He likes to be in his living unit and goes to work regularly. He wanders around less. It is easier for the environment and the family to hold him.

But the bizarre sexual behaviour described above continues to be a problem. For example, he steals underwearnot only to wear it but also to damage itby cutting out the nipples from bras. He is also preoccupied with blood and pricks himself with needles:'Have I got blood everywhere?' This kind of pathology seems to have come to the fore since the other manic-like forms of behaviour have diminished. He also talks more about himself.

Discussion

TRANSFERENCE

As we reviewed the case, it occurred to us that over the past year many diagnostic labels had been used: ADHD, manic-depressive disorder, autism, perversity, organic disorder, psychosis. They are not just labels. There was also a question about his psychic structure, that is, psychotic or perverse? This is partly to do with the variety of symptoms involved as well as a certain disharmony in the clinical phenomena, but is perhaps also a matter of transference.

James differs in two ways from our other clients. First of all, there is his verbal capacity, especially his power to convince and overwhelm others with logical and consistent reasoning. 'You can't resist him', has become a cliché. It is rather uncommon to find a person with a mental handicap who out-argues you. Unconsciously we have overestimated this verbal dimension. Second, we cannot deny the fact that he affects us in our own lives, our desires and conflicts. 'I want to look after her, after the sick ones, after the helpless ones', and 'I love her, I will do everything for her.' We recognise our own Don Quixote ideals as human beings and certainly as social workers.

Our images of James were coloured by our latent denial of his mental handicap; his social and verbal skills confirmed his wish not to be a person with a mental handicap. And so at a certain level, we denied the underlying psychopathological process.

THE PSYCHOPATHOLOGICAL PROCESS

To understand this process, I shall review the history again, and in particular the three periods before hospitalisation. I ask the following questions: What is the main theme of each period or phase? Which anxiety and which kind of behaviour is the most peculiar?

Three periods

In the first period he was dominated by the thought that he had to manage everything because there were so many things that could go wrong. He was anxious about what might happen but he had no fear of danger. He took many risks but could not foresee the consequences. He was always trying to control things, to reorganise, to look for solutions to problems which were real but not as dramatic as he supposed In a shop, he opened a packet of biscuits to see if the contents were as described. If the electrician had temporarily left some wires uncovered in a hole in the wall, he would fill in the hole.

In the second period, he had to look after Daisy. He was her tutor and her saviour. He had to stay with her because something might go wrong; so he chained her bicycle to the wall and threw the key away and tied his bathrobe around hers. He was obsessed with her, but only when she was present. When she was not there, he was calmer.

In the third period, which was just prior to his admission to the psychiatric hospital, he was preoccupied with the question of what it meant to be a woman. He wanted to feel like a woman, so he asked the female tutors very intimate things about women; he became very intimate. At first most of them wanted to give him educational information about sexuality and reinforce his interests. But he also wanted to dress like a woman. He found panty hose and sanitary towels soft and warm. On the other hand, he was destructive; he mutilated himself and damaged underwear as a female attribute.

Significant themes

In fact, the process is cumulative. In the third period, the theme of the first was still present. It was clear that the themes and anxiety had become increasingly focused. At first, he was preoccupied with everything, then with Daisy, and then with himself, his body. His field of interest has become smaller and more centred on himself.

We wish to call these themes delusional thoughts. There is still a link with reality, but the main characteristic of these thoughts is their form. What he says is the truth. You cannot argue with him. But it is all locked up in his own logic. Let us not forget that intellectual disability colours the construction of a delusion. As delusions are cognitive disorders, it might be forgotten that people with learning difficulties can have delusions. His aggression increased; at first, only when other people made remarks, then in his protection of Daisy and finally in his self-mutilation. We thought that this was the result of an increased amount of anxiety.

His behaviour, in each period, was uninhibited, but was characterised by compulsivity: he had to control everything, including
Daisy and his own body, because nothing could be taken for granted.
Everything and everybody could move and change. The distance
between him and others had become minimal and he seemed to lose
control over his own body (blood). The circle was closed.

Interpretation

His delusional thoughts increasingly concerned his own person, his
own body. He became increasingly anxious and aggressive. His
compulsive behaviour risked turning into self-mutilation. I will now
try to integrate the above findings with certain concepts from the
psychoanalytic theory of psychosis.

Freud points out that at a certain moment in the psychotic process
there is a withdrawal of libido from the objects to the ego; psychosis
is viewed as a regression to primary narcissism, which has not been
renounced completely (Freud 1914).

In the last period James was preoccupied with his body. The
female 'things', like the dresses and the underwear, referred to the
dynamic movement of 'opening' and 'closing', of 'opening' and
'covering the holes'. They were not used as a fetish, but as a surro-
gate for what was lost.

Obsession with faeces can refer to the compulsive way of controlling what can be lost: the use of sanitary towels to contain what has
left the body. This is a kind of ultimate anal fixation.

We presumed there was a lot of basic anxiety and great fear of the
body falling apart. In Kleinian terms, he was trying to differentiate
between the good and the bad object because he could not integrate
the whole object with his good and bad feelings (cf. the depressive
position). This differentiation is so difficult and so artificial that the
result is fragile and can lead to a further fragmentation of the ego
(Klein 1946).

Looking back at his early years, we had to take into account his
relationship with his twin brother. From the start, there was a great
difference between them. James had a difficult birth and eating
problems, with mental disability as a result. His brother enjoyed
good health and grew up as a normal person. Nevertheless, there had
always been a great physical resemblance.

The girl he was obsessed with had the same name as his brother's
girlfriend; they even shared the same hobby, photography. The eye
was always present. We found it again in the glasses which James did
not want to wear when he was upset. We also found it in the father's
hobby, painting.

Probably, James' twin brother functioned as a mirror. On the one hand, there was a confrontation with their physical resemblance, but on the other hand, there was a great difference from the start. One recognises parts of an imaginary identification in James' attempts to have the same life as his brother. Even the transference problem in the diagnostic process, as described earlier, had an imaginary character.

But the psychic structure described above refers to a massive defence against fragmentation, as if there has not been an (imaginary) experience of the body as a unity. This may explain his preoccupation with the literal differences between the sexes. It is a horrifying difference; there has not been any symbolisation or even any imagination. I want to finish with the following dialogue as an illustration of this deficient process.

James: 'How many boys and girls are there in the institution?'
Monitor: 'There aren't boys and girls here, there are only adults, men and women.'
James: 'But how ... what's the difference between them, between girls and women? How can they do this, how do they become ... I don't know.'

REFERENCES

Freud, S. (1914) 'On Narcissism. An Introduction', in James Strachey, ed., *The Standard Edition of the Complete Psychological Works of Sigmund Freud*, 24 vols, London, Hogarth, 1953–73, vol. 14, pp.67–102.
Klein, M. (1946) 'Notes on some Schizoid Mechanisms', *International Journal of Psychoanalysis*, 27: 99–110.

11 The Brothers and Sisters of Handicapped People: Suffering which can be Relieved

REGINE SCELLES

As a clinical psychologist working in a Service for Specialised Care and Education at Home, I detected the suffering of the brothers and sisters of handicapped children whom I followed, occasionally witnessing an escalation in the seriousness of their symptoms. Sometimes, after being particularly good, over-concerned about the well-being of their parents and of their deficient sibling, they would become aggressive, inhibited or, on the contrary, hyperactive. Sometimes their school results would suddenly deteriorate and sometimes they were depressed. Some of the very active ones would make the handicapped children 'work' intellectually or physically, thereby entering into rivalry with the professional staff and their parents.

In certain non-French-speaking milieux, one of the children, generally the eldest, would serve as 'translator' and 'coerced intermediary' between the family and the treatment centre. The importance of this 'child translator' for the treatment could be such that whoever was assigned this role could not get out of it unless one of the other siblings replaced them.

If staff took interest in the way in which parents were affected by the birth of a handicapped child and reflected on how to help them cope with this painful trauma, they did not do as much where the impact of the handicap on the non-handicapped children in the family was concerned. For example, a circular letter giving notification of a handicap[1] and distributed to maternity wards does not mention the brothers and sisters of a baby born with a deficiency. The fact is, when parents or staff notice signs of suffering in the siblings, they tend to say nothing, as in most cases they do not know what to do.

Marcelli[2] considers that the reactions and suffering of brothers and sisters depends on how parents deal psychically with the presence of their handicapped child. Ferrari et al. make a connection between the lack of research into the siblings of handicapped children and the silence of parents on the subject: 'This silence (parental) concerning siblings is of course a defence aimed at protecting familial and parental narcissism and deserves as such to be respected.'[3]

If parents say nothing because they fear that their deficient child will be experienced as having a contaminating influence on the siblings or will tarnish even more the image others have of them as well as their self-image, it also has to be recognised that they are rarely encouraged to speak about this aspect of family life with staff. It is generally only after vain calls for help have been received from children and when sufficiently severe symptoms manifest themselves and can no longer be ignored, that staff intervene.

If one asks oneself how a child is affected by the handicap of a brother or sister, one is obliged to think about *handicap* and *fraternal ties*. That also means thinking about how an individual deals psychically with the confrontation with this person who is *different* from him (or her), (in the relationship each has with the norm), and who is *similar* (in that he is human, has the same parents and belongs to the same generation).

As all children do, the brothers and sisters of handicapped children face psychic conflicts which are born of the complex relations they have with their parents and each one of the siblings. Furthermore, on several occasions during the course of my clinical practice, it appeared that attributing responsibility to the handicapped child for the outbreak of symptoms served the other children by masking the role played by other family members in the genesis of their symptoms (parental divorce, jealousy of another child in the family, and so on). Therefore, it is necessary to consider what is said by subjects who have a handicapped peer within the more general context of theories on fraternal ties.

By going beyond a simple description of observed facts, psychoanalytic theory allows us to account for intrapsychic dynamics and the manner in which they are affected by aspects of external 'reality', and to analyse the vertical and horizontal dimension of fraternal relations as well as the interaction which occurs between them.

For the brothers and sisters, a handicap signifies the impact that this affliction has on the dynamics of the psychic life of each family member and on the family as a whole, the limits and sufferings it generates in their peer, the way they perceive it in the eyes of others and finally the way they are affected by it themselves.

On the basis of cases involving brothers and sisters, often very young, that I have seen in my clinical work, and of research interviews conducted mainly with adults, I will show that the processes of identification and separation between siblings are problematic. Furthermore, inability to speak about their feelings and questions concerning the condition can compromise their future, sometimes seriously.

SIBLING TIES

If the relations between parents and children exert a determining influence on the future and psychic structuring of subjects, it is no less true that the identity, social relationships, affective and professional life of the latter also bear the stamp of fraternal ties experienced in childhood.

Brothers and sisters belong to the same generation; each one of them is born at a precise moment in their parents' history. Their resemblance with one or other of the members of the wider family, the circumstances of their conception and birth gives each one a special place in the family. Each child metabolises and integrates the projections he receives, and adopts a stance towards his siblings, themselves objects of parental projections.

When Freud (for whom fraternal ties is a minor theme compared with other issues like the incest taboo) speaks of the 'family complex', he sees it as an extension of the Oedipus complex.

> A boy may transfer onto his sister the love which he formerly felt for his mother whose infidelity so profoundly hurt him ... The little sister substitutes her older brother for her father who no longer shows her the same tenderness as before, or she substitutes her youngest sister for the child that she had desired in vain from her father.[4]

As a result, fraternal relations could only be evoked in analytic treatment as a defence overshadowing an oedipal problem causing guilt and suffering.

Freud affirms the existence of a primary propensity for aggressiveness in human beings. For him,[5] hate and fratricidal wishes come first and fraternal solidarity is a formation reaction which induces the rivals – objects of hate – to become allies. He analyses the 'hordal myth' as follows: in order to prevent fraternal rivalry from leading them once again to kill their father, the brothers share the prohibition against patricide, turning their hate and jealousy into solidarity. In exchange, each of them appropriates symbolically a bit of the paternal power by identifying with their begetter. It is because they cannot rival their brothers and sisters without causing damage that the transformation of their hate into solidarity and complicity is necessary.

Brusset[6] observes that in small groups a reactualisation of fraternal transference often appears which is different from oedipal transference in the sense that it involves an individual's narcissistic problems, personal identifications, bisexuality or conflicts linked with activity and passivity.

The role of siblings in the psychic maturation of individuals has received renewed interest as a result of the research of Burlingham, Freud[7] and Bowlby.[8] According to the latter, if the satisfaction of the need for food is indispensable for a child's survival, social contacts are necessary for developing his intelligence and establishing satisfying social relationships. These two needs do not proceed from each other as Freud and Spitz supposed.[9]

For Lacan,[10] the setting-up of triangulation – me/my brother who I am jealous of/my mother – object of my love – obliges a child to substitute specular ambiguity for the rivalry involved in a triangular situation. Before becoming conscious of the existence of a brother or sister, a child recognises that he is not his mother's whole world, that others solicit her attention and need her too. Seeing her act independently of him, a child realises that he does not have unlimited power over her. Frustrated by this, he consoles himself by becoming attached to other persons, distancing himself from his mother while at the same time experiencing a *rapprochement* with her; for, like her, he loves other people and is loved by them in turn.

GUILT AND THE DYNAMICS OF SIBLING TIES

The hate and guilt mentioned by the brothers and sisters of handicapped people cannot be dissociated from the meaning and function these feelings have in our culture.

Guilt does not necessarily relate to a 'real' fault. In effect, when confronted with something which is beyond him, which he does not understand, which happens unexpectedly, an individual will try to control what is happening to him even if it sometimes entails arranging things so that he, or someone close, feels responsible for it. Indeed, chance and absurdity are anxiety producing because they take away the power of the individual to prevent the error from repeating itself and make him painfully aware of his powerlessness to control and foresee what happens to him.

The impact of guilt on the psychic life of brothers and sisters cannot be understood without reference to the manner in which they succeed in dealing with fraternal aggressivity and without taking into consideration their difficulty in not submitting to a tyrannical superego, an inaccessible ego-ideal which makes any revolt or vindication illegitimate.

When a child becomes autonomous and feels capable of exerting a certain amount of control over his environment, he finds it more difficult to put up with restrictions imposed on him by adults. These restrictions provoke his aggressivity against which he can defend himself by identifying with the aggressor (Spitz; A. Freud). Freud mentioned this phenomenon in connection with what is known as 'the bobbin game'.[11] He recounts that when his daughter went out, his grandson would amuse himself by throwing, out of her sight, an object which he had first taken the precaution of tying to a string, allowing him to bring it into sight at will. By imitating heartless adults who would disappear and leave him alone, the child identified himself with the aggressor and became conscious of object-permanence, the bobbin reappearing whenever he so wished. In other words, even if it was only in imaginative play, he exerted control over the trauma and felt enhanced for facing it without too much suffering.

It is by identifying himself with different people that a child learns what he has to do to please his parents (ego-ideal) and what he must not do (superego).[12] The superego allows the individual to compare what he does with what he should do but also has an impact on his ego-ideal. In other words, a child who follows familial rules and accepts punishment for his misconduct, feels proud of himself and integrated within the family. This is what leads Freud to say[13] that the superego has three functions: self-observation, moral conscience and the function of an ideal.

MAUD: MY SHAME, MY GUILT, AND THE SHAME AND GUILT OF MY PARENTS

Maud, who was five years old when Solène was born with cerebral motor disability, has the strange feeling that she experiences guilt which belongs to her parents. 'It is as if, like them, I had to pay, sacrifice myself for a thing I didn't understand at all. It was as if I was doing that because I saw what they were doing and thought I had to do the same.'

My parents' guilt

As a child Maud was convinced that a 'good family' of a handicapped person had to act as her parents did. As an adult, after having therapy, she has come to understand that it was because they were oppressed by the burden of their guilt that her parents punished themselves by depriving themselves of pleasure; paid for their 'errors', mortified themselves and obliged their non-handicapped child to do the same. They never spoke to her about it but on several occasions she heard conversations in which they mentioned their fear that they were responsible for what had happened to her sister.

Her mother reproached herself for having taken aspirin and, although the doctors had reassured her about this, she continued to believe that this medicine might have harmed her child. Her parents didn't want a second child so soon, but when Solène's mother wanted to have an abortion, the doctor refused to carry it out for religious reasons and Solène's mother gave up the idea. Her parents now feel guilty not only for not having wanted the child but also for not wanting it to be born. Finally, when she was pregnant, her mother refused to have her fortune told by a gypsy and the latter is said to have put a curse on the baby.

So her mother failed to manage her birth and protect her child and was unable to impose her will on the doctor either. Speaking as if it were a matter of fact, Maud refers to the 'handicap' as a 'punishment' or consequence of her parents' not wanting the child to be born.

Maud's guilt

Although, in a way, Maud has inherited guilt from her parents, she also feels guilty herself.

When she knew that Solène was in bad health, Maud remembered that she had not wanted this birth and that she had been very difficult with her mother during the pregnancy. Her silly behaviour and aggressivity were designed to attract her parents attention so as to make them somewhat forget the coming baby. After the event, she thought that it was these bad thoughts, this bad behaviour which had harmed her sister and made her parents sad. She says that now these thoughts have gone and she regrets not having been able to get rid of her guilt sooner. She does not want to think about how she would be today if the extent of her suffering had not pushed her in adolescence to get into therapy. In spite of the help this has been, she is still not certain today that thinking badly of someone, having a grudge against someone, does not affect them negatively in reality. 'If I had been able to express all these bad thoughts at the time, I certainly wouldn't have paid so much for the birth of my child.'

Anna Freud[14] shows that a child is anxious when he sees the damage which seems to him to be the result of his more or less conscious desires. While studying the behaviour of children during the Second World War, she noticed that they were made so much more anxious by the sight of damage caused by bombs that they had to struggle to channel their own destructive wishes. In this case, the presence of a comforting person, such as the mother, could help them to differentiate between an external and internal danger.

If a child has to learn progressively to control his aggressivity, he should not, however, totally inhibit it and should have the chance to express something of his feelings of hate without being afraid of hurting in reality the object of his resentment. In a recent programme on 'cot deaths', a young girl of twenty-five explained that she felt responsible for the death of her little one-month-old brother which happened when she was nine. And it was only when she was eighteen that she managed to give less importance to guilt in her psychic life. Until then, she had feared that any aggressive thought towards a person would do them harm and lead to their death, to the extent that when her parents had another child, she over-protected it and forbade herself to have aggressive wishes towards it. When this defence failed, it triggered great anxieties in her.

Like Maud, this young woman shows the difficulties that children have, and sometimes adults too, in giving up the conviction that their thoughts are all-powerful and can have effects in reality. Convinced that wishing someone dead is tantamount to killing them, an individual can come to prohibit himself from playing creatively with his fantasies, his desires and his feelings. This thought-inhibition, this power attributed to ideas can prevent him from using his intellect and lead to failure at school. He thus sees this as the only way to avoid being assailed by the fear of seeing his 'bad thoughts and desires' come to light; or, worse, having consequences in reality.

SELF-ESTEEM AND ESTEEM FOR OTHERS

Parents

Maud reproaches her parents for not having helped her manage her sister's handicap and for having prevented them from developing a sisterly relationship. This was particularly because they could not stand her being aggressive with Solène, or expressing the jealousy she felt towards her. Thus, they prohibited any kind of physical play which they feared Solène would suffer from; only maternal and tender support were permitted.

A brother who wasn't as we dreamed

A handicapped child is not a brother or a sister children can be proud of. They are not always sure that they love or are loved by the child in question and hold it against themselves for having uncertainties, not always knowing what to do, how to be with them. In the case of two siblings, they sometimes guiltily accuse the deficient child of having taken the place of the brother or sister they did not have but who they needed.

I am not 'good enough'

Whereas her sister had just undergone an operation and was suffering – which no one seemed able to relieve – Maud resented her for yet again monopolising her parents' attention and arousing everyone's compassion. She wished she could be sick so that she could be taken care of at last and hated herself for being unable to feel sorry about her sister's lot. Once again, then, she was aware of the gap that existed between what she wanted to be and what she was really like. The resulting lack of self-esteem showed itself clearly one day when, seeing her Christmas presents, she began to cry. Maud did not feel she deserved them, felt sad and prey to her complicated feelings: she enjoyed these tokens of love but felt ashamed of appearing to be a 'nice girl' in front of others while she herself harboured 'bad thoughts' towards her sister. She had difficulty in accepting these tokens of attention which contrasted starkly with the way in which her parents otherwise abandoned her. She thought her parents preferred her sister and that they were relieving their conscience by offering her gifts; so by refusing them she showed that she was not fooled by what they thought.

Maud's parents never spoke to her about their guilt, their shame, their suffering, for fear of making her sad, losing her confidence or being judged badly by her. By acting in this way, they convinced her that one should not speak about one's doubts, one's anxieties and that one should pretend to be stronger than one is in order not to disappoint close relations. So she did the same: she did not ask any questions, said nothing of her confusion, of her feeling that she was bad and not very likeable, and this continued until she began therapy.

None of her brothers or sisters mentioned earlier openly asked their parents to console them and relieve their suffering – which is understandable in the light of Maud's case. While her mother was doing the washing-up in the kitchen with her back turned, Maud began to cry saying she was feeling sad at the idea that her younger sister would never be normal. She no longer knows what her mother said but felt that she ought to stop crying because by showing her suffering she triggered her mother's as well. Her mother wanted to act *as if* she was not sad. If she had insisted, she would have risked making her unhappy and feeling guilty for it.

As a child, it would have been good for Maud if her mother had cried with her and told her that she had the same emotions, but her mother could not do that. When Maud understood this, she learnt not to talk about her suffering any more and not to ask her parents for help in coping with it. So while Solène's handicap made her mother unhappy, it also deprived Maud of the possibility of being consoled.

Philippe, the younger brother of a twenty-one-year-old woman with Down's syndrome, gives a different explanation for the reasons that led him not to complain, although he remembers that his parents used to worry sometimes when they saw him sad and without any friends. He would have felt guilty for seeking more affection from them and would have felt he was getting it at the expense of his sister.

An ideal beyond reach

The brothers and sisters of a handicapped child often have the painful feeling that they have to compensate for their disabled sibling. Thus, in order to repair the narcissistic wound of their parents, they try hard to embody an ideal which is necessarily beyond their reach. This is what happened to Laurent, born ten years after Loïc who has a mild motor and intellectual handicap. Laurent has the feeling that his parents hoped he would embody the hopes and qualities that his brother did not have due to his condition: 'I was supposed to succeed for the two of us.' For him, brothers and sisters functioned like communicating vessels. What is taken from one goes to the other, for the amount of 'idealness' is constant. The handicapped child has 'the least' and the others 'too much' and the parental ideal invested in the former, but not actualised, is transferred to the latter who thus have to live up to an ideal which is beyond them.

However, it sometimes happens that this ideal, even when it is very high, stimulates the children and pushes them to exceed expectations to satisfy and console their parents. This is Martin's case, the eldest of six siblings of whom the fourth is autistic. 'I told myself that I couldn't let myself disappoint them. They had had a very difficult time of it with my brother and there was no question of my letting them down.'

A PROBLEMATIC DIFFERENTIATION

Partly because of their similar size, a child who looks at his brother sometimes has the feeling that he is looking at himself. Brusset writes:

In the sibling group, more so than in the family group, differentiations are progressive and relative for a long time; phenomena of shared identity, consanguinity, specular double, and projective identification, are constantly at play in childhood relations with their alliances and reversals, scruples and complicities.[15]

What is true for all brothers and sisters is also true for those who have a deficient sibling, but the latter have to face specific conflicts. In the mirror a child sees what in 'reality' is only a reflection; and what he feels and experiences in his body cannot be seen. He cannot see his back nor can he see himself in profile. In other words, he has sensations that he cannot see and sees things which are different from those he feels. Zazzo[16] has shown that a child differentiates himself more quickly from his image perceived in a mirror than he does the image of another person from the real person. The reason for this discrepancy is that children can feel in their bodies what they see in a mirror whereas they perceive nothing of the sensations of another person. In other words, in the one case they confront the image perceived by their interoceptive sensations, and in the other, they do not.

Before the age of two, a child does not have the cognitive means to differentiate himself clearly from the other so the birth of another younger baby can endanger the faltering construction of his individuality. He is afraid of becoming the other who he is imitating; putting himself in the position of the other, he assimilates his feelings and attributes his own to the other. He thus demonstrates a confusion between himself and the other, which Wallon calls ' syncretic sociability'.[17] For example, a child cries when it is another child who has hurt himself and the one who is doing the hitting says in good faith that he has been hit himself. It is by experimenting with contrasting attitudes (for example, aggression/submission) that a child gradually differentiates himself from the other. During an intermediary period, there can be moments in the same child where he demonstrates confusion of 'me-other' and other moments where he affirms himself as 'I'.

If a child has succeeded in differentiating himself from the other, the birth of a younger child can help the older ones to affirm their individuality. Imitating a sibling not only no longer makes a child fear he will lose his autonomy and identity, but can also enhance him by giving him the opportunity of putting his abilities to the test and filling the role of the elder child. Acting *as if*, he can have what the other *has got* without fearing he will become what the other *is*, since the 'barrier' which separates him from the other is sufficiently watertight that he can resemble him without fear of confusion.

In the case of siblings comprising a handicapped person, it is a matter of knowing whether resembling the other involves the risk of becoming 'like them'.

Tania: 'the wrong model'

Tania, who has an older brother, Allan, with cerebral motor deficiency as well as a little sister, Sophie, explains:

> I thought that if I had a brother, it was so that we would both be the same. And that frightened me a bit. Now, it's over. When I was shown a big mirror to look at myself in and when they explained to me that that was me and that he was handicapped, I understood that it was him who was handicapped. I felt reassured, freer. For my sister it wasn't the same. As soon as she was born, she started imitating me and not Allan.

It needed adults in whom she had confidence to help her differentiate herself from her brother by confronting her with her own image, but it did not reassure her completely and she continued to wonder 'whether it's what is outside which is different from us or whether it's also the thing inside which is different'.

It is in order to answer such questions, without her parents' knowing, she walks like her brother and imitates his athetosic movements. She wants to feel in her own body what Allan feels so as to understand better who he is, to be able finally to differentiate herself totally from him and to acquire the certainty that she is not, and never will be, like him. By imitating him she proves that she can be 'like him' and then behave again as a 'normal child'. She thereby reduces the difference between them while making sure that something will always distinguish her condition from that of her brother's, since he cannot imitate her.

Philippe: reducing the difference between us

Philippe wants the mirror to confirm that he does not look like his sister who has Down's syndrome 21; all the more so since he sometimes feels, with accompanying anxiety, that he has the same attitudes and gestures as her. For Philippe, as for Tania, his sister's mild handicap furthered his fear of resembling Sabine.

Philippe is convinced that the intrapsychic and interpersonal conflicts engendered by his sibling relationships have been, and still are, in part insoluble because the 'handicap' and the 'normality' which make him different from his sister are a focus for jealousy which cannot be talked about amongst the siblings or in the family. Sabine envies the way he is validated by others; his friends envy his capacity to form relationships with people from the area, as well as his strength and autonomy. This makes him feel guilty for being normal. He knows that even if he can pretend to be less than normal, his sister cannot be normal. Thus, although he can soothe Sabine's 'legitimate' jealousy by failing at school or by falling sick, she cannot do likewise. Which is why Philippe has the painful feeling that he has a debt towards his sister that he will never be able to pay.

In the cases of Philippe and Tania, these difficulties in knowing where they stand in relationship to their deficient sibling are considerably increased by the fact that both are convinced of having a handicap which is less conspicuous than that of their brother or sister.

Cathy: my sister in me

Cathy speaks as follows of the bond which exists between herself and her older sister, Samantha, who has Down's syndrome 21. 'I was a Siamese sister, I was and still am, right, even if I've blanked it out, if I've let go of it a bit, I mean, Sylvie, she's ... I was saying only a few months ago: if she left now, half of myself would leave with her.'

Cathy's sister is inside her, like a baby is inside its mother, but she is also stuck to her and consequently to the outside of her. As they are Siamese twins, their separation can only take place with the full recognition of their separate integrity and identities and will necessarily involve a wrench which will leave its scars.

Once a week, she spends an evening with her sister. Sylvie told her one day that she would prefer to listen to her favourite music than to play with her. So Cathy said she would not stay, and to her great surprise her sister did not change her plans, which triggered very ambivalent feelings in Cathy. She is happy that her sister encourages her to free herself from her, but at the same time she experiences it as a rejection, a refusal to recognise everything she has sacrificed and continues to sacrifice for her. She is afraid and thrilled at the void that she will certainly experience if her sister shows her desire to live more independently from her.

OTHERS: A MIRROR OF MYSELF

Brothers and sisters are affected differently by the way 'others' look at their handicapped sibling. Third parties who sometimes make them suffer by asking questions, by their curiosity, can, however, be useful by putting their intrapsychic and interpersonal conflicts into words.

If the way in which parents manage the confrontation between their handicapped child and third parties influences the way their other children behave in society, it is a matter of influence and not determinism. In effect, depending on their intrapsychic difficulties, each individual reworks psychically the models offered by his parents. This depends on how children deal with their relationship with their handicapped sibling and, in particular, on whether they have been able to recognise what they share as well as what makes them different. If this separation is clear, then aggressions from third parties are experienced as affecting the other and dealt with as such; if it is not, they feel attacked *just like* their handicapped sibling.

Seeing in the look of others what one has in oneself is reassuring for certain brothers and sisters who thereby have the feeling that their way of envisaging the relationship with the handicapped person is 'legitimate', since other people think and act like them. So, Philippe appreciated that the psychologist who was following him told him that he should not have been brought up with his sister whom he reproached throughout his childhood for being there. He then began to speak with this woman about his shame for not being able to bear his sister's handicap. He was not afraid of disappointing her for she had brought the subject up herself.

On the contrary, it is also clear that for other brothers and sisters or for the same, but at different moments in their lives, this mirror image is shattering. Cathy remembers her suffering, her shame, her painful feeling of impotence when she watched in silence children from the area making fun of Samantha, bullying her in the sand pit while her sister never defended herself and did not even appear to grasp the meaning of the aggression of which she was the object.

It is not cowardice which prevented Cathy from defending her sister, but the fact that all of a sudden she understood that her darkest premonitions were being confirmed: her sister was definitely not normal, was incapable of defending herself alone and was the object of mockery which had repercussions on the entire family. Her being different was therefore a flaw for which she had to take responsibility. She knew vaguely that if she had been in her friends' shoes, she would have done the same thing; but at the same time, as Samantha's sister, she owed it to herself not to do it. So, it was because she felt at once close to the aggressors and the object of aggression that she was incapable of acting, able only to feel a painful sense of shame.

DEFENCE MECHANISMS

In order to face these difficulties, children employ more or less effi-cient or rigid defences which evolve with time. In this chapter, reference is made only to those which are most often found where brothers and sisters are concerned.

Idealisation

In many cases, in order to manage feelings of shame and guilt, the families of the people we met employ processes which are intended to create the idea of an ideal family taking up position against a persecuting environment. The defensive aspect of this image can come to light for brothers and sisters during therapy or when they move away from their families and distance themselves from the family group.

Turning aggressivity against oneself

MASSIE: DYING

Sometimes the only escape from suffering for brothers and sisters is self-punishment. Thus, Massie,[18] the sister of a haemophiliac, recounts the times when her brother suffered haemorrhages: she felt responsible because, without anybody knowing, she sometimes hit her brother and was jealous of the solicitude and tolerance which his parents bestowed on him. 'So my thoughts turned sour and I told myself: one of these days I might die and then they'd see. That would make them cry.'

Massie wanted to die in order to punish herself, to show her strength, to force her parents to think about her and to take her suffering into account. She wanted them to recognise her value, her need to placate her guilt, her shame and her desire to be mothered like her brother.

NOT WANTING TO BE 'NORMAL'

Philippe punished himself by not exploiting his capacities. He was a brilliant student in his final school year who had memory and attention difficulties and failed his baccalaureate. The moment when this symptom appeared is extremely significant. In fact, getting his baccalaureate would have meant choosing a profession and affirming himself as an autonomous individual.

He had a severe depression, was hospitalised and began a therapy which enabled him to understand the meaning of his symptom. Through this failure, he was expressing his desire not to increase his sister's jealousy by demonstrating too ostensibly his normality and his fear of not being able to live up to the hopes placed in him. By not being able to choose a sufficiently prestigious profession, he was punishing himself for having enjoyed and benefited from being normal and was asking to be taken care of. Describing himself as having been a sensible and good child who was not mothered enough, the prospect of becoming an adult made him realise that he could never again receive the attention, care and mothering which he lacked as a child.

SPEAKING WITH ONE'S BODY

Nadia remembers how her mother, when she was pregnant with her little brother who has Down's syndrome 21, asked her if she wanted her parents to keep the baby. She is convinced that it is because she said 'yes' that her brother came into the world. She was training as a midwife when I met her and she said that it was only much later that she became aware of the guilt she felt at the idea that she had had to play this role in the birth. Nadia then described her brother as adorable, and said her parents had faced up well to their situation while she herself actively took care of him.

In the final year at school, she felt unable to take any exams. She was 'paralysed with a hard lump in the stomach'. It is difficult not to make a link between the 'lump' which Nadia gets in her stomach when she is asked questions and the baby in her mother's womb which was born because she had answered her mother's question. So her guilt had to manifest itself in her body for her to start a therapy and understand the role that her brother's handicap played in her life.

DISPLACEMENT OF AGGRESSIVITY

Tania prohibits herself from reproaching her parents for not taking enough care of her and says they are doing what they can. Nor can she let herself reproach Allan for taking up too much of his parents' time, for any aggressivity towards him makes her feel too guilty. On the contrary, she has a very difficult relationship with her younger sister, Sophie, of whom she is jealous and with whom she has violent verbal and physical exchanges. She says that sometimes she has felt like killing her. She recounts:

> My life is a bit bizarre, because I am between the two; I've got a big brother who I get on well with, and I'm my little sister's big sister so I should be able to get on well with her like with my big brother, but no, we can't stop squabbling.

The contrast between her relations with her brother and parents which are exempt from aggressivity and her extremely violent relationship with Sophie leads one to think that part of her affects towards Allan and her parents are displaced onto Sophie, whom Tania can attack without too much guilt. It is possible that a part of Tania's feeling of 'bizzarreness' can be explained by the fact that she feels her sister is invested with affects that do not concern her. Although she does not reproach her brother or her parents for anything, she accuses her sister of not being grateful for the help she gives her. By condensing in her sister everything which concerns the other members of the family, Tania can say, without feeling too guilty, how she feels about her position within the family.

TRANSFORMING AGGRESSIVITY INTO ITS OPPOSITE: SOLICITUDE

Wilkins[19] shows that, in certain circumstances, brothers and sisters feel enhanced and reassured by taking part in the education and care of the handicapped child. They thus find a way of making themselves useful and have less tense relations with the person concerned. Stoneman et al.[20] note that the more a child accepts tasks such as child minding and helping with the bodily care of the handicapped child, the more his relationship with the latter will have a positive affective tone. This can be interpreted in two ways: either parents can easily make demands on their non-handicapped children because they know that the relationships between the siblings are good; or the children, who find themselves obliged to take on responsibilities for their handicapped sibling, adapt to the situation and inhibit their aggressive tendencies. In the second case, these inhibited aggressive tendencies can pre-exist requests for help or they can result from them. The protocol employed in their research does not allow us to know which of the two hypotheses is pertinent.

While certain children suffer from not being able or not knowing how to console their parents in their sadness and their pain, others succeed in helping them learn how to smile again and to have hope: either by mothering them, or by chivvying them; or again, by trying to be 'model' children to make them forget their pain; or by giving them a vision of the handicapped child which enables them once again to feel competent with him.

Participating in the care of the handicapped child is for some children a way of feeling they are 'a better brother or sister'. In this way they alleviate their guilt and improve their self-image and the image others have of them. Moreover, by identifying themselves with whoever they are caring for or educating, they do themselves good by doing good to others, like a child who consoles his teddy bear when he is sad.

Caring for and educating their handicapped sibling 'proves' as well that they are different from him since they have a superior position to him which puts a comforting distance between them. Nevertheless, when the deficient child is better and refuses to be under the tutelage of his siblings, the latter must establish a more equal relationship with him, sometimes involving suffering and thinking again about the differences and similarities which exist between brothers and sisters.

Although helping their parents and their handicapped sibling alleviates the children's distress, it nevertheless deprives them of their right to be supported and mothered and obliges them to take on roles and responsibilities which are costly at a psychic level. Here, we find again what the psychoanalyst Bowlby called 'a compulsive tendency to care for others'.[21] A child can thus develop its identity around this function of caring and his altruism allows him to keep his inner disarray hidden. At the same time, by proving sometimes to be more competent than adults in caring for the handicapped sibling and making him obey, the 'caring child' enters into rivalry with them and evacuates in this way some of the aggressivity they provoke in him.

Boszormenyi-Nagy[22] has studied families where one of the children becomes 'the parent' of their father, their mother, or of their siblings. He considers that, on a temporary basis, the experience is positive for the child who feels valued. However, if it goes on too long and is not sufficiently gratifying, the child finds himself alone and feels he is both a 'bad child' and a 'bad parent'.

STRATEGIES OF AVOIDANCE

Philippe is ashamed of his sister and cannot stand the looks or the questions he has to face when he goes out with her. So, to fight against this unspoken suffering, he first tries to act as if he is not part of the same family as his sister by walking in front of or behind her in the street, for example. But being unable to bring himself to break with the family, he rebels and behaves aggressively towards the 'normal, stupid and nasty children' who make fun of his sister and, indirectly, of him. However, he cannot and does not want to reject 'the normal ones' for that would reinforce his fear that he, too, is the bearer of a handicap. So he excuses the behaviour of 'people' by their lack of information and ignorance which makes it possible to see their hurtful attitudes as something passing and circumstantial. Finally, by identifying himself with his sister's aggressors, he makes fun of handicapped persons too, thereby expressing his difficulty in finding his place and in knowing who he is in relation to his sister.

As none of these strategies led to an alleviation of his suffering, he decided to limit his social relationships and to keep them separate from his sister. It is as if, after trying out various defensive strategies, Philippe made up his mind to follow the example of his parents, that is to say, to isolate himself socially and to fall back on a suffering which no contact with the outside world could appease.

Philippe avoids speaking about his sister with his friends to create some distance, not to mention a rupture, between them. Although he is happy to preserve a space where his suffering is, for a time, put on hold, he blames himself for symbolically eliminating his sister from his life, comforting himself with the idea that he is incapable of putting up with her socially.

This defence which is adopted by many of the brothers and sisters we met shows both themselves and others that they feel ashamed of their handicapped brother or sister. Moreover, suspending social relationships so as to avoid situations which give rise to shame, does not prevent brothers and sisters from feeling threatened by an unexpected meeting.

CONCLUSION

Whilst parental reactions account in part for the way in which the non-handicapped children deal psychically with the presence of a deficient child in the family, sibling ties possess their own specificity and dynamics which affect each one of them in a special way.

The tendency of children and parents to avoid speaking about emotions around the handicap also prevails within the sibling group. It is as if, in these families, not speaking about the way each person reacts subjectively to the handicap was part of an implicit pact which it would be dangerous not to respect. However, silence which encloses a feeling, a question, an emotion, is a source of anxiety and fear and leads to the setting-up of rigid defences and the generation of symptoms.

To improve the bad image which certain brothers and sisters have of themselves, it sometimes suffices that they can tell an adult that they think and feel things which are not in line with what they would like to think or feel or with what they imagine others would like them to think and feel. It is less a matter of giving answers which sometimes neither doctors nor parents have, than to say that one hears and shares the worries and uncertainties of the child. This work of verbalisation and explanation helps brothers and sisters to become conscious of what separates them from their deficient sibling, legitimates their desires for independence, and allows them to affirm their right to be different.

Brothers and sisters do not suffer so much from attending medical consultations, waiting in hospital waiting rooms, visiting the institution where their deficient sibling is in care, as from always figuring as spectators in whom nobody really takes an interest. Each child must be able to choose whether or not to accompany their deficient sibling to the care centre. In those cases where they choose to go, then parents and professional staff should take an interest in the way they react to this situation. If the doctor not only enquires about their parents, their handicapped brother or sister, but also addresses them, then they will know that their suffering and the complexity of emotions that assail them can also be heard. They will benefit from a sense of security based on the knowledge that adults are capable of understanding and supporting them, of devoting time to them and caring about what they are going through. Even if they still say nothing, they will know that it is possible to express themselves and will make use of this knowledge more easily when they need to.

NOTES

1. Ministerial circular (1985) 'L'accueil de l'enfant né avec un handicap, rôle des maternités', 29 February.
2. Marcelli, D. (1983) 'Etude clinique de la fratrie de l'enfant handicappé', *Sem Hop*, 12: 845–9.
3. Ferrari, P., Crochette, A. and Bouvet, M. (1988) 'La fratrie et l'enfant handicappé: approche clinique', *Neuropsychiatrie de l'enfance*, 1(January): 20.
4. Freud, S. (1916–17) 'Introductory Lectures on Psycho-Analysis', in James Strachey, ed., *The Standard Edition of the Complete Psychological Works of Sigmund Freud*, 24 vols, London, Hogarth, vols 15–16.
5. Freud, S. (1913) *Totem and Taboo*, S.E. 13, pp.1–162.
6. Brusset, B. (1987) 'Le lien fraternel et la psychanalyse', *Psychanalyse à l'université*, 12, Paris, PUF, pp.5–43.
7. Burlingham, D. and Freud, A. (1949) *Enfants sans famille*, Paris, PUF.
8. Bowlby, J. (1978) *Attachment and Loss*, London, Hogarth.
9. Spitz, R.A. (1968) *De la naissance à la parole*, Paris, PUF.
10. Lacan, J. (1938) 'Le complexe, facteur concret de la psychologie familiale', in *'La vie mentale'. L'Encyclopédie française*, VIII, Paris, Larousse.
11. The game of *'fort-da'* described by Freud with reference to his eighteen-month-old grandson.
12. Freud, S. (1923) 'The Ego and the Id', *S.E.* 19, pp.3–66.
13. Freud, S. (1933) 'New Introductory Lectures on Psycho-Analysis', *S.E.* 22, pp. 3–182.
14. Freud, A. (1936) *The Ego and the Mechanisms of Defence*, New York, International Universities Press.
15. Brusset, B. (1981) 'Transfert fraternel et groupe', in M. Soulé, ed., *Frères et soeurs*, Paris, ESF, pp.113–41, p.128.

16. Zazzo, R. (1986) 'Les dialectiques originelles de l'identité', in P. Tap, ed., *Identité individuelle et personalisation*, Paris, Privat, pp.207–21, p.217.

17. Wallon, H. (1968) *L'évolution psychologique de l'enfant*, Paris, Armand Colin.

18. Massie, S. (1976) *Pas à pas*, Paris, Stock.

19. Wilkins, R. (1992) 'Psychotherapy with Siblings of Mentally Handicapped Children', in A. Waitman and S. Conboy-Hill (eds) *Psychotherapy and Mental Handicap*, New York, Sage, pp.25–40.

20. Stoneman, F., Brody, G.H., Davis, C.H. and Crapps, J.M. (1987) 'Mentally Retarded Children and their Older Same-sex Siblings: Naturalistic In-home Observations', *American Journal on Retardation*, 93: 174–83.

21. Bowlby, *Attachment and Loss*.

22. Boszormenyi-Nagy, I. and Spark, G.M. (1973) *Invisible loyalties, Reciprocity in Intergenerational Family Therapy*, New York, Harper and Row.

12 Sexuality and Handicap from the Perspective of Psychoanalytical Anthropology

OLIVIER-RACHID GRIM

INTRODUCTION

What does the idea of perspective imply? A perspective can signify a field of vision which opens itself to the thought or activity of someone. It is also a particular way of seeing things, an aspect under which they present themselves. Perspective equally expresses the idea of a certain distance, but within the eye's reach. The 'perspectivist perspective' – if I dare use this expression – that is, the doctrine in which all knowledge is relative to our general view of the world or to our situation and personal tendencies, is, for me, what psychoanalytical anthropology could be; where I would consider myself as a researcher at the beginning of his work, a novice who is setting out the premises of his research.

Psychoanalytical anthropology, referred to as an 'alternation between the couch and the tropics' by Jean Paul Valabrega (1967, p.167), enables the anthropologist, thanks to psychoanalytical anthropology, to shed light on the problems posed by data gathered in the field of ethnology and enables the psychoanalyst to have access to the same data and to enrich himself, whether it is a matter of artistic manifestations, collective behaviour, beliefs, rites or myths. Furthermore, according to H.J. Stiker (1996, p.5), anthropology and psychoanalysis, while having a similar concern for language, even if their approach is different, have in common the question of origins: 'Where do we come from? From one? From two? From below? From above?', and so on. What does the question of origin and the solutions related to it signify?

Hence, the common strategy which consists in turning back the clock – which for some leads to myth and for others to phantasy – leads Jean Paul Valabrega to say that, on the one hand, the question of phantasy is correctly stated only from the anthropological point of view and, on the other hand, that the fluctuation from myth to phantasy and phantasy to myth conveys a reality where precisely the foundations of psychoanalytical anthropology are anchored. This necessary link between the cultural, the familial and the individual leads these two specific and autonomous disciplines to 'converse', to use the expression of Claude Levi-Strauss (cited by Stiker 1996, p.6), thereby creating this third term.

Concerning the notion of handicap – since here it is a question of a handicapped person's sexuality, mainly in its function of organising psychic and social life – I do not know at the moment which of the terms, 'handicap' or 'disability', I prefer. From a historical point of view, one may prefer disability which, generally speaking, is a neutral term which does not designate a particular status. It has the advantage of taking into account the aspect of monstrousness. However, it has the drawback of placing more emphasis on weakness or physical pathology, whereas the term 'handicap', which covers a large variety of states, emphasises more the aspect of deficiency, particularly if we bear in mind the definition given by Simone Korff-Sausse (1996a): 'an invalidating affliction affecting psycho-somatic integrity'. In any event, the question remains unanswered for me at this stage of my research.

FROM PRIAPUS TO CYRANO: THE THWARTED LOVE AFFAIRS OF THOSE WHO HAVE A 'NOSE'

If the monster recognises himself in the mirror ...
then he will become more human.
(Richard Mielgo-Rivi)

Without doubt, we delight in suffering from the complex of Roxanne, the name of the bewitching idiot who, in Edmond Rostand (1897), prefers the inane beauty of a stupid fop to the genuine love of a boorish ruffian with an impossible nose. Fortunately, war and death are vigilant and keep good company – which might be the brief moral of this heroic comedy.

Cyrano Savinien-Hercule de Bergerac, first cousin of a certain Pinnochio, an Italian hero with unlikely origins which are thought to go back to Priapus, is endowed with a nasal appendix which makes a freak of him.

Considered variously as a diabolical freak, a sign of exteriority for the ancients, an object and instrument of science in the eighteenth century, a simple anomaly for nineteenth-century anatomists, 'this morphological misfit' – to use the expression of Georges Canguilhem – 'is in our eyes, a monster' (Canguilhem 1962, p.29).

Cyrano exhibits this nose, this abnormality, with as much pride as pain; he shows it to the world with the same arrogance and provocation as his illustrious ancestor who exposed his attributes to whoever wanted to see them. Priapus, the last in line of the gods, according to Fernand Compte (1988), is a little bearded man lifting his apron full of fruit above his inordinately large and erect phallus.

While generally considered to be the son of Adonis or Dionysus, in certain versions of the myth Priapus is the son of Zeus and Aphrodite. All the gods are startled by Aphrodite's beauty and Zeus seduces and takes possession of her. But Hera, the jealous wife of the supreme god of Olympia, is afraid that the fruit of this corrupted love will turn out to be as beautiful as his mother and as powerful as his father, so she sees to it that the child is born ugly and deformed. When Aphrodite sees Priapus, she is utterly ashamed of her new-born son and, fearing she will be the object of ridicule, turns her eyes away and abandons him in the mountains where he is rescued and brought up by shepherds.

Priapus' sexual organ makes him legendary. He is seen to be the protector of orchards, scaring off robbers – particularly female ones who might approach him – with his virile attribute, threatening them with sexual violence, and above all verbal violence, for Priapus is impotent. The lands he supposedly keeps watch over are poor; the symbol of fertility which he represents is inefficacious and robbers do not appear. Occasionally, he becomes desperate and begs potential aggressors to trespass so that he can find relief by punishing them.

He courts the nymph Lotis (Hestia, in another version) but fails miserably as usual. One day he finds her sleeping. Delighted with this god-send he prepares to rape her but an ass which happens to be there starts braying and wakes the beauty. Priapus is forced to flee, exposing himself to the ridicule of all. He is a rather ridiculous god who suffers repeated set-backs. He is likened to the ass, considered as a lewd animal. Together, they take part in the cortège of Dionysus. Both are ithyphallic there, as if they were competing for a prize in obscenity. It is recounted that they held a competition to see which of them had the biggest member. The ass won, and being unable to accept this, Priapus is said to have killed it.

Until the Roman era, statues of Priapus were crudely carved in wood from fig trees, smeared in red and placed in orchards. From being a symbol of fertility, he gradually turned into an obscene scarecrow.

However, Cyrano, unlike Priapus, fights with all his strength against attempts to reduce him to his unusual features – he is more than just his nose and proclaims this loud and clear with truculence and sensibility.

But 'this peak, this rock, this cape, this peninsula!' – in other words, this blow dealt by fate, this evil legacy, this divine malediction, this injustice – bars him at once from access to mutual love and above all from carnal consummation. How, with a nose like that, is even a mere kiss possible? Thus, Cyrano is condemned and condemns himself to loving by proxy all his life.

The length of the nose auguring the length of the penis is a classic part of popular imagery and works marvellously here: sharply addressing a 'busybody' with respect to his singularity, Cyrano asks: 'Does it swing like an elephant's prehensile trunk?' (Act 1, scene 4).

Cyrano in love! That is as conspicuous as a nose in the middle of a face, concludes Jean Clair for whom the nose – contrary to the eye – 'is what constitutes the most wild, the most primitive, the most animal' (Clair, 1992, p.47). One only has to contemplate a few of the iconographic documents that he has brought together in his book *Giacometti's Nose* to be convinced, if it is still necessary.[1]

Would too much sex kill sex? Were Cyrano and his unfortunate companions caught in a double-bind? That is, between showing their singularity and, thereby, taking the risk of being reduced and of reducing themselves to the latter, or trying to dissimulate it and in so doing blocking the epistemophilic drives which, psychoanalysis teaches us, take their root precisely in sexual curiosity (Freud 1905).

This crucial question is illustrated abundantly in the clinical experience of handicap. Thus, many of the children we follow no longer have the energy required to struggle against the effects of this double-bind, imprisoned as they are by a *priori*. 'Madam, your son will be able to walk at such and such an age ...'; 'Sir, your daughter will probably never speak ...'; 'don't dream, he certainly won't make ENA or Harvard ...'. Motricity, language, intelligence – at least the idea we have of them – are wrapped up in knowing and pertinent observations with the allure of deadly prophecies occasionally punctuated with comments like: 'I would be curious to see him again in ten years' time ... .' To see what? No doubt the disastrous effects of those words. Let us follow the rather more distant approach of Dominique Decant on this subject:

[A]ttributing a child with a position in a given nosography, attributing him with such and such a psychopathological functioning already induces a whole list of associations ... This indeed is at the origin, whether one likes it or not, of expectations or refusals concerning the development envisaged by parents or caretakers and greatly affects the progress or impasses of the therapeutic treatment of the child. (Decant 1988, p.2)

But worse still, because never put into words and always present as a subliminal image, is: 'Dear parents, your child will have no children because God or nature or both are against it; your child is proof that our "creators" are fallible and this proof must be got rid of, otherwise what will become of us!'

Even if due to historical discontinuities and ruptures,[2] humankind, from antiquity to the Enlightenment, has not been able to utter such words on themes as recurrent as monstrosity, sexuality and procreation, these imaginary words nevertheless bear witness to a clinical reality where one can sense a veiled phantasmatic with ancient resonances consisting both of evil and transendence which finds a similar echo in the very real words of parents when they say: 'But what have I done to the good Lord to deserve that, why me?'

'Monsters do not reproduce', says Michel Tournier (cited by Korff-Sausse 1996b, p.38). No doubt, but how far are we responsible for this sterility? What are our secret motivations; indeed, even our unconscious ones? Would it not be better to admit that we do not want them to reproduce?

Cyrano says to Christian on the subject of love: 'While I could speak it all if only my face were more expertly planned' (Act 2, scene 10).

Children do not grow on trees, in spite of the invention of test tubes, and the whole problem of the Cyranos of this world is contained in this observation and these two lines. The stigma is such and the interdiction so strong that the sexuality of 'those with large noses' gets reduced to a minimum and humanity can sleep soundly as if Darwin's 'nature' had, in this precise case, found a sophisticated subterfuge so that, once again, only the fittest reproduce.

Paradoxically – since it has no direct influence on this question of continuity – the ludicrous idea of seduction and the no less ludicrous idea of a 'thing' done uniquely for pleasure is shelved, and for good reason. Let us return to Canguilhem when he writes of the monstrous: 'It is inverted magic' (Canguilhem 1962, p.31), provoking at the same time fear and utter terror, curiosity and fascination. One can imagine in the proscenium that seduction and pleasure between monsters arouses in us these twin sensations, without forgetting that, meanwhile, in the wings, one of the two monsters in action could very well be us, as Tod Browning[3] shows in his own way in his film *Freaks* (Grim 1995), where, against the background of circus life, he tells of human loves from the most angelic to the most monstrous, leaving it up to each of us to decide who is the most angelic and who the most monstrous.

If it is accepted that the function of the artist, whatever his medium, is to open our eyes to *truth*, then it may be said that Hans

Rudi Giger (1991), a Swiss painter, illustrator and sculptor, reveals through his tormented work some of the dark recesses of the human psyche.

Freud's concept of the *unheimlich* is illustrated in a striking manner by these 'bio-mechanical' beings as they are referred to by Giger. Simply seeing them plunges the spectator into a disturbing impression of the *déjà vu,* as the artist himself says: 'sometimes people come to see my work and only see the horrific aspects. I tell them to look more carefully and then they are able to see that there are two elements in my paintings: something horrible and something pleasant' (Giger 1979).

Furthermore, Ridley Scott was not mistaken in entrusting him with the creation of the monstrous creature in his film *Alien.*[4] It is interesting to note in passing how the monster's sexuality and repro- ductive cycle are represented: from an abandoned egg-trap, it fertilises its victims by the mouth, its hybrid offspring then being born from their host's abdomen. This monstrous procreation and birth, which leaves its imprint on the imaginary solutions invented by children who pride themselves on resolving the fundamental puzzle about how babies come about, shows us how obsessed we are with restricting the monster – even if an imaginary one – to a pregenital sexuality.

If the latter nevertheless achieves genitality, it can only do so by wearing a mask with a human face and being recognised as such socially. The cowl makes the monk, as the film *Species* shows,[5] where we see a hybrid creature – also created by Giger (1995) – got up as a very beautiful woman in order to marry an earthling. However, making love and procreating condemn both it and its monstrous offspring to extermination since they are considered to be a threat to humanity. This imaginary space into which desires and drives which are difficult to control can be projected (Belmont 1974), fits in well with the contemporary idea of a collective fear and fascination for the potential mutation of our species. This theme is also partly respon- sible for the world-wide success of TV serials like *The X Files,*[6] and can explain the umpteenth version of *The Island of Dr Moreau,*[7] adapted from the novel by H.G. Wells. Moreover, this fear of mutation linked to sexuality might partially explain the 'monstrous' act which consists in surgically 'incising' the eyes of children with Down's syndrome: plastic surgery which aims amongst other things at hiding from everyone's eyes the extreme alterity which bars the way towards anthropogenesis and, therefore, potential genitality.

In this respect, Joseph Boruwlaski, an eighteenth-century Polish gentleman and famous dwarf who answered to the sweet-sounding name of 'Joujou', recounts in his memoirs how, for a long time, everybody considered him to be a child, including Isaline, for whom he was consumed with love:

> [*Isaline*] '... you are a child and I can only laugh at your extravagance ...'

> [*Joseph*] I admit that I was not expecting this reply; it humiliated me. I had a lot of difficulty in making her understand that I did not love her as a child and that it was not as a child that I wanted to be loved ... (Boruwlaski 1788, p.102)

He finally married her and they had several children. This marriage was found shocking and incited the general reprobation of all. They had to leave the court of their protectress Countess Humieska who had kept them up till then.

Two centuries later, Michel Petrucciani, who has become a '*monstre sacré*' of jazz, certainly owes his 'humanisation' purely to his musical talent, which has served him as a kind of mask. This phenomenon would in itself merit a deeper study to the extent that one can imagine that music saved him from 'the infra-human'; that is, something almost animal, to lead him towards the more-than-human; that is, something between the human and the divine – the mid-way stage enabling him to have a child. In this case, music has had the same function as the exposure of children did in myths, as Nicole Belmont explains (1995, pp.41–2): music, like exposure, is intended to provide proof of belonging to humanity. Behind all this, one can imagine on the one hand, the exceptional strength developed by the parents of this 'extra-ordinary' musician – in the literal sense of the words – to inscribe him within the succession of generations and consider him as a link in the potential chain of transmission, and, on the other hand, the considerable energy that he has been able to muster in order to achieve procreative genitality. And the latter, precisely where – for our personal comfort – most of them are fixed at pregenital stages condemning them to pursue paths of perverted sexuality where handicap or disability are eroticised in sado-masochistic relationships. This is shown in another way by the mythical figures of Dracula and the Minotaur whose extreme orality leads to cannibalism, whereas Cyrano's leads to poetry.

One then observes the setting up of a perverse cycle which leads a disabled person who is barred from genitality – and is, therefore, less well-equipped in this area, regardless of the nature of his handicap – to entice like a victim designated by predators who, behind the mask of social norms and morality, give themselves over to condemned sexual practices, as Nicole Diederich shows (1997). Her observations of the sexual abuse of which disabled and deficient persons are the victims is so alarming that it renders banal any fiction of monstrous sexuality, be it mythical, romanesque or science fiction.

At the same time, where these issues are concerned, it seems difficult to avoid falling into an easy ethnocentrism – perhaps it does not matter – which makes us judge such practices as abnormal; just as it seems equally difficult to yield to the lure of cold objectivity which, while pretending to be scientific, would allow us to describe and analyse horrors which would concern us as observers only in a very distant way. All that remains is for us to abide by the laws of the Republic and respect their implementation.

It will have been understood by now that it is not the monstrousness that is exceptional in the sense of being a rare phenomenon but, on the contrary, humanity which falls cruelly short. It is not a question of establishing a logical equivelance, a linear connection between monstrosity and handicap, but rather of considering the figure of the monster as an anthropological starting point, a grid which enables us to study the social representations linked to handicap and infirmity. For we have to defend ourselves, and, when the choice is made of trying to avoid a socially imposed Darwinism, to struggle against a perpetual triple movement in which we are irrevocably caught which combines what radically separates and differentiates us from monsters with what we have in common with them. We then become like the Minotaur who, in the labyrinth of Baudrillard (1993), wanders between total indifference and extreme fright without hope of salvation.

If in the anthropomorphic bestiary of La Fontaine we happily cry out 'let's get the ass', to do the same here with the motif of the monster is to have a misplaced sense of economy. As Gilbert Lascault writes, 'the monster in art designates what we do not want or are unable to recognise in ourselves' (Lascault 1973, p.13). Which, in other words, brings us back to the issue of counter-transference.

NOTES

1. The devil embodied (p.58); erotic Japanese mask (p.63); erotic Japanese print (p.63); engraving by Franz von Bayros (p.64).
2. Stiker, H-J. (1996–97) Complementary lectures – 'An Anthropological review of disability: from disability to handicap, XVIII–XX century', Paris, Ecole des Hautes Etudes en Sciences Sociales.
3. *Freaks*, a film by Tod Browning, produced by Irving Thalberg, 1932 © MGM.

4.   *Alien*, a film by Ridley Scott, produced by Gordon Carrol, David Giller and Walter Hill, 1979 © Twentieth Century Fox. Giger received an oscar the same year for special effects.
5.   *Species*, a film by Roger Donaldson, produced by Franck Mancuso Jr. and Dennis Feldman, 1995 © MGM.
6.   *The X Files*, televised cult serial created and produced by Chris Carter.
7.   *The Island of Dr Moreau* has been adapted for the cinema several times: in 1933 by Erle C. Kenton; in 1959 by Gerry de Leon; in 1977 by Don Taylor; and finally, in 1997, by J. Frankenheimer. All the productions use the same 'emerald green' in their poster, a colour which is identical to the clothes of the buffoon. Might not this emerald green symbolise fear and monstrosity?

REFERENCES

Baudrillard, J. (1993) *Transparency of Evil: Essays on Extreme Phenomena*, London, Verso.

Belmont, N. (1974) 'Comment on fait peur aux enfants', *Topique*, 13: 101–25.

Belmont, N. (1995) 'Les rites de passage et la naissance, l'enfant exposé', *Dialogue*, 27: 30–44.

Boruwlaski, J. (1788) *Memoirs of a famous dwarf, Joseph Boruwlaski, Polish gentleman*, London.

Canguilhem, G. (1962) 'La monstruosité et le monstrueux', *Diogène*, 40: 29–43.

Clair, J. (1992) *Le nez de Giaccometti, faces de carême, figures de carneval*, Paris, Gallimard, collection Art et Artistes.

Compte, F. (1988) *Priape, Les grandes figures des mythologies*, Paris, Bordas.

Decant, D. (1988) 'Place et fonction de la théorie dans le travail avec les psychoses infantiles et l'autisme', *La revue de l'ANECAMSP*, 7: 1–7.

Diederich N. (1997) 'La vie affective et sexuelle des personnes "handicappées mentales", Difference de sexe, différence de devenir?', *Sexualité et handicap, Contraste* 6: Ier semestre.

Freud, S. (1905) 'Three Essays on the Theory of Sexuality', in James Strachey, ed., *The Standard Edition of the Complete Psychological Works of Sigmund Freud*, 24 vols, London, Hogarth, 1953–73, vol. 7, pp.125–245.

Giger, H.R. (1979) Alien, *Métal Hurlant*, hors série no.43bis.

Giger, H.R. (1991) *Poster Book*, Taschen.

Giger, H.R. (1995) *Species Design*, London, Titan/MGM.

Grim, O.R. (1995) 'Freaks ou la monstrueuse parade', *Contraste*, 3: 216–21.

Korff-Sausse, S. (1996a), 'Figures et devenir de l'étrangeté, approche psychanalytique du handicap', thèse de psychopathologie fondamontale et de psychanalyse, Université Denis Diderot Paris VII.

Korff-Sausse, S. (1996b) 'L'énigme des origines, quelque réflexions psychanalytiques sur handicap et sexualité', 'Handicap et inadaptation', *Les cahiers du C.T.N.E.R.H.I*, 71: 34–5.

Lascault, G. (1973) *Le monstre dans l'art occidental, un problème esthétique*, Paris, Klincksieck.

Rostand, E. (1897) *Cyrano de Bergerac*, Oxford, World's Classics, 1975.

Stiker, H.J. (1996) *'Rapport après soutenance de la thèse de Simone Korff-Sausse: Figures et devenir de l'étrangeté, approche psychanalytique du handicap'*, Université Denis Diderot Paris VII.

Valabrega, J.P. (1967) 'Le problème anthropologique du phantasme', in *Le désir et la perversion*, Paris, Seuil, pp.163–206.

13 Encountering the Real[1] in Handicap

MONIQUE SCHNEIDER

The metamorphoses which follow upon a handicap cannot be confined to the destructuring and restructuring which affect the person who is the main victim; a shockwave can be traced around the sensitive point which affects both parents as well as therapists confronted with an issue which will not leave them intact.

At the same time as assumptions which underpin daily life are shaken – assumptions, moreover, which go unnoticed except when they are confronted by something which renders them derisory – it is also familiar theoretical axioms which suddenly appear to vacillate. Such an encounter is thus particularly likely to bring out the vulnerable points in the analytic process. The research conducted by Simone Korff-Sausse in her thesis and in her book[2] is particularly enriching for analytic theory. Is it not true that the confrontation with handicap enables us to get in touch with the dead areas of analytic discourse?

ON THE NEAR SIDE OF (EN DEÇA DE)[3] GUILT

The unexpected arrival of a handicap essentially carries with it a boomerang effect, to the extent that the initial questions concerning the existence of the handicap immediately get directed towards whoever is in the position of witness or parent. Guilty anxiety seems then to cover other possible reactions; and we need to think about it here, not in order to question its importance but to uncover the psychical strata involved. How are we to understand the feeling of guilt which is so pervasive?

The first aspect of an answer concerns the analytic process itself. In Freud's dream about the injection given to Irma, the theme of guilt is closely bound up with the interpretative process itself, as if interpreting was essentially a matter of attributing some kind of responsibility. This correlation is, moreover, apparent in the words

Freud addresses in the dream to his patient: 'If you still get pains, it's your own fault.' The work of interpretation which follows describes a trajectory during which Freud switches from accusing the other – in this case, the suffering patient – to accusing himself, an accusation which turns into an attempt at self-defence. At this stage, it is essentially a matter of circumscribing the guilt by ascribing it to past acts. Freud then draws up an impressive list of medical errors.

Before ascribing suffering to initiatives which can be questioned *après coup* – which can be justified up to a point – the sense of responsibility can be found to operate at a more fundamental level. In *La violence de l'interprétation*, Piera Aulagnier outlines a form of implied responsibility, not primarily at the level of acts but rather at the level of sensorial encounter. By forwarding the postulate of self-begetting, she draws attention to the correlation established between all perceptive data and psychical movement at the primal stage, which constitutes the world as a ' fragment of specular surface'. This phenomenon of specularisation giving rise to the pictogram is analysed as follows:

> Any creation of psychical activity acts as a reflection for the psyche, a self-presentation, a force generating this image of something in which it is reflected ... If we admit that at this stage, the world – the non- psyche – has no existence apart from the pictographic representation created at the primal stage, it follows that the psyche encounters the world as a fragment of specular surface in which it contemplates its own reflection.[4]

At the primal stage one cannot speak, therefore, of being face-to-face with an object; thus, in the meeting of mouth-breast, it is the 'good mouth' which experiences itself as creating the breast, as if it were an extension of it. In this way the image of 'a complementary object-zone' is forged. From the moment one postulates – in the primal process as distinct from primary and secondary processes – a fundamental connection between what is perceived and the perceiver, the risks linked to a bad sensorial encounter take on an abyssal character:

> The desire to destroy the object will always be accompanied in this primal process by the desire to annihilate an erogenous and sensorial zone as well as the activity of which this zone is the centre. The perceived object can only be rejected during this stage by renouncing the visual zone and its own particular activity.[5]

The interest of such a theoretical construction is to emphasise the extreme nature of what one might call the bad encounter. The reac-

tions of rejection which accompany confrontation with a disconcerting object do not only concern the status of the object. The
perceiver himself (or herself) experiences a kind of eclipse, or fall into
oblivion. To the extent that, if we refer to the postulate of self-begetting which animates the primal register, the reality met with is experienced as self-engendered, responsibility ceases to be related essentially to contingent acts and becomes radically co-extensive with
perceptive life as a whole. If one adopts this outlook, one is led to
think that those who are destabilised by confrontation with handicap
are not only the parents who can ascribe the responsibility to filiation,
but also, all those who by noticing the handicap find themselves
caught in the act as it were, as if the act of perception immediately
created as decisive a bond as filiation.

SPECULARISATION AND AGGRESSIVENESS

The correlation between rejecting the other and self-mutilation
which exists in the primal register, will necessarily be checked or, at
the very least, partially thwarted, if one refers to less fundamental
agencies which characterise primary and secondary processes. The
correlation between perception and specularisation will not, for all
that, be suspended. It is in order to avoid the destructive effects of
the emerging specularisation that a strategy of avoidance is adopted,
as a result of which, the similar other in whom one does not manage
to recognise oneself, becomes the object of a process of de-realisation. Why de-realisation instead of a more aggressive response; one
motivated by potentially destructive aims? If we hastily oppose
aggressiveness and love, there is a risk of failing to recognise the
specific strategy which can be employed in a confrontation with that
which appears to be monstrous. In effect, in the encounter with a
person who is initially considered as dissimilar, aggressiveness itself
is diverted, making place for more devious forms of undoing. In the
Lacanian analysis of specular experience, aggressiveness is considered as a necessary component of a confrontation – even if it is purely
visual – in which a human being comes face to face with his double,
with one of them feeding off the other's being. Such aggressiveness,
far from being destructive of the bond between them, is thus an
integral part of the process of recognition by which the other is put
in the position of being similar; a recognition which leads indissol-
ubly to the establishment of a bond and the apprehension of a threat.

What becomes of the emerging specularisation when the other
reflects an image which I can only apprehend as the origin of an act
of delegation? Aggressiveness is thus deprived of its potential for
expression insofar as the transferential component which sustains it

is paralysed. In *The Interpretation of Dreams,* Freud draws out the two vectors which sustain the murderous wish motivating the fratricidal impulse by resorting to a French expression: '*ôte-toi de là que je m'y mette*' (get out of the way! give me some room).[6] In this expression, emphasis is often put on the annihilating wish, '*ôte-toi de là*', without necessarily taking into account the vector which makes possible the primary wish '*que je m'y mette*'. Understood in this way, annihilating wishes do not primarily consist of a refusal of recognition but presuppose a minimal recognition of the similar other one wishes to be rid of. When the fratricidal impulse is integrated within a context of rivalry, it comprises, both for oneself as well as for the rival, the possibility of occupying the same position.

What strategies can one resort to when this minimal specularity necessary for aggressive functioning runs up against an impossibility, that is, of the '*miroir brisé*' (broken mirror) which Korff-Sausse speaks about. Confronted with the potential inscription of a taboo-position, the person faced with a handicap and deprived of his habitual means of defence, will resort to a more extreme defensive measure involving the multifaceted characteristics of denial and undoing. Nevertheless, this impulse towards impossible identification, specific to the encounter with the other who cannot be speculated, cannot be magically suppressed. This other, who cannot face himself in the mirror, will then invade me to the extent that specular impossibility will prohibit me from positioning him opposite me. Thus, he will become an invading, vampire-like non-object, shaking the foundations of identity.

Obviously, the question must be raised as to how the handicapped person will perceive this structure of aggressiveness which has been neutralised because it is impossible. In his work, Johan De Groef[7] insists on the way in which the subject anticipates this impossible specularity by adapting himself in advance to the other's desire. The subject has perhaps understood that the pact of aggression to which the witness of the handicap sometimes feels driven, is the reverse side of a denial of existence. One of the axes which structure his relationship with the other in the event of a conflict is as a result invalidated.

THE SOCIALISED CREATION OF A PSEUDO-REALITY

What is the destiny of an encounter which does not allow the other a place within a structure of conflict and rivalry which, however violent, is nevertheless helpful in establishing specularity? The figure who abandons the mirror space will be condemned to being the object of denial, whose forms we can try to define. A retort which makes use of denial is certainly not specific to an encounter with handicap but constitutes a form of defence against trauma. 'Nothing can happen to you' (*Es kann dir nix g'schehen*): this is how Freud formulated the reaction of the ego when faced with potential catastrophe. Such a megalomaniac negation can, moreover, be turned into an accusation revendicating guilt, when the subject is faced with catastrophe. In '*Père, ne vois-tu pas ... ?*' (Father, don't you see ... ?),[8] a text consecrated to a reading of *The Interpretation of Dreams*, it seemed to me that the collection of dreams presented by Freud were organised around a traumatic fall during childhood, around which there was a blank which is repeatedly blotted out as if the trauma had just occurred, not by openly polarising a representative field but by perforating or tearing the screen on which a network of traces seeks to appear. This destructive work which depends on abolishing potential inscription can, however, be checked by resorting to a revendication of megalomaniac self-accusations. In the account he gives of his haemorrhagic fall in childhood, Freud reproaches himself with the words: '*Es ist dir recht geschehen*' (you deserved that), a remark which echoes '*Es kann dir nix g'schehen*'. The self-vindictive retort is certainly terrible, but nevertheless helps to restore omnipotence undermined by trauma. His self-accusation re-establishes a cruel, inflexible order, but one which is nevertheless likely to become the object of relentless fascination. It is in this way that a vast area of trauma which puts a check on anticipatory processes can , be re-elaborated in a phantasmatic enactment of destruction.

Is such a game which is inherent to the enactment of destruction possible with the representation of handicap? Does not handicap fundamentally elude the catastrophic register which is likely to be recuperated within a theme of murderous almightiness? Having presented a series of dreams during which he abandons himself to a kind of murderous celebration, Freud says that he has the impression 'of being the sole scoundrel [*einzige Bösewicht*] among the noble souls around him'.[9] By claiming uniqueness in this way, even as a scoundrel, Freud turned an eventual self-reproach into a triumph. Is such a reconversion imaginable for the person who, both on the level of perceptive complicity as well as filiation, finds himself phantasmatically assigned to the position of the one through whom the monstrous is revealed? If such a reconversion is not unimaginable, it nevertheless remains extremely difficult to conceive of.

Given the apories (insoluble rational difficulties) involved in attempting to inscribe handicap within a perceptive participation, the most banal form of defence consists in massive irrealisation, which is not limited to a few individual strategies but is part of a collective retaliation in the form of a 'negative pact' which René Kaës sees as fundamental to the formation of the group. The efficacy of such a pact is detected at the very heart of the analytic movement and Kaës gives the example of the words addressed by Freud to Fliess after the operation on Emma Eckstein during which Freud committed a professional error. However the alliance between the two men was strengthened by an exonerating statement: 'As far as blood is concerned', wrote Freud to Fliess, 'you are absolutely not to blame.' Far from rendering impossible the beginning of a new field of exploration, such a denial essentially ensured the maintenance of a command structure as if he had just limited the dimension of responsibility which is equally inseparable from the constitution of the group. Kaës insists on both the instituting and relative function of such a pact.

> We can only think and come together in Groups on the basis of extreme negativity. But whereas the purpose of thinking and forming groups is partly to reduce the infinite quantity of this negativity, to limit it and welcome it as the necessary condition for contact with the unknown and with otherness, we work towards filling the space opened by this castration with substitutes and omnipotent objects.[10]

The basic denial should, moreover, extend itself to a series of retroactive denials, for the dimension 'negative pact' can only be justified if it is itself hidden: 'We should, moreover, agree', continues Kaës, 'to forget that we have our own 'oubliettes' so as not to be faced with the thought that they contain waste or corpses.'[11]

To the extent that the *raison d'être* of such a pact touches upon the register of the uninscribable, the difficulties met with in the perception of handicap – a perception based on a relative measure of adoption, given the strangulation which affects the aggressive impulse – is there not a danger for whoever incarnates the non-similar, of becoming one of the privileged objects of the negative pact?

ENTERING AN IRREALISED FIELD

While the decree promulgated by the negative pact takes the form of a decree of non-existence, anyone who contests this non-existence can only occupy the position of the aggressor in the pact thus finding himself, with respect to the socialised sphere, in the virtual position of a revolutionary suspected of organising the group's subversion.

From the moment one finds oneself aligned with what represents a danger for the group, is it possible to have recourse to measured responses? Is one not condemned to resort to over-investment to the extent that guilt-inducing negotiation, inasmuch as it leads to an acceptance of localised responsibility, presupposes belonging to a community which is in itself problematic for those who are perceived as incarnating a permanent wound for the group's narcissism?

Being excluded can then sustain a megalomaniac phantasmatic analogous to Freud's when he claims he is 'the sole scoundrel'. A difficulty which has already been pointed out, crops up again: if one can phantasise that one is at the origin of something destructive, it requires even greater acrobacy to represent oneself as being at the origin of what risks being attributed to the monstrous. In this respect, Frankenstein, the hero of Mary Shelley's novel, comes to mind. It is often forgotten that the name Frankenstein refers to the learned author who created the monster and not the monster himself. This assimilation says much about the 'position' of the person who, tied by the self-generating activity implied in any sensitive encounter apprehended at the primal level, finds himself caught up – vis-à-vis the reality of handicap – in a demiurgic phantasmatic relationship. He becomes the creator of a neo-reality and it is understandable that this challenge can inspire (I refer here to the thesis of Korff-Sausse) artistic works.

The subversive impulse – which cannot be separated from the attempt to avoid withdrawing far from the field of visibility – can take on other forms than those which accept the dimension of aggression inherent to the status of being not-similar. The testimonies of parents indicate a greatly increased sensibility as if the reality of handicap constrained those who are trying to come to terms with it to invent another temporality to escape from the programming intentions which dominate the socialised universe, and to invent another value system which allows for the unpredictable. Here, we are closer to a Ferenczian theme where what is excluded is transformed into a saviour or 'guardian angel' than to Freudian dynamics which toy insolently with the contingency of the monstrous. Freud's irony with regard to Dr Herod, sometime paediatrician, is a case in point. Somehow or other, it seems difficult to confine oneself to ways of thinking which, according to the hypotheses advanced in the Esquisse, obey the law of 'small quantities'. Does over-investment not constitute the minimal price to be paid for maintaining a position in which breaking the pact is a possibility?

Does such a condemnation to excess, however, represent a durable position? It is clearly necessary to have recourse to a rhythm which implies moments of sober realism, the essential thing being to maintain a critical stance towards normative thinking which defines the criteria of normality. Whoever is regularly confronted with the necessity of inscribing that which, compared with the implicit

contract which regulates ordinary life, is uninscribable, will certainly
be led to resort to retaliation which under more ordinary circumstances would be stigmatised either as being maniac or as being too
idealistic. In order to judge this recourse to what borders on the
pathological, it is important to remember Freud's remark concerning
cultural activities in general: art, religion, and philosophy can have an
analogical relationship with the pathological but at the same time
defuse it by making it part of it a process of sharing. By qualifying as
'Zerrbild'[12] (the torn image), an image literally 'torn to pieces' in
which the major social productions are caught in a specular relation
with the pathological – even if this is based on a defiguration – Freud
draws out the violent dimension which sustains both pathological
choices and cultural creations, as if both were fed by some kind of
tamed monstrousness.

THE ANONYMOUS THREAT OF DEATH WEIGHING ON A CHILD

The umbilical cord which is able to link the threat of the monstrous
to aesthetic creation is, moreover, operative if one thinks of one of
the phantasmatic corner stones which underpin the creation of
psychoanalysis. Chapter VII in *The Interpretation of Dreams* is in effect
largely inspired by words taken from a poem by Goethe. 'Father,
don't you see ... ?' The dream of the dead child who is burning,
which is re-dreamed by several people, is presented by Freud as if the
source was 'unknown'. This is a strange phenomenon of blindness –
but is not blindness called for by the poem? – if one recalls that
Goethe is the author most often quoted by Freud throughout *The
Interpretation of Dreams*. Goethe's relationship with the dead child
was to be the subject of a text of Freud in which he studied Goethe's
autobiographical text *Dichtung und Wahrheit* (Fiction and Truth).
Whilst, in his psychoanalytical study, Freud based the theme of the
child 's death on a particular struggle as if it was necessary to establish a confrontation between the child dethroned by a rival and the
new arrival, Goethe describes a much more complex trajectory which
is attentive to the multiple forms linked to the advent of the
monstrous. It is essentially the text of Goethe – to the extent that it
contains the germ of what will appear in 'Erlkönig (The King of the
Aulnes)' – which will help us to recapture the effects of mutilation
and transfiguration which come in the wake of a traumatic threat. In
Goethe's text, the account of the catastrophe which struck the
children is itself situated within a cosmic frame of reference; that is,
the Lisbon earthquake, the scandalous and absurd nature of which is
underlined by Goethe: 'Nature's unbridled arbitrariness [*ihre
schrankenlose Willkür*]'.[13] Such natural violence is immediately

regarded as a sign of the 'monstrous' (*ungeheuer*), as if the frame of reference within which domestic events lie had itself been blown to pieces. The particular story which is the main subject of the narrative is thus related from the outset to what normally should have served as his foundations, that is, the ground beneath him which suddenly subsided resulting in a catastrophe which was an 'event of world-wide importance' (*Weltereignis*): 'sixty thousand human beings who a moment before were calm and untroubled, go down together [*gehen miteinander zugrunde*]'.[14] The attention given to the cosmic dimension is important at a time when sensibility to individual life journeys tends to minimise the traumatic violence experienced on a transindividual level. However, this shaking of the foundations will, in the child's mind, put in question the ground of trust itself:

> The child who was obliged to hear all this repeated was extremely troubled by it. God, the creator and protector of Heaven and Earth, whom the first article of the Faith described as being so wise and merciful, had not conducted himself at all as a father, confusing the just and the unjust in the same loss.[15]

Before turning to strictly individual life journeys, the narrator focuses his attention on increasingly narrow circles: following the cosmic shock, came the 'family suffering' (*Familienleiden*)[16] – smallpox – presented first as a misfortune which fell upon all the brothers and sisters. Whereas Freud tries to include the unexpected death within a fratricidal pair, Goethe introduces a catastrophic temporality which cannot easily be reduced to the theme of guilt alone. The destructive element seems to occur at the same time as the failure of a primal agency provoking an effect of depersonalisation: 'Just as in summer a family walk can be spoilt ... by a sudden storm, in the same way ...',[17] disease seems to fall upon the family as if analogous to a natural and blind force:

> Disease was rife in families, killed or disfigured many children ... The scourge also reached our house and struck me especially violently. My whole body was covered with spots, my face was covered and I was blind for several days suffering terribly.

What is the object of the scourge? There is a considerable gap between the enactment as interpreted by Freud in 'A childhood memory of *Poetry and Truth*' and Goethe's text. Freud is in fact mainly concerned to separate the agent who on the level of phantasy has the destructive role and the victim, the younger brother who is bullied by the eldest, which confines the interplay of life and death to a confrontation between two protagonists. While leaving open the possibility of a phantasmatic fratricidal struggle playing itself out behind the scenes at the time of the little brother's birth, it is important not to simply reduce this interpretative schema to the unexpected onset of illness and to approach the more indirectly destructive phenomenon which can be seen when something catastrophic occurs. The differentiation of their respective identities first occurs for reasons other than personal ones, as if the person who suddenly fell sick stood for the family as a whole, for Goethe speaks of 'family suffering' (*Familienleiden*). It is only later, during the course of the narrative, that the circle tightens around Wolfgang himself who is disfigured by his illness:

> Finally after some time had passed sadly, a kind of mask fell from my face [*fiel es mir wie eine Maske vom Gesicht*], without the postules leaving any marks on my face, but my features had changed noticeably [*merklich verändert*]. The others were sufficiently merciless to remind me of my former state. In particular, there was a distinctly lively aunt who up till then had worshipped me, but who now could hardly see me without exclaiming: 'Pooh, what a nasty nephew you've turned into!' [*Pfui, Teufel! Vetter, wie garstig ist er geworden*].[18]

Before the duality between the elder and younger brother manifests itself, a phenomenon of split personality appears first of all in the effects of the sickness itself. With the second layer of skin which formed after the postules, we witness the fall of what had temporarily served as his face: '... a kind of mask fell from my face'. Before losing the other, there was the equivalent of a loss of the self, the loss of his face. A fall which was all the more disconcerting as the face which was normally behind the mask was itself 'visibly changed' *(merklich verändert)*. Insofar as the relationship one has with one's self-image constitutes a substratum of identity, it is the primal identity which seems to get swept away by the fall of the mask-face. His aunt's remark confirmed this rupture of recognition of the self by the other. The real face is now only referred to by referring to the past: 'my former state', says Goethe.

During the narrative we witness a succession of losses or rather an intertwinement of different losses. The sickness from which the youngest brother suffers comes in the wake of the elder brother's illness; as if, due to the latter's illness, a part of the sibling relationship had died, while mourning for the other is included in the preliminary mourning for oneself:

While speaking of this family illness, I also want to remember one of my brothers, three years younger than I, who fell sick from the plague and suffered a lot ... He hardly outlived his childhood. Among several brothers and sisters born after me who did not live long either, I can only recall a very beautiful and pleasant little girl who also died soon after, so that after a few years, my sister and I lived alone.[19]

Can such devastation – at the level of unconscious transcription – be imputed to fratricidal rivalry, as Freud hypothesises in his reading of Goethe's text? Without completely invalidating Freud's hypothesis, returning to the literary text nevertheless restores a psychic stratum disrupted by the irruption of the catastrophic.

Before individual identities, is it not the global unity represented by the phratry as a whole which is threatened, as if the family suffered the equivalent of a loss of the face linked to the feeling of vulnerability concerning its roots. Are we not witnessing here the equivalent of an earthslide which occurs as a result of ground movements linked to the earthquake?

There may well be a feeling of guilt, but it is important not to be taken in by its defensive and secondary character. It is extremely valuable in reintroducing individual responsibility at a point where the catastrophic has been experienced as a blow affecting the support itself and not just the scene contained within it. The trauma related to the catastrophic in effect breaks up, disrupts, the system of co-ordinates within which destruction occurs; before subjective conflicts, one witnesses the equivalent of a ground subsidence which relates to more global units than those which are incarnated in an individual: family, nature, the order of the universe – all props which collapse. Revendications of guilt may, indeed, arise but to stem and limit the feeling that the fruitful substratum which relates to archaic states of shared narcissism has collapsed.

It is certainly not fortuitous if immediately after retranscribing the family loss, Goethe introduces a dimension which confirms the fundamental importance of the relationship with the earth. The grandfather who plays the part of powerful guardian of the garden now looms into view. At the point where psychic survival is disturbed, attention is turned towards the conditions of infra-human life, anonymous and vegetable, marked by the slow, cyclical temporality of the seasons. In analytic experience, after the irruption of the catastrophic, it is necessary to be attentive to attempts made to rediscover complicity – a kind of animistic or cosmic fraternity – with what is alive, thus making possible a sleepy survival.

Immersal in the chtonic dimension represents, however, only one of the vectors introduced in Goethe's text. Poetic creation intervenes to build a bridge between the catastrophic and initiation to an aura of sacred terror. It is not without concern, that in the poem 'The King of the Aulnes' one can find traces of a signifier which in the biography was connected with the presentiment of death. Just as in a puzzle, one of the verses of the poem lays out and isolates verbal elements which are similar to the term used to designate the family illness: *Windblatter: 'In dürren Blättern saüselt der Wind'* ('The wind rustles in dry leaves'). The verse thus transmutes terror into a magical and disturbing murmur; the character of the king taking upon himself the powers of sickness as if the mutism brought about by the monstrous catastrophic could only be reconverted by what, through the power of the poem, provokes this ambiguous effect of combined wonder and stupefaction.

Is it this night-time effect that Freud is sensitive to when, reinserting in his theoretical text the words attributed to the child in the poem – 'Father, don't you see ... ?' – he suppresses the name of the author of the poem in order to re-establish a more anonymous community before making any subjective claims. Whether it is a matter of attention given to the chtonic dimension or on the access to nocturnal speech, it seems that the impact of the monstrous cannot be circumscribed within the limits of personal subjectivity and that it requires that common ground be taken into account.

NOTES

1. Translator's note: this is a Lacanian concept not to be confused with reality. It is linked to the symbolic and imaginary orders but stands for what is neither symbolic nor imaginary and remains foreclosed from analytic experience. For further reading see, for example, Lacan, J. (1973) *The Four Fundamental Concepts of Psychoanalysis*, London, Penguin, 1977.

2. Korff-Sausse, S. (1996) *Le miroir brisé. L'enfant, sa famille et la psychanalyse*, Paris, Calmann-Levy.

3. Translator's note: the French prepositions *en deça de/au delà de* do not have neat equivalents in English but have the rough meaning of 'on the near side of/on the far side of' or 'short of/in excess of'. For further reading, see Bowie, M. (1991) *Lacan*, London, Fontana Press.

4. Aulagnier, P. (1975) *La violence de l'interprétation. Du pictogramme à l'énoncé*, Paris, PUF, p.58.

5. Ibid., p.63.
6. Freud, S. (1900) 'The Interpretation of Dreams', in James Strachey, ed., *The Standard Edition of the Complete Psychological Works of Sigmund Freud*, 24 vols, London, Hogarth, 1953–73, vol. 5, p.463;. *Die Traumdeutung*, Studienausgabe, Frankfurt am Main, Fischer (1977), p.466. I have analysed this structure of confrontation in *'Père, ne vois-tu pas ... ? Le père, le maitre, le spectre dans* L'Interprétation des rêves, Paris, Denoël, 1985, pp.165–95.
7. De Groef, J. (1997) 'Du sei wie Du. De l'amour et de la passion', *Le Coq-héron*, 145.
8. Schneider, M. (1985) *'Père, ne vois-tu pas ... ? Le père, le mâitre, le spectre dans* L'Interprétation des rêves, Paris, Denoël; 'L'analyse du travail d'effacement à l'œuvre dans le trauma est poursuivie', in *La part de l'ombre. Approche d'un trauma féminin*, Paris, Auber, 1991.
9. Freud, S. (1900) 'The interpretation of Dreams', p.464; *Die Traumdeutung*, p.467.
10. Kaës, R. (1989) 'Le pacte dénégatif dans les ensembles transsubjectifs', in A. Missenard et al., *Le Négatif, figures et modalités*, Paris, Dunod, p.118.
11. Ibid., p. 114.
12. Freud, S. (1913) 'Totem and Taboo', *S.E.* 13, p.73.
13. Goethe, J. (1975) *Fiction et vérité* [*FV*], Paris, Aubier, p.26; *Dichtung und Wahrheit* [*DW*], Frankfurt am Main, Inseltaschenbuch, 1975, p.37.
14. *FV*, p.26; *DW*, p.36.
15. *FV*, p.26; *DW*, p.37.
16. *FV*, p.30; *DW*, p.43.
17. *FV*, p.30; *DW*, p.44.
18. *FV*, p.30; *DW*, p.44.
19. *FV*, p.30; *DW*, p.45.

14 A Psychotherapy from the Beginning to the End?: A Case Study

RICHARD RUTH

Thomas Ogden (1994) has rightly argued that writing is a form of resistance – what we write on paper reflects not just the depth and clarity of what we know, but perhaps more importantly the limits of what we know. Around the edges of a text, infusing the texture of a text, and in the preconscious resonances of a text, lies a dialogue between the conscious and the unconscious of the writer. One problem is that it is in the nature of a text to kill the dialogue, to turn active thinking and live movement into something static, with pretensions of authority that can only be defensive and thus distorting.

This has to be all the more true when we write about a case, about a piece of analytic work we have done with a patient, and perhaps true in an especially crystalline way when writing about work with a patient with mental retardation. Such patients typically have secondary as well as primary mental handicaps (Sinason 1986), with defensive and characterological structures organised around ego-dystonic reactions to the disability. As all analytically engaged patients do, they try to make us feel what they feel, often using projective mechanisms. Thus, in synergy with the elements of resistance inherent in preparing a written case report, an analyst writing about work with a patient with mental retardation has to cope with an awareness, or the possibility or phantasy of an awareness, that lingering introjects of the patient remain unmetabolised in his/her mental apparatus, muddying judgement and distorting lived history.

These problems are unsolvable, and perhaps the more interesting for that. At least they can be acknowledged.

Mindful of the inherent risks I have tried to elaborate, I wanted to write about my work with Patrick (not his real name, but resonant with it) for several reasons. As this meeting reflects, there is now a substantial body of experience in productive analytically influenced work with people with mental retardation. Experiences have been replicated in different settings. We are perhaps at a point where we can plunge with more foundation and focus into the work of extracting lessons, refining theory, and exploring the implications of what we are learning. Not unrelated to this, there is the question of how to talk about what we can offer, about what kind of connections and relations we would want to have with the broader world of mental retardation. Talking about a case which began on a naturalistic note – that is, a patient was referred by someone who felt he needed help and his family sought treatment too – and which had a chance to develop relatively freely as well as to terminate when the time was ripe, might contribute to both sets of questions.

HOW THE WORK BEGAN

Patrick is the son of Chinese immigrant parents in the US. He has moderate to mild mental retardation, the uncertainty in level being attributable to the fact that he has never really co-operated with a psychological assessment. As is often done, both parents adopted English names when they came to the country. Why they chose to give their children Irish names, I was unable to ascertain. He was referred to me when he was twelve, and I saw him twice a week for a little more than five years.

The proximal issue that led to the referral was that Patrick had begun refusing to go to school. Related to this, he was wilful, demanding, sometimes violent toward his parents (hitting both of them, throwing things at them, breaking things near them), and little interested in learning or doing what he was asked to learn or do. Acknowledged by both his parents and his school, but seen as less pressing and focal, were observations that he was often sad, bored and lonely, with feelings of emptiness and much confusion about where his life was going or what he wanted or needed to do. There were clear, problematic issues in Patrick's environment, and many would have been tempted to focus on these rather than on his inner life and its dynamics. Both parents were unsatisfied with their lives, and had problems of their own.

The mother, a medical technician, felt she had never achieved the status and regard she desired, and seemed to experience and use her child's retardation as a container for her lost and lapsed aspirations. Once Patrick approached puberty and seemed less willing, perhaps less able, to serve in this capacity, as symbolised by his school refusal, she turned to essentially manic defences – a constant round of social activities, a tendency to pick and sustain arguments with Patrick. Her sense, often expressed with an inescapable element of covert pleasure, that Patrick persecuted her, seemed like a tenuous connection with her own projected contents.

The father, who was a dentist, came across as depressed, with an autistic personality style. He felt that his life had never become what he imagined he may have wanted – he could not really articulate what that might have been, and I suspect he did not know and had never known. His intention was to lose himself in work and to die young; his primary defences were schizoid rather than manic, somewhat complementing his wife. Patrick's misbehaviour seemed to embody covertly his split-off desires.

Neither parent had ever recovered from the birth of a retarded child, and neither seemed to experience Patrick in a whole-object mode of relatedness. Each identified with a different fragment – the mother with the part of him that was not retarded, leading her to push and make demands on him all the time; the father with the part that was dead and hopeless, the heart of the handicap, leading him never to expect or try much with Patrick. Father could not tolerate awareness of Patrick's alive parts, nor mother awareness of his dead parts. The marital relationship lacked intimacy, and seemed more like a minimally satisfactory business relationship. Mother was more westernised, father more Chinese. Neither ever learned much about mental retardation, or seemed very motivated to cathect their ideas about Patrick intensely enough to try to really prove or disprove them. When they would fight for services for their son, the fight would be listless and soon peter out.

Early on, a pattern had been laid down. When Patrick would not do what the school or the parents wanted, when he would assert a bit of rebellion or seem immobilised by confusion – it fascinated me how easily the two stances shifted to and fro so easily – the mother would bribe and cajole him, and then the father would undercut the power and efficacy of the bribe. When Patrick was first brought to me, the bribes had become excessive, and had stopped working at all well.

Both push and pull factors led me to think individual work with Patrick would be most effective. In the initial consultations, the discord between the parents and the limited capacity of both to grasp the dynamics at play made me pessimistic that work with or through them could be readily effective or sustained. The tendency for Patrick's needs and perspectives to get lost in their arguments and failed efforts to control or help him made me feel he needed space to get to know himself, to develop an identity, to interact with someone who might believe in his eventual ability to think. Furthermore, his fierce hostility toward me in our initial meetings made me feel there was an alive spark beneath his surface dullness with which it might be very useful to work. He would refuse to get in the car to come to sessions, or to get out of the car once he was at my office, sit and glare at me, saying little and lapse into the most persevering and empty phrases.

ESTABLISHING A WORKING ALLIANCE AND SPACE FOR WORK

I have little idea why Patrick decided he would be willing to work with me. In a way, I see this as validating my original positive prognosis. There was an 'inside' to Patrick in which he was able to work out a decision to collaborate in the treatment, at least in the sense of entering and staying in the field, cathecting both the process and the object Other. At least this fragment and moment of a depressive position was there from the start.

I see child, adolescent and adult patients in the same room. Each child has a locked box; adolescents and adults do not, generally speaking. There are a few larger toys and games visible for the use of those who choose them. My first sense that Patrick was already feeling a cathected transference relationship with me, and thus the beginnings of an alliance, came when, a few weeks into the treatment – which, up until then, had consisted of painful, wearying sessions of glaring and few words – he asked if he could play cards. What was triggered in me, quite powerfully, was an awareness of how carefully Patrick had been scanning the visual environment of the office, including me as a part of it – he had seen the cards, while it had appeared to me that he was seeing nothing. He seemed to be trying out at the level of bodily sensation what he could not yet establish at the level of mind and affect, some element of relationship – and the first card games were very much interactions primarily of body ego, with the passing and placing of the cards much more important than their numerical meaning (which Patrick would often get wrong) or the rules of the simple games he chose (which he often lost track of entirely). His preferred game, not without symbolic evocations, was War.

A rhythm set in. Patrick or I might toss out some attempt at verbal interchange, but it would not last long or go far, or feel very satisfying. Then, he would pick up the cards, and a sense of aliveness would return. I was surprised one day to realise that this felt like a working alliance, as it was quite different from what I was used to thinking about as an alliance with other patients; but the more I thought about it, the more it was. Patrick and I had met each other inside his retardedness, and were communicating and working there. Slowly, of course, he came to talk while he played, as children often do in play therapy when they take up clay or drawing; and the talk often became very rich and poignant. But it felt like it was never the heart of the alliance.

As in any therapy that does not involve an adult arriving of their own accord, establishing space for my therapeutic work with Patrick was an issue. For long months, he would refuse school frequently and get into frequent, awful, sometimes violent conflicts with the parents. Once he destroyed a loved and expensive toy, and then several compact discs; on another occasion, he killed a pet rabbit in a fit of frustration. Often he was angrier and more upset after sessions than before. It was not illegitimate for the parents and the school to wonder what, if anything, therapy was doing. I wondered too. All I could tell them was that I thought there was a good likelihood that, over time, therapy could help Patrick get to a place where he would go to school, and accomplish other important things as well, and that, in the meanwhile, there was value in putting up with things as tolerable within certain liberal limits, in getting to know what he wanted to do and why he wanted to do it. I was also very clear that there was an unknown we would all have to be able to live with, and communicated this to the parents, to the school, and to Patrick. Patrick looked at me as if I were odd when I said this to him, and I was not at all sure he understood what I meant, though I suspect that a part of him understood a part of what I said.

What ultimately seemed to help the parents was when they perceived there was a space inside of me that could conceive of work with Patrick as a rich and alive possibility – that I seemed to be thinking about Patrick, and bearing the thinking. Their willingness to help create the conditions of external space – transporting him, waiting during his sessions, paying, accepting the obligation of regular, long-term appointments – seemed to flow from their introjection of this sense of internal space.

PATRICK'S USE OF PLAY

For a very long time, Patrick seemed to use non-play play. He would use the cards as a primitive structure for interaction between us, but not really follow the rules of the game, or even cathect the cards as play objects the way young children might develop a pleasure in playing with pots and pans. There was no fantasising about the cards that was at all discernible, no proto-thinking to accompany the non-play.

During the long period of time that these conditions held, my sense was that Patrick was occupied more than anything else with his sensations, and some volitional processing and metabolising of these. In a way that I have come to think might be characteristic of numerous people with mental retardation, I think he had to learn how to play with his own unreliable and hard-to-get-to-know sensory experience as a prerequisite to more effective engagement with the subsequent developmental line of play in the way we more usually think of this term. He delayed developing a secure cathexis of mastery strivings until he felt really ready for this. I came to respect this quite deeply as representing his decision to approach development on his own terms, with a rhythm and pace congruent with his desires and character, and with his retardation. I think something important that therapy did for Patrick was to sustain space in which he could do this.

When Patrick did begin to play, it was always retarded play, but rich retarded play – never uninteresting. Two of his favourite activities were throwing a Nerf ball at a poster in a parody of basketball, and speaking in foreign accents.

At first I thought his ball play was similar to what boys often do when they imagine themselves as professional athletes, but it was not. Patrick would indicate his awareness that he was not athletic, not able to be at all like a professional athlete even on the level of humour or fantasy, and that his throwing game was the game of someone who was cognitively limited and uncoordinated. He was not doing what younger, non-retarded boys do. What he was doing, then, was playing, mentally as well as physically, with the notion of having mental retardation and what that was all about.

Similarly, in his use of accents, he seemed to be recognising that his range of vocabulary was limited – saying the limited phrases accessible to him in different ways, he was among other things confronting, and communicating his awareness that his communications were limited. He was also showing me – and showing me he would remain incapable of articulating verbally or more directly – that he had a tendency to copy form over developing content, that his mode was one of concreteness and copying rather than abstraction. He was playing with awareness of these kinds of things.

I suspect Patrick was simultaneously also trying to work out what he thought about his bilingualism – Patrick spoke English primarily, but Cantonese at home – and about the cultural differences between us, in a kind of transitional space, using the accents to play with notions of language, foreignness and culture in an indirect way rather than commenting on them directly. The retardation seemed it would have made it difficult, if not impossible, to capture his thoughts and feelings about these kinds of issues in communicable words. His play with these concepts, using accents, had a quality of whole-object, well-cathected mental activity, unlike his parents' more split-off ways of thinking about being Chinese (having two names; talking about some things only with other Chinese people and others only with non-Chinese; introducing discussions of elements of Chineseness in their conversations with me, and then telling me that I seemed to understand a lot, but they doubted I could ever get anything like a complete understanding).

THE EMERGENCE OF LANGUAGE

In the third year of therapy, Patrick's language began to flower. This was gratifying, to the parents and to me, and to Patrick only to a much lesser extent; but it also seemed very predictable, almost routine. It paralleled a sense of an often discussed phenomenon in child therapy, that if therapy can help life remain bearable, development will eventually happen. Patrick began to name feelings, to report events in his life, to colour in his previously telegraphic and schematic narratives.

More than this phenomenon of therapy as a holding environment, however, what seemed focally significant was the willingness of the therapeutic space to permit Patrick to experience his discovery of language *in his preferred style as a person with mental retardation*. That is, there was no impetus, as he found in school or on family occasions, to use language 'normally'. For example, Patrick was able, when prompted or when he wanted to, to speak in full sentences, with articles and subjects and predicates in their assigned places; but he often preferred not to, and the result had a poetry to it, a poetry specific to mental retardation and its voices.

At a later point in the treatment, Patrick's freed-up language development seemed to plateau. His parents and his school seemed acutely aware of this; he did not. Therapy at this point served not to protect him from a sense that his parents and school were feeling loss and disappointment, and attempting to project this into him, so much as to create a space internally in Patrick and in the therapeutic field, where the issue of what he said or did not say was treated with analytic neutrality and curiosity. What he had to say was experienced as congruent with his identity as a teenager with mental retardation; it was enough, and it could be appreciated and explored within its own frame of reference, without a need to compare it to non-retardation for a sense of identity.

The awareness and tracking of these dynamics happened principally in my own thinking, and then were introjected by Patrick, but the effect of the introjection was visceral and observable. What was important was the emergence of a language of mental retardation, which is the only whole-object kind of language it seems likely Patrick will ever have. When he speaks at times more 'normally', it is a false-self kind of speech. When this 'normal' kind of language use was also encountered neutrally, and not celebrated, a capacity for self-creation seemed to be facilitated in Patrick.

SUSTAINING THE ALLIANCE AND SPACE FOR WORKING WHEN PATRICK BEGAN TO GET BETTER

It is not only the parents of children with mental retardation who experience their children's development and emerging identity and autonomy as embodying annihilatory wishes directed toward the parents but, as Mannoni (1967, 1973) has discussed, this has a particular shape and power in many such parents. Thus, when Patrick began to go to school, to fight less often and less viciously and to regulate his affects better, the therapy that had come to constitute a vital life space for him was threatened.

I became aware of this one day when Patrick and I had been laughing uproariously during a session, and the mother was able to hear some of the laughter through the doors. This had led her to go out and buy food for us, announcing at the end of the session with a big smile that she had brought 'treats for the boys'. The items she had selected for both of us were not just unappetising, but things she must have covertly sensed would be contrary to our tastes, not to mention violative of what she had already learned were the analytic ground rules.

The mother's act, as the incident was analysed over time, was multidetermined. She perceived us as acting non-retarded, and was attempting to let us know that we *were* retarded nonetheless (me symbolically and by identification, Patrick by not even momentarily escapable or tolerable fate), and that we were infantilised by being so. Simultaneously, she was expressing jealousy that we had the pleasure of retardation – only people with mental retardation, in this construction, laugh out loud – while she did not, and was attempting to be allowed to share by a projected act of oral incorporation: if we would eat her food, then she would be inside us, and could share in our pleasurable retarded laughter. She was also attempting to put toxic contents into the therapeutic field and into us – communicating this by letting us know, among other things, that she had listened to the secrets of the private therapeutic space, and had taken them in. The extremity of her act, which did not escape us, let us know (or made us wonder whether we really agreed with her) that we had pushed her to an edge, had threatened her existence, and thus engaged us with wondering whether what had felt like a free, contented moment had constituted or been transformed into dangerous ground.

There was a very real possibility at this point that the mother would decide Patrick was well enough and no longer needed therapy; and a sense that there was very little Patrick or I could do to influence her decision. She had long decided not to have any treatment of her own, and did not seem inclined to change her mind. Arguing with her seemed pointless: to me, I thought it would covertly communicate that her concerns were rational, accurate and valid in ways I did not experience them to be so; and to Patrick, it seemed both impossible to even think about arguing with his mother in favour of therapy, and that it would be violative of elements of his identity to even fantasise doing so. Instead, there developed a sense between Patrick and me that the mother (the father had long since abandoned any claim in these matters) would do what she would do, and he and I could only think about it, continue our work and play and conversation in the time and space available to us, and work at bearing the uncertainty in the environment.

Once again, it was this sense of internal space for thinking that seemed to help generate, and regenerate, the working alliance and therapeutic space. Patrick and I developed a renewed sense that the process between us had deepened and become more intimate, and the mother seemed to perceive this and to introject an element of soothing. Our ability to bear her sallies seemed to help her bear our continued work, and in particular to bear that Patrick would remain retarded – indeed, in some important ways, would seem more retarded than ever – as he began to feel more comfortable with his identity, and more able to relate with a sense of mutuality as he became more grounded in this comfort.

THE DECISION TO END THE TREATMENT

Few child treatments end neatly or gently. My work with Patrick was no exception.

Symptoms had abated but were not absent. Patrick could still have tantrums and refuse reasonable requests, though in both cases far less frequently than had been the case, and the tantrums had an edgy quality, less intense than they had been but at times barely within tolerable bounds. He went to school regularly, but would keep the parents on edge by threatening not to do so with some frequency. He would sometimes refuse to go to planned extended family events or religious activities, seemingly as a way of showing he still had the capacity to refuse.

In school, Patrick was more co-operative with the curriculum he was being taught, which could be the interesting subject of another chapter. His classes were often boring, odd or had an empty feeling about them, teaching him how to do things he already knew how to do or that seemed pointless, but he would do what was asked of him more often than not. Again, this was not across the board; he would refuse activities that seemed really noxious to him often enough to let the faculty know he was still capable of doing so. They responded to this by praising his performance more, as if to devalidate by dishonest praise from a non-retarded person what was honest and authentic in Patrick's stance.

Patrick had an increased range of interests – music, collections, pet snails and fish, karaoke, movies (which had formerly terrified him, because of their multisensory intensity), watching sports and nature programmes on television – and a few friends. He liked doing things with his friends only in very secure contexts (nothing spontaneous, for example) and relatively infrequently; he seemed to need a lot of build-up time, and then a lot of metabolising time to process the experience. He had the sproutings of some interest in females, though this tended to frighten him, and he would decathect and pull back quite easily. He did a few simple jobs the school found him for money, performing adequately but not more than adequately, as he did not seem to want to do more.

Patrick was very much a teenager with mental retardation, far from what a teenager without mental retardation would be like. He was clueless, at seventeen, about what he wanted to do in the future, but the future was still far off, as he would remain in school until he was twenty-one. He seemed secure, effective and quite comfortable in maintaining his ground – no one was going to get him to think very far ahead; perhaps because he felt grounded in his ability to think about where he was.

Several factors seemed to suggest that it could be time to finish therapy. The level of symptoms was consistently bearable, and seemed like an effective compromise solution. When I would think about whether Patrick's life seemed good, satisfying and interesting, my sense was that it was. I began to feel that, while Patrick seemed to enjoy coming to sessions, there was a palpable lessening of intensity in his feelings about me, about being in therapy, and about the discussions and play in the sessions. The need and tie had both weakened. I could imagine Patrick not being in therapy and not feel counter-transferential or withdrawn when thinking this. He seemed to be experiencing me with less of a quality of over-determination. In other words, his moves toward a relative, adequate resolution of a transference neurosis did not feel like the resolution of a transference neurosis, just as his establishment of a working alliance had not at first felt like the establishment of an alliance, because both were a version of these phenomena chosen by a person with mental retardation within the parameters of his own abilities and operating style.

Perhaps most importantly, Patrick had developed an identity, even at times a pride, in his retardedness. In his therapy, as in his life-course, libido that had been withdrawn back into the system ego from an object experienced originally as non-accommodating, and then subjected to the processes of splitting and projection, was now being used non-narcissistically. Patrick was enjoying his retarded life. The radical choice, but the one that felt most authentic, was to acknowledge that the space that had been the space of therapy needed now to be the space to live out his retardation.

One way to deal with the problem of writing as resistance in a chapter of this sort seems to be to acknowledge, by way of conclusion, what is still fragmentary and unmetabolised in my understanding of my work with Patrick. I felt like I recognised major elements of the therapy – the establishment of a working alliance, the beginnings of resolution of a transference neurosis – after the fact, and wonder whether and how this may have constrained what we were able to accomplish. I also wonder whether at critical points I may have deviated from a neutral stance between body and mind – whether my sense at times that body-ego phenomena were primary led me to neglect simultaneous dynamic phenomena, and vice versa; and I wonder whether my sense that medication was not likely to play a useful role with Patrick may have had elements of a similar violation of neutrality among operative agencies.

I have wondered whether this was a therapy that ended too soon, and in particular whether I may have resisted thinking about whether something more like analysis than therapy might have been indicated for Patrick. Toward the end, I recall having a sense that if we were to go further, phenomena that had been worked through to a partial but satisfying degree would need to be re-excavated – for example, it felt that further work on what went through Patrick's mind when he thought about himself as retarded (he hated the term) might be useful, but might involve major upheavals – and that this would be painful and destabilising for both Patrick and his family, and might not work. I am not sure whether I was being objective, or just frightened, or specifically frightened of a secret that had been projected into me for safekeeping – that it is too frightening to think too much about being retarded, as the possibility of that line of thinking lives in Patrick and as fragments of it live in me – and that I had abdicated my responsibility to analyse these projected contents.

What feels, oddly, most grounding and most frightening to me is my sense that what Patrick's therapy needed to do was to help him become more fully retarded – that to the extent it did this, it succeeded, and to the extent it did not, it had elements of failure. The metaphor continues to intrigue me: is our task less to help people minimise their elements of retardation, and more to help them discover the depths, possibilities, truths, uniquenesses and qualities of their retardedness? I continue to play with these thoughts and wonder where they will lead to, and what they fully imply.

REFERENCES

Mannoni, M. (1967) *The Child, his Illness and the Others*, London, Penguin.
Mannoni, M. (1973) *The Retarded Child and its Mother*, London, Tavistock.
Ogden, T. (1994) *Subjects of Analysis*, Northvale, NJ, Jason Aronson.
Sinason, V. (1986) 'Secondary Mental Handicap and its Relation to Trauma', *Psychoanalytic Psychotherapy*, 2: 131–54.

15 A Psychoanalytical Approach to Mental Handicap

SIMONE KORFF-SAUSSE

My research into a psychoanalytical approach to the handicapped child has two bases:

- from a theoretical point of view, it is grounded in psychoanalytical theory. I refer in particular to the concepts of trauma, the process of mourning and the construction of self-identity emphasising the importance of the mirror-role of the mother (and society) as described by Winnicott (1967)
- from a clinical point of view, it is derived from my own practice as a psychoanalyst, partly in a centre which treats young handicapped children and their parents, and partly in a nursery school where a third of the total number of children are handicapped.

First of all, I think it would be useful to clarify what the characteristics of these institutions in France are, because they determine the methodology and theoretical orientation of my research.

CENTRE FOR EARLY SOCIO-MEDICAL ACTION

The role of the CAMSP[1] in France is to provide care for infants up to the age of six who have a handicap, as well as their families. The handicaps treated include motor handicaps (CMI, spina bifida), mental deficiencies of diverse origins (Down's syndrome, encephalopathies, retarded psycho-motor development linked to varied etiologies or unknown etiologies), sensor handicaps (deafness or blindness) and children with multiple handicap. These handicaps are often associated with disorders in personality and communication. In certain cases, autistic pathology is in the foreground.

AN INNOVATIVE NURSERY SCHOOL

This is a child care centre[2] which works with twenty children from the neighbourhood, aged one to six, a third of whom are severely handicapped in some way. This blending of 'normal' children from the community with the seriously handicapped, ill or autistic is an innovative concept of integration. By studying the interactions between 'normal' and handicapped children, we can observe the processes of identification at work in young children, whether handicapped or healthy, who are confronted with their differences. This experiment makes it possible to avoid the isolation of an infant who is 'not like the others' when he (or she) is seen as an exceptional anomaly within a group of healthy children.

The term 'handicap' is not very satisfactory, giving rise to problems of definition, boundaries and translation. The children I am talking about are afflicted with a variety of handicaps, but they have in common the experience of being confronted by a type of peculiarity that is imprinted on their psychosomatic existence and affects their autonomy, psychic life and social adaptation. Thus, in my opinion, the typology of the handicap does not appear to be pertinent as far as psychoanalysis is concerned.[3] We should not interpret the psychic modes of a child by relating them to his type of handicap, but be attentive to the psychic processes the child uses to confront his peculiarity, no matter what his handicap is. In other words, I do not believe that any given handicap has its own specific psychopathology.

This methodology is closely related to the approach during the 1970s which created care centres and provided a framework for this kind of therapeutic work with handicapped children. In effect, the CAMSP were created with the idea of offering early and global medico-psychosocial help to children and parents faced with whatever type of handicap. The aim, on the one hand, was to support the parents' educative efforts on behalf of a child who profoundly affects their own narcissistic and identity problems while, on the other hand, maximising the potential for fulfilment of a child with a severely limiting handicap.

Children are often taken into care during their first year. At that stage:

- specific aetiology is not always conclusive
- psychic and organic factors are intertwined
- early intervention enables action to be undertaken
  - with regard to the child's first stages of identity formation
  - with regard to the parents during the years immediately following the discovery of the handicap

- the duration of the period of care, spread out over several years, provides for the study of the psychic processes as they evolve
- the complexity of the symptomology requires the existence of a team referred to as 'multidisciplinary' and capable of dealing with multiple factors: medical and social problems, speech therapy, motor or psychomotor re-education, the psychological support of the parents, and the psychotherapeutic follow-up of the children. It is very important for parents that a variety of therapeutic services are available under one roof so that they can have ready access to the different people and services which their children are in need of.

The discovery of the child's handicap is viewed as being a traumatic event for the parents. However, this hypothesis requires some precision: on the one hand, the concept of trauma is perhaps too general to take into consideration the specific nature of different clinical situations; on the other hand, there are successive interpretations of trauma in Freudian thought.

At first, the psychoanalyst runs the risk of being overwhelmed himself (or herself) by the extremely painful counter-transference feelings evoked by a handicapped child. The irremediability of a handicap constitutes a limit to the hope for the care which can be given by the analyst. The psychoanalyst is faced with his own powerlessness over the organic and psychic reality of the child and the trauma this represents for the parents. Many analysts, therefore, turn away from this clinical experience because their own feelings of omnipotence and omniscience are undermined. However, my observations have shown me that, on the contrary, the psyche is capable of elaboration even when very serious, absurd or violent traumas are concerned. One can mention in this connection other traumas and extreme situations such as war, torture and natural disasters which make similar demands on the psychic resources of the 'normal neurotic'. Therefore, I think that the psychic process, from both the parents' and the children's side of the story can, nonetheless, become the object of a psychoanalytic approach, even if the symptoms are largely organically determined.

These patients are facing an unthinkable and unbearable experience. In these cases psychoanalysis exceeds the traditional limits of analysis – as with somatic, psychotic or mute patients – and is forced to look for other conceptual tools. Initially, there are no representations. The handicap has left the child with the stamp of abnormality and has apparently generated a sense of stupor in the parents, creators of this abnormality. This study investigates how, and over what time period, that which at first sight appears clinically to be irrepresentable will nevertheless in time link up with representations.

Further, it explores the manner and form in which this 'uncanniness' makes itself felt as well as its psychic evolution.

THE PARENTS: TRAUMA AND MOURNING

The handicapped child transmits an image of deformity to his parents; a broken mirror (*miroir brisé*) (Korff-Sausse 1996) in which they recognise neither themselves nor the awaited child who is supposed to ensure their continuity. Through their child their narcissistic impulses have been hurt because, as Freud (1914) wrote, 'the child brought into the world by the mother is a part of her own body and is thus an object of narcissistic love'. We know the famous saying of Freud about His Majesty the Baby who ought to be protected from all the frustrations of life. How are we to make the connection between this projection of narcissism and the reality of a damaged baby often stamped by a serious medical diagnosis? Classically, we speak of mourning for the imaginary child: the gulf between the imaginary and actual child is so great that a real period of mourning is necessary to make a place for the handicapped child.

My observations indicate that after the shock of discovering their child's handicap, the parents – at least initially – show an incapacity for the symbolisation which is essential for mourning: that is to say, the ability to put something in the place of the lost object. This is a grief which cannot be dealt with. Never completed, the process of mourning keeps reappearing during the child's life, especially with each important new stage (like the change of school or institution). One cause for the impossibility of mourning is the continuing existence of the imaginary child. The gulf is too great for the actual child to find his place. The imaginary child and the actual child thus co-exist, which is an enormous burden for both the parents and the child. In the back of their minds, the thought may emerge that it would have been better if the child were dead as mourning for it would be less difficult to bear than mourning the imaginary child – a process that can never be completed, as the real child is a constant reminder of it. In her work on mourning illness, Maria Torok (1968) writes that when the mourning process is not completed, the lost object is incorporated into the psyche. In this way, it is not lost and remains deeply embedded in the psyche as a 'commemorative monument' which 'stamps the ego with so many tombstones'. This phenomenon explains the fixed and static quality of time which is so characteristic of the relationship between the parents and their handicapped child.

The idea of grieving seems inadequate, however, to account for this clinical material. The handicap constitutes an event which embodies something unthinkable and horrifying. The handicap of a child calls to mind the idea of the uncanny *(unheimlich)* described by Freud (1919). Among the figures of the uncanny, Freud presents that of illness linked to the idea of deficiency: 'The uncanny effect of epilepsy or madness has the same origin. The layman sees in them the working of forces hitherto unsuspected in his fellow men but, at the same time, he is dimly aware of them in remote corners of his own being.'

The handicapped child holds out a mirror unmasking our own proper imperfections, reflecting an image of ourselves which we have no desire to see. This child has been stamped as strange. From being strange, he may become a persecutor, for he exposes our own strangeness. 'He played a dirty trick on us', said a father of his Down's syndrome child. According to Freud, that which appears strange in reality is familiar: 'For what is uncanny is in reality nothing new or alien but something which is known of old and long familiar and which has become alienated from it only through the process of repression.'

Is this strange child the expression of an ancient repressed figure? In other cultures, the figures of ancestors are believed to be reincarnated when a child is born; above all, when the child is marked by some difference.

At first, what has happened is beyond comprehension or words. Reactions of denial and somatic manifestations are very frequent. They are signs of the temporary impossibility of metabolising this shock which necessitates a painful psychic restructuring. All parents describe this period as vague, empty, blank. 'During many months, I had no imagination. Total blackout. Impossible to see this baby as a little girl. And as an adult, that was unthinkable.'

Behind the telescoping of these emotional states, both violent and contradictory, is hidden the inexpressible and inadmissible death wish. This situation holds in check the ability of the ego to assimilate emotions and incites a psychic state we can link to fright. We know that Freud differentiated between fright, fear and anxiety. Fright is the state which occurs when one faces a dangerous situation unprepared, it accentuates the surprise factor. Ferenczi develops at length this aspect of trauma in terms of fragmentation, atomisation and partial destruction of the mind following a trauma: 'An unexpected, unprepared for, overwhelming shock acts as if it were an anaesthetic. How can this be? Apparently by inhibiting every kind of mental activity and thereby provoking a state of complete passivity devoid of any resistance' (Ferenczi 1931, p.239).

The shock of discovering the handicap has a destructive effect on the psyche. This in turn creates an open wound in the psyche itself which unceasingly and vainly tries to close. The customary mechanisms of defence are held in check and pathological mechanisms may appear. 'Nothing is the same any more', say the parents.

But Ferenczi also suggests that these mechanisms are survival strategies. I wonder actually if the parental pain and the accompanying inability to think could not be considered as a way of short-circuiting an unbearable link. It would have, therefore, a double function of blocking the thinking process, and also of protecting the survival of psychic life, similar to hibernation. One can refer here to the theory of Bion (1963) who postulates that at the beginning of psychic life (which he places before birth, during the intra-uterine period), there is an emotional experience which searches for a way to be represented. 'Thoughts searching for an apparatus to think them.' The psyche develops the capacity to think these corporal and emotional experiences in an intersubjective relationship. Parents will be confronted by this situation: an unthinkable thought occurs to them and, according to Bion's terminology, the subject is led to create an apparatus which allows him to think 'thoughts which have already emerged'. The work of the psychoanalyst will be to promote this linking process and facilitates expression there where there was only silent pain.

Indeed, in the light of psychoanalytic work done with certain parents over time, it would appear that the condition of being dumbfounded is transitory. The psychoanalyst can in fact notice a process of repression or, more likely, an uncontrollable return of the repressed. The birth of an abnormal child discloses brutally and objectively precisely what was the object of repression. It would then be a failure of the process of repression. Indeed, parents cannot forget. Forgetting is impossible. The events surrounding the birth and diagnosis are burnt into the memory with a red-hot iron. It is always as if it were only yesterday. Time has stood still.

But what is the nature of the repressed fantasy reactivated by the discovery of a handicap? If every baby brings to the light of day his parents' sexuality, a handicapped baby would be testimony to an abnormal sexuality. A monstrous birth unveils in broad daylight a faulty conception. The handicapped infant violently stirs up questions about filiation. Who is responsible for this defect? Invariably, this question is asked. Parents push the responsibility onto each other or protect each other by not speaking about it at all. The grandparents are also actively involved in this questioning about the origin of the handicap. Brothers and sisters are also deeply affected and doubt is cast on their own future as mothers and fathers.

With the idea of 'differed action' (*nachträglich*), we are able to clarify the different stages of the process and attempt to restore, as

Freud did with Emma (1895), the associative links between the current and real event of discovering the handicap and what has been violently and painfully mobilised in each parent on the level of fantasy. The traumatic event is not traumatic in itself but has reactivated an earlier event. The psychoanalytic approach consists in retracing the paths leading to an earlier event or fantasy by favouring its re-emergence which always comes as a surprise. A mother came to see me after the birth of her Down's syndrome girl. She was depressed, petrified. No words, no tears. It was impossible for her to begin the mourning process which would provide a place for this child who evidently insisted on this, with troubling behaviour. After several interviews, the tears came, but in an unexpected way and not due to her child but *vis-à-vis* her own mother, lost at the age of nine. She had never shed a tear over her mother's death, being obliged – or feeling obliged – to react to the sorrow and solitude of her father, and not reacting herself to the loss. Over several months, she cried during each session, surprised to see this resurgence of emotions, within the transference setting. She had never suspected so many unknown emotions and realised how much her own hidden grief prevented the elaboration of her grief concerning her daughter's handicap. She was not able to speak to her child nor her family about the Down's syndrome until the day she was able to speak to herself about her mother's death, which had been announced to her indirectly and weeks after it happened. She said: 'It's as if I announced my mother's death to myself in one of my sessions here.'

The birth of an abnormal child awakens a sense of culpability, even if it is in complete contradiction with objective medical knowledge. The mother of a blind child could not prevent herself, despite the diagnosis of a genetic illness, from attributing the cause of the blindness to a medication taken during her pregnancy. Apart from this reproach, a fantasy came to light whereby she had wanted to destroy this foetus, a fantasy connected to a real abortion she underwent at the age of seventeen, in secret and in shame. Was it not this shame – which she succeeded in hiding at seventeen – that was now revealed with her son's handicap? Was she not being punished through this child for an adolescent sexual relationship with a man who resembled her father, an allusion to incest? Reality and fantasy blend. Past and present are confused. The borders between the psychic and the organic falter dangerously. We see the vacillations in certitude which characterise the uncanny as Freud describes it.

One could bring together these examples with Freud's last theory of trauma (1938) attributing to trauma a negative and positive function. Although he did not mention it, he was in fact inspired by the ideas of Ferenczi and postulated that if analysis could bring the patient to relive the unsettling trauma, 'a new sort of resolution of the trauma, more positive, more long term, could take place'. A repetition of the trauma could, therefore, promote a more favourable integration into psychic life of what would otherwise remain split-off like 'a State within a State' and as such would become, according to Freud, 'an inaccessible party with which co-operation is impossible' (1938, p.76).

Freud introduces with the idea of 'differed action' an important notion: the psychic apparatus is made of successive stratifications which interact in both directions. Not only does the present event interact with the past, it also modifies it. At the moment of a present event, an old trauma re-emerges which could suddenly give place to a revision, a rewriting of the moment, provoking a reorganisation. The consequence of this idea from a clinical point of view is that what is called 'psychological support' is not sufficient for the parents. Therefore, the therapeutic aim must be seen as an elaboration, or rather a re-elaboration.

These theoretical advances allow us to see in an altogether different way the psychic effects produced on the parents by the arrival of a handicapped baby. Rather than the image of a family turned in upon itself in a frozen immobilised state, we see the possibility of a reorganisation around and connected to this pathogenic event. After a period of pain and stupefaction, of pathological defence mechanisms (splitting, denial), of an absence of demand ('What good will it do to speak with you if it won't cure the handicap?'), the psychic functioning held temporarily and partially in check begins working again. The psychoanalyst's job is to promote this mobility.

THE CHILD: A QUESTION OF IDENTITY

A handicap affects the child's identity. In fact, how does a child bearing an abnormality assimilate this image of a body and a mind stamped by strangeness? Being estranged from others, he may become estranged from himself. How can the child construct the narcissistic foundation of the personality when he is not the one who was expected or hoped for? A psychoanalytic approach enables us to study the ways in which identity formation occurs in this respect.

In my own professional experience, a child acquires a sense of his abnormality at a very early age. This is true even with very deficient children. This results from the coming together of two different factors. First, perceptions from the external world: relations with parents and society. Second, internal perceptions: awareness of the differences between the child's limited physical and mental faculties and the innate sense of what constitutes normal development that all humans experience (Bion's 'preconception').

Being able to stand up, for example, is a fundamental stage in the evolution of an individual. Verticality inaugurates a new perspective on the world and oneself. At a certain age, children who are not able to stand – due to a motor or mental deficiency – suffer serious harm to their self-identity. When such a child is able to stand up, either thanks to his own motor faculties, or with the help of mechanical means, we observe a spectacular and immediate change in his attitude with respect to others and the world in general. A child in a nursery school who was silent and unresponsive to others, became talkative and even demanding. Another child in a nursery school who seemed uninterested in group activities due, so it was believed, to intellectual deficiency, turned out to be very interested in playing with others once he was equipped with a suitable apparatus by a physiotherapist.

The knowledge of his difference from others involves all aspects of his handicap – not only those which are obvious to the eye, but also mental deficiency. This discovery is more difficult to accept or even conceive of when it concerns the mentally deficient. One prefers to believe that the child is not aware of his difference and to hold on to the image of the child as a 'happy idiot'. However, my observations show that all children, even those with serious intellectual impairment, try to find out who they are and where they come from and, consequently, to know the peculiarities which distinguish them from others. Neither problems of communication, comprehension difficulties, troubles with motor co-ordination, nor writing difficulties escape this undertaking.

Very early on, a child begins to understand reality, his own reality with its disillusionment and frustration, the failures and differences between what is expected and what one is able to do. He compares himself with other children. He measures the effort necessary to accomplish what he wants to do and what is expected of him.

The discovery of being different implies experiencing moments of depression. I would place the peak of this phase at about three or four years old, at the onset of the Oedipus period when the child becomes conscious of two differences which constitute his self-identity: sexual and generational differences. Handicapped children pass through periods of instability and arousal, alternating with refusal and discouragement. These are the different manifestations of a real depression often camouflaged and rarely perceived by the family. In fact, this depression is unbearable for adults, since it awakens their own depression which has been repressed and blanketed by reactive behaviour. The parents are blinded by their own guilt which translates into a desire to make the child progress. They become rehabilitators, with their own therapeutic ideal. The child is constantly under pressure. The parents have difficulty in allowing for moments of relaxation, laziness or a desire to do nothing. This intolerance is exacerbated when the child becomes an adolescent and manifests the need for regression and revolt, typical of this period.

It is difficult to find a balance between denying the handicap and respecting the need for illusion which everyone has. One oscillates, on the one hand, between the risk of letting an illusion of 'normalcy' take root and, on the other, the imperative of not destroying hope which would break the dynamic of evolution. Certain parents, or handicapped children themselves, fight against everything and everyone, irritating professionals who do not like to be put in question, contradicted or fought against. Illusion is essential but disillusion is a necessary step. There is a high price to pay for those who get caught up in a compulsive defence mechanism of trying to escape the restructuring of psychic pains required in confronting the painful reality of the handicap.

Laurent has a very serious physical handicap but normal intelligence. He claims that he is going skiing like his brothers or asks for rollerskates. The denial of his handicap, as well as his refusal to accept physical re-education brought him into psychotherapy. Like many children at the first session, he collapsed literally into uncustomary passivity. Escaping from the customary pressure of anxiety, the child invests himself deeply in this relationship with another person who is simply at his side, a witness to his regressive activities and moments of depression, and who asks nothing from him. Laurent spent entire sessions painstakingly breaking things or playing with water and modelling clay. These moments of 'silent communication' (Winnicott 1963) are to be respected and considered as a necessary passage before tackling the work of interpretation. Winnicott says: '[I]n practice then, this is something we must allow for in our work: the patient's non-communication as a positive contribution.' This links up with the experience of being alone while with someone else, also described by Winnicott (1958). It provides a special quality to the therapy, especially for handicapped children, as the starting point giving access to the depressive position and the quest for self-identity.

In the oedipal myth, the oracle requires Oedipus to ask himself about parentage. At the oedipal stage, all children ask themselves the same question: 'Who am I? Where do children come from?' With handicapped children, the same questions are intertwined with those concerning the handicap. 'How and why do parents have handicapped babies?' And from there: 'Why am I handicapped? How does one become handicapped? Does one remain handicapped? Will this go away when I grow up? What have my parents done to me or what have I done to my parents?'

The child asks questions but no one hears. For one thing, because these questions are formulated in a camouflaged or deceptive way. Like messages in code, they necessitate interpretation. For another thing, because adults prefer not to hear questions which raise the issue of their own powerlessness (we are not able to cure or repair a handicap) or ignorance ('Why am I handicapped?'). These are questions without answers. Questions which lead to other questions. To the question 'why', more or less disguised by the child, the adult simply does not answer, or answers in such an ambiguous way that the confusion is only increased. When Thomas wants to know why he has to go to the re-education centre, adults reply: 'If you work well with Mr So-and-so, you will be able to walk.' But maybe Thomas' physical handicap will never permit him to walk. In the child's mind, the impossibility of walking one day will be due to his own responsibility of working well or not working well with Mr So-and-so. This type of answer feeds into the guilt the child already bears due to his handicap. Could this be an attempt to alleviate the guilt of the adult?

The need to understand always implies the notion of causality. Due to their craving for understanding and their omnipotent thinking, every child assumes total responsibility for whatever occurs. Stéphane, five years old and physically handicapped, plays during his psychotherapy sessions with trucks. They do not go very well. 'This car doesn't work', says the child who cannot walk himself.[4] 'It has had a terrible accident, it's broken down.' Then, a little later, it's the red light that prevents it from going ahead. Sliding from inability (the breakdown) to the forbidden (the red light). At that moment, the fact of not being able to walk was translated into the realisation of the oedipal punishment. In his fantasy, he has been deprived of the use of his legs because his father was mad at him for sexually desiring his mother. With children, as with adults, there is a search for meaning which is then revealed on a totally different plane than that of rational thinking (genetic accident, prematurity, and so on).

The handicapped child is afflicted with a double wound. On the one hand, he is faced with the frustrations inherent in the handicap. On the other hand, he must also carry the weight of another wound, this time symbolic: the wound inflicted on his parents' narcissism. He not only has to face his handicap, but also the anguish it incites in his parents and in the eyes of others.

When studying the formation of self-identity in handicapped children, it is necessary to keep in mind the central issue of perception by others. In fact, all children construct their self-identity through the eyes of others. What image can the handicapped child identify with when he is always defined by what he is not and what he does not have? The study by Winnicott (1967) on the mirror-role of the mother will serve as a guideline in this investigation. 'During the emotional development of an individual, the precursor for the mirror is the mother's face': this is the central idea of Winnicott. To see oneself, through the look of another person, the mother, is to feel one exists. The mother's look has a reflexive function: what the infant first sees reflected in his mother's face will be the foundation for the knowledge of his own self-perception. 'What does the baby see when looking at the mother? Generally, he sees himself. In other words, the mother's face looking at her baby generally expresses what she sees.' One could then ask what the handicapped baby sees. A look of depression, evasion or uneasiness? He reads in that look the wound he has inflicted on her and seeks desperately, like Narcissus, a mirror to see himself in.

The look is essential but it can also be dangerous. Rejecting or empty, it can topple towards persecution. We turn finally then to the 'psychological profile' of the Down's syndrome child or the deaf child or the blind child or the physically handicapped child. Everything which constitutes an individual is reduced to one single element, his handicap, which screens out all the rest. In a day care centre which receives handicapped children along with other children, Stéphanie, who is a five-year-old with Down's syndrome, finds herself for the first time face-to-face with another little girl who also has Down's syndrome: 'Here's Stéphanie!', she exclaims. Has she been reduced to a handicap? She is glad to recognise another child similar to herself, but she also identifies herself entirely with her handicap. Her name and the diagnosis are confused. Handicapped before being a child. Often, the first words expressed around the crib are medical. A diagnosis is pronounced before the baby has even been given a name.

In this game of looks or perceptions projections operate like ping-pong balls, in the way Winnicott would speak of lack of perception resulting from the reflection one receives of oneself. This situation sometimes occurs when the handicapped child finds himself alone among a group of normal children. He receives every projection there is about abnormality and absorbs every fantasy relative to oddity and death. This position is very difficult to uphold because there is a risk of accentuating the difference. My observations at La Maison Dagobert show that handicapped children integrate better into a group when there are two or three of them. Contrary to what one might fear, they place less value on their differences and identify more readily with the other children.

Others see only a stigma (Goffman 1963) that attracts and diverts attention at the same time. All handicapped people speak of the unbearable attention paid to them by others: inquisitive or fleeting, too obvious or excessive, never right. A look expressing an indecent fascination. Or a look revealing phobia and rejection. But there is also a libidinisation of the look and eventually a perverse use of the handicap.

The mythological figure of Priapus illustrates the connection between abnormality and sexuality. The mother of Priapus, Aphrodite, goddess of beauty and love, could not bear the vision of this ugly child and had to turn her eyes away. The child deprived of the mother's look will be reduced to provoking laughter and mockery in exhibiting his sexual hypertrophy, source of his shame and rejection. Handicapped children often have this kind of exhibitionist behaviour. Reduced by the eyes of others to their handicap, incited by fear or fascination, they vacillate between two contradictory attitudes: concealing and hiding their difference or showing and accentuating it. Isabelle, a mongol child of five, makes up her eyes with large red and blue lines with coloured pens: is she trying to mask or emphasise her slit eyes that are characteristic of mongoloids?

The handicap is never integrated, once and for all, into the personality; it never takes on a sense of finality. It is submitted constantly to reinterpretation in accordance with libidinal development. One can compare the process with how the child tries to interpret his handicap, using infantile sexual theories. Just as objective sexual knowledge does not prevent children from having irrational or personal theories on sex and birth, in the same way the handicapped child will also try to explain his handicap. Thus, Mireille, a five-year-old Down's syndrome girl, says: 'Antoine [her brother] has a penis and I am a mongoloid.' At this moment, she has assumed that her handicap is the equivalent of a sexual difference. She asks herself if girls are mongoloid and boys are not, if mongoloidism is reserved for children and if, when one gets older, the condition disappears. The specific conflicts linked to the handicap always reappear within the limits of fundamental neurotic complexes of the human psyche and the individual's history: separation, object loss, sexual difference, the oedipal conflict and death. The psychoanalyst is confronted by these contradictory elements in this clinical material: on the one hand, a specificity which it is important not to deny, on the other, an evaluation of these conflicts which follow the customary paths of elaboration of psychical conflicts.

The psychoanalytic therapy of a handicapped child offers a privileged environment where it is possible to carry out psychical work where depression, instead of being misunderstood, can be taken into account; where questions, instead of being deflected, can be formulated with an adult who will accept silence without feeling obliged to offer an answer. One could describe this therapeutic process according to Bion's (1965) model of alpha-function.

This evolution is not always comfortable, either for the analyst or the child, or the family. On occasion, it produces symptoms or an increase of anxiety, signalling a psychic metabolisation of raw reality. The psychoanalyst may feel counter-transferential scruples, being the one who provokes painful open-ended questions. But as Ferenczi puts it concerning work done with trauma recall: '[D]on't let yourself be impressed by suffering; in other words, don't suspend suffering prematurely' (Ferenczi 1931). Bion (1963) reiterates this idea by saying that analytical experience tends to increase the patient's capacity for suffering.

I will finish with two short clinical cases. Beatrice is a young girl afflicted with a slightly debilitating physical handicap which allows her to live in an 'as if' state where the handicap is present but not really significant. She presents herself as an automaton, well re-educated to speak, walk, and work at school, but living outside herself. She does not inhabit her own body. She is aware, however, of the medical diagnosis but this is only a strange thing she can do nothing about. It is through language that self-identity makes itself known and most of the time the handicapped child does not hear the words needed to express what he is or has. Lacking words, the handicap remains within the personality as an object and source of splitting and denial. Beatrice was such a case. As Ferenczi (1931, p.240) wrote: 'the absolute paralysis of motility also includes the inhibition of perception and (with it) of thinking. The shutting off of perception results in the complete defencelessness of the ego. An impression which is not perceived cannot be warded off.' It required several months of therapy before one day Beatrice asked the question: 'What's really wrong with me?' Asking this question opened the door to an awareness of her disability with a capacity for feeling the sadness, disappointment and rage that would flow from it. It is as if her ability to imagine and desire had been blocked because, in any case, her desires were unattainable. She was caught in reality, with no interior freedom, no space between the possible and the impossible.

It took me a certain amount of time to understand that behind the façade of David's aggressiveness and hyperactivity lay a profound depression. His behaviour was the expression of his concern about his severe illness. His extremely anguished parents could not approach the subject at all. David had his own way of asking questions concerning the 'unspeakable' nature of his illness. But he brought his questions anywhere and everywhere in such a violent and inadequate way that no one heard. What is more, everybody was either so busy or anxious to protect David from himself, to contain him, that their thinking capacity was largely put out of action. The child was drawing the adults into a game of risk and repetition they could hardly resist. Using this aggressive and destructive behaviour, David challenges the adults and arouses in them the very attitudes that conform to his fantasy. 'I feel broken, rejected, unloved and so I continue to break and reject things, make myself rejected. Don't my parents reject me because I'm ill, an invalid, not handsome? Would they not have preferred a child in good health? It's not me that they wanted.' He puts parents and nurses to the test. 'Do you really love me? You can see very clearly that you don't love me because you reject me all the time.' The psychotherapy sessions were also invaded by this emotional outpouring impossible to channel and I too found myself faced with a desperate sense of impotence. It was only when he was able to make me feel the depth of his depression that I could help him verbalise the anxieties linked to his illness, the frustrations of his treatment, his uneasiness concerning his parents and the fear of death. Only after this, did he relax. In psychoanalytical terms, the words that cropped up or appeared suddenly in the transferential space (this term includes for me 'transference' as well as 'counter-transference') led David to progressively elaborate on his fantasies concerning his illness and to gain a certain amount of breathing space related to it. Thinking about one's illness is not going to change it, that is true, but it will allow a child to live, not as someone prey to the blind forces of nature, but one who has a destiny and is ready to take responsibility for it.

NOTES

1. Le Centre d'Assistance Educative du Tout-Petit, 27, rue du Colonel Rozanoff, 75012 Paris, created in 1971, was the first organisation to offer early socio-medical action to handicapped children and their families. The CAMSP statutes have been defined and other centres have multiplied as result of a law passed in favour of the handicapped on 30 June 1975.
2. La Maison Dagobert, 30, rue Erard, 75012 Paris.
3. Such an approach could be linked in theory to the work of Georges Canguilhem (1943).
4. In French, the word 'marcher' is used both for 'walk' and 'work'.

REFERENCES

Bion, W.R. (1963) *Elements of Psycho-analysis*, London, Karnac, 1984.

Bion, W.R. (1965) *Transformations: Change from Learning to Growth*, London, Heinemann.

Canguilhem, G. (1943) 'Essai sur quelques problèmes concernant le normal et le pathologique', in *Le normal et le pathologique*, Paris, PUF, Coll. Quadrige, 1991.

Ferenczi, S. (1931) *Final Contributions to the Problems and Methods of Psycho-analysis*, New York, Basic Books, 1955.

Freud, S. (1895) *The Origins of Psychoanalysis. Letters to W. Fliess, Drafts and Notes: 1887–1902*, London, Imago, 1954.

Freud, S. (1914) 'On Narcissism: An Introduction', in James Strachey, ed., *The Standard Edition of the Complete Psychological Works of Sigmund Freud*, 24 vols, London, Hogarth, 1953–73, vol. 14, pp. 67–102.

Freud, S. (1919) 'The Uncanny', *S.E.* 17, pp.217–56.

Freud, S. (1938) 'Moses and Monotheism', *S.E.* 23, pp.1–137.

Goffman, E. (1963) *Stigma*, London, Prentice Hall.

Korff-Sausse, S. (1996) *Le miroir brisé. L'enfant handicapé, sa famille et le psychanalyste*, Paris, Calmann-Levy.

Torok, M. (1968) 'Maladie du deuil et fantasme du cadavre exquis', in *L'écorce et le noyau*, Paris, Flammarion, 1987, pp.229–51.

Winnicott, D.W. (1958) 'The Capacity to be Alone', in *The Maturational Processes and the Facilitating Environment*, London, Hogarth, 1963, pp.29–36.

Winnicott, D.W. (1967) 'Mirror-Role of Mother and Family in Child Development', in *Playing and Reality*, London, Tavistock, 1971, pp.11–119.

Winnicott, D.W. (1963) 'Communicating and Not Communicating Leading to a Study of Certain Opposites', in *The Maturational Processes and the Facilitating Environment*, London, Hogarth, 1963, pp.179–92.

16 At La Maison Dagobert a Handicapped Child is no less a Child for that ...

CECILE HERROU

La Maison Dagobert is a child care centre which has the capacity to work with up to twenty children, aged one to six, at any given time, a third of whom are handicapped in some way. In all, there are eighty to ninety children registered with the centre. These children are often severely handicapped and/or have parents who present symptoms which are viewed as complicated by the personnel who refer them to us. Many of the children would not be admitted elsewhere for these reasons. Our concern is to push back the barriers which work against their integration rather than to interfere with work which is already being done. The children come for at least two half-days a week; some of them for up to four whole days. They are invited to take part in a variety of *ateliers* (small activity groups). Everyone can take part, whether they are very small or very handicapped, thanks to a system of individual accompaniment.

La Maison Dagobert is situated at the heart of the ancient Merovingian kingdom. Although trousers sometimes get put on back to front as with the 'good' king Dagobert in the popular song, children are, nonetheless, treated as whole individuals. It is the mildly handicapped children who welcome the other children from the neighbourhood. Indeed, La Maison Dagobert was founded on the self-evident principle that, like other children, those with a handicap, whatever its nature or degree of severity, need to live together with others: with their families, as well as with children of their own age. We know how important it is to learn to cope with separation; that is, being able to go away, come back, meet up again with others is very important in life. Who has not felt uncomfortable at the sight of a mother with her grown-up handicapped child, a feeling provoked less by the handicap than by the 'monstrous' relationship of these two persons forever locked into a state of mutual dependence? La Maison Dagobert seeks to reduce a legal inequality caused by the natural inequality induced by handicap. It offers a place to an excluded child, without, however, creating a more pernicious form of exclusion by leaving the child alone with others. The contact with all the other 'healthy' children would only accentuate their isolation.

Nevertheless, the record concerning the integration of very young handicapped children is far from satisfactory. Generally speaking, attitudes have evolved over the last thirty years. Nonetheless, restrictions persist: this is almost systematically true for autistic children with behavioural problems, tolerated with difficulty by the community at large; multiply handicapped children; children with breathing difficulties; those with severe epilepsy and even children who are developing normally but suffering from metabolic irregularities which require strict diets. If it is true that for their well-being and optimal development, all children need to have contact with other children, it follows that it is unacceptable to exclude some because they have a disability. La Maison Dagobert seeks to demonstrate that we can live (well) together whatever – even thanks to – the individual particularities of some. Another obvious fact which informs our work is that although the anxiety induced by handicap must be taken into account and respected – for it is understandable – it must also be treated. La Maison Dagobert aims to reduce these fears by sharing its experience. Everyone knows that living together is not always easy but it is from this faculty for adaptation that the satisfaction and pleasure of living together come, whatever our differences may be.

As long as the idea of integration exists, its corollary, exclusion, will persist. There can be no will to work towards integration unless exclusion is a possibility. La Maison Dagobert hopes to abolish this risk and speaks of 'non-exclusion'. Independently of its founding ethical principles, it has understood that when given expression and recognition, extraordinary life-experiences can be remarkably enriching for thought, aestheticism, desire and pleasure, provided that one makes the effort of facing what one believes to be the horror of the unknown. It is a question of realising that vulnerability is our common lot, whether we are in fact afflicted with a recognised handicap or not. As one handicapped person put it so well, what frightens those who are 'normal', is not the difference between them (for they are radically different, and so not threatened), but the resemblance. Admitting that means we do not need to deprive ourselves of the only real defence available in face of this archaic anxiety: the pleasure of sharing other people's experiences and, in so doing, breaking down constricting social barriers. We thereby enrich

our vision enormously. Very young children do not deprive themselves of this freedom. La Maison Dagobert shows that as adults, we
can rediscover our natural reflexes.

How does La Maison Dagobert ensure that the children and their
families are made really welcome? Much could be said about its way
of working and, in particular, numerous accounts of shared experiences could be related, but here I must be content with providing a
simple outline.

If one had to pick out one essential factor which makes it possible
for somewhere like La Maison Dagobert to function, it would be the
following: it is vital not to deprive ourselves of the *diversity*, flux, and
exchanges which must not be fettered by hierarchies, arbitrary terri-
torial claims, imaginary positions and fictive roles. No one has a
monopoly on 'know-how' and the capacity to listen. In this context,
beyond the more or less troubled personal stories of each person,
desire and pleasure are expressed by all and sustain our institutional
life; in short, life itself.

In order to encourage a state of mind which allows each team
member to make his (or her) full contribution, it has been necessary
to break with practices commonly employed in centres which work
with handicapped children.

Those who 'officially' represent the policy of integration – paedia-
tricians, paediatric nurses, day nursery managers, psychologists –
that is, those who have thought about the conditions of admission for
handicapped children to centres for young children, often express the
opinion that 'each person must have a clearly defined role, whatever
their job is'. This point of view is not shared by those who really 'have
the children in their arms' and even less by maintenance staff.

For the only way to really work with these extraordinary children
– indeed, with *all* the children, for none of them are ordinary – is to
encourage the expression of different standpoints while not impeding
potential changes, so that a wide range of possibilities and responses
are available to meet the needs of the children as well as their
families.

Anxieties are often fed by silent responses to more or less explicit
questions under the pretext of it being a 'professional secret'.
Inadequate knowledge of what a 'professional secret' entails nour-
ishes a confusion between a child's medical history and his situation
of being disabled. The latter needs to be talked about openly to avoid
fabricating secrets which are known to be destructive not only for the
child and his family, but also for the institution which gets embroiled
in them.

In these centres, where it is not a matter of re-educating but of
enabling the children to live together under the best possible circum-

stances for their well-being and general development, it is clear that the children as well as the adults must be able to choose their interlocutors and eventually change them, since transference phenomena have an important part to play. The paediatric assistant, the maintenance staff, the cook or the gardener should not have the feeling that they cannot speak and communicate with the children (whether handicapped or not), or with the parents, on the grounds of incompetence. It is the prohibiting attitude of those who claim to 'know' towards those who are 'considered ignorant' which fosters incompetence.

Another leitmotif which is sometimes expressed by the very people who present themselves as theoretical proponents of integration is that 'integration should not take place at any cost!' At its best, this affirmation is unhelpful; at its worst it is dangerous because it does not take into account the capacity for change in individuals and institutions. I would respond to it by saying that whatever the gravity and nature of their handicap, handicapped children should be taken into care *at any cost*, and that we have a responsibility to adapt to them so that they in turn can develop their own capacities for adaptation. That means being open to the thoughts of others as well as realising that fear can be overcome.

It is therefore a matter of developing a way of working which allows everyone to feel comfortable with their own viewpoints and the actions which result from them by trusting in the co-operation and interaction of professional staff. Everybody has their limits which must be respected, but the capacities and limitations of one person are not necessarily those of another. Which is why, as is often the case, it is a monumental error to require all the team members to decide unanimously in favour of taking on a handicapped child. The decision to take on a handicapped child should not be the responsibility of individuals but should depend on the organisation's regulations. It should be explained that each and every person has a right to their reticence and fears ... but also to their knowledge and their desire to get involved, whether they be paediatric assistants, doctors or managers ... and it must be ensured that everyone receives the support they need.

Moreover, each person's weaknesses are minimised and their strengths maximised to the extent that we allow them to be ... the functioning of the institution depends on this system of interdependence which helps to contain fear and to maximise competence by relying on diversity. The so-called weaknesses or impossible aspects of a colleague are to be understood as the symptom of a particularly acute comprehension of a difficult situation and will be analysed by the team as a whole for the good of the child, his family, and professional staff.

The capacity to be welcoming is not an exact science and is within everybody's possibilities. The competence of each person is revealed in the mutual trust that exists between staff and implies a constant process of questioning our practice and our own sense of alienation.

We have created a setting where power, in the sense of 'the power to act', 'the power to take decisions', is shared by all. Power is shared and appropriated in function of the needs and requirements of the children and their families. To achieve this, there is neither a hierarchy of tasks (some being valued more than others), nor of persons (due to their qualifications) which would rigidify the institutional system. Potentially, each person is in a position to make decisions, to submit their ideas, their thoughts, their point of view to others; in fact, to play a leading role. Everyone is required to do certain tasks; for example, to take part in educative activities, to hold interviews, to chair the weekly meeting, to give support to a child or a parent, to meet with specialists, to share their experience during training courses and conferences, whatever their original training may have been. The *capacity* of everyone on the team to possess *knowledge* revolves around the emergence of multifaceted knowledge and experience. The fundamental principles or, shall I say, the founding 'myth' of La Maison Dagobert boils down to the creation of a 'container' based on a systematic policy of non-exclusion with regard to people, their ideas and their experiences. Like any living institutional 'myth', it has evolved over the years through contact with those who have adhered to it.

Even if La Maison Dagobert has not been accorded the status of a treatment centre as such, the rich therapeutic effects it offers have not passed unnoticed. These are institutional therapeutic phenomena which have to be induced rather than impeded ...

17 Psychoanalysis and Mental Handicap: Experience from the Tavistock Clinic

VALERIE SINASON

I started this work in a significant way in 1980 when I joined what was then called the 'subnormality workshop' at the Tavistock Clinic started by an adult psychoanalyst and psychologist called Neville Symington. My father, Professor Stanley S. Segal OBE, was in the field of mental handicap – in fact both Paul Berry and Christian Gaedt from Germany have worked with him – and both in my spare time and in my previous life as a teacher, I had been involved in that work but not psychoanalytically until I joined the workshop. Symington attracted a lot of psychoanalysts who were interested in his work but once they had taken on one patient, their interest stopped.

Looking at analytic history, as far as it is recorded, it seems that in a lot of countries one analyst would take one patient on – usually with a mild handicap – and would be fascinated that therapy could work but then, somehow, could not bear to take on a second. It is people who have been involved in mental handicap before their psychotherapy training, who have either had someone with a mental handicap in their family or someone who has worked in this area, who keep the work going.

For example, Judith Usiskin, who was an occupational therapist working with handicapped adults before she began the child psychotherapy training, has taken on the main work at the Tavistock together with me. We have succeeded in making more child and adult psychotherapists take on one patient, but, again, the practice of working with the severely and profoundly multiply handicapped seems to rest mainly with those who were already involved.

It is quite interesting to think how universal the fear of getting close to this sort of damage is. In one international conference on mental handicap where the participants – for the most part psychiatrists – were all specialists in the field, psychotherapy was spoken about the least, whereas organic syndromes and thinking about organic meaning had the largest amount of space. Even in the field of the psychiatry and psychology of mental handicap it is painful to think of meaning. So this small group of ours which has got larger over the last fifteen years, is very unusual in terms of not being frightened of the mentally handicapped, not being frightened of grief, loss and damage, and also of being able to stand thinking about meaning.

MIRRORING

The first theoretical ideas that I came up with turned out to be very similar to Dietmut Niedecken's (this volume) in terms of her idea of death-feigning (which I initially misheard as 'failing'). I missed her talk because of my analytic training case. I was not able to leave until Friday afternoon. Her idea is, that around the organic handicap, something gets added on to do with the internalising of the death wish of the mother or society towards the infant. This gets taken inside and becomes another layer which can be more damaging than the organic handicap and is what I have called secondary handicap.

So, in a way, one of the beauties of a conference like this is that in our separate areas we have all come up with quite similar ideas concerning what we have noticed. It is really important that we put them together so that we have shared knowledge, being able to bring in each other's work as corroboration. In some of the discussions at this conference, mention was made of the infanticidal introject, that is, the disabled child breathing in the death wish towards it of those around and of how the mother's eyes are the first mirror in which we are what we see looking at us. Therefore, the theme of the handicapped baby taking in a sense of deathliness, of otherness, of something that inspires guilt, pity, confusion, disturbance or whatever, seems to be something we have all picked up in our work.

The task of psychotherapy has often been to differentiate the primary organic handicap from the secondary one with the result that the handicapped person is spared the pain and shame of what their real handicap is and what their real feelings of pain about it are.

I think the heart of this pain is that a man and woman have come together and instead of producing something as beautiful as the best of themselves, something has come out wrong. I find the title of the film about deafness, *Children of a Lesser God*, wonderful in terms of expressing hurt at a handicapped creation and the internalisation of being the product of a damaging intercourse.

Since nearly all my work has ended up being with sexually abused and abusing handicapped children and adults, I have found that the inherent feeling of sexual badness is there, spoiling every stage of psychosexual development. Especially the awful feeling that you cannot work through the Oedipus complex because, as one girl with Down's syndrome said: 'Daddy doesn't want to marry me because I've got Down's syndrome.'

I do think that in working with learning disabled adults the sexual transference is the most unbearable to deal with as those kind of daring, erotic thoughts come out of the shell. It takes a long time before it feels safe to bring that verbally into the transference and speak about it without causing more hurt.

For example, I work in individual, family, group and marital therapy with mildly, severely and profoundly handicapped patients, both children and adults.

In one adult group, one woman with Down's syndrome had a job as a nursery assistant in an infants' school. It was not really a proper job; it was helping to tie shoelaces and wipe noses and take children to the toilet. She was very proud of it. After the group had been working for two years she said: 'I won't get no man, no one in my school to go out with.'

Another woman in the group said: 'There are man teachers in your school, aren't there?'

'Yes.'

'So why you say you can't get a man? There is man teachers.'

There was a terrible pause as the whole group looked at me, and I said, 'You're all looking at me; maybe you're wondering if I would be the one to say for everybody that it would be a very abnormal professional man that wanted to have a handicapped woman as a girlfriend.' And then thinking: they are all going to attack me; I am a sadist; what have I said? But the sigh of relief that went round the room was enormous.

They had put the fragility and the fear of naming the difference into me. Again, as Evelyn Heinemann was describing, the therapist is at times in the position of being an auxiliary ego and sometimes the group voice until the group can speak for themselves. I am now going to give some examples across the age groups of some of the main themes that have come up for me in therapy. I shall start with a fifteen-year-old adolescent with Down's syndrome who picked up a toy mirror in the therapy room.

Now, with adults and children – I work with both – I can have a room that has got a doll's house and toys and drawing paper without worrying politically whether I am being rude to adults. People who only work with adults feel worried whether they are breaking a boundary by bringing something else into the room. But I found it particularly important to have a mirror, and I found that a lot of patients were in homes where mirrors had been removed. Not only did the mirror stage not work but the eyes were registering a death wish. Fear of the different appearance of the handicapped patient meant that sometimes, for protective reasons, the parents took on the handicapped person's shame, so it was not because they thought their child was ugly, but they were acting out the shame the handicapped person felt. So again, like our question about what is the mother and what is the child, it is important to see who is carrying out what for whom.

She picked up the toy mirror, looked at her face, put a toy crown on her head and looked at her face again. She took the crown off, then put a necklace on and looked in the mirror. I said she did not look pleased with what she saw in the mirror. She did not appear to hear me. She was deep in her own thoughts. Then she picked up a veil and wound it around her head, round her eyes, covering her whole face with it. A second later she took it off. Then she covered the mirror with the veil so nothing could be seen in the mirror. There was a painful tension in the room. Then she threw the mirror violently, but it was plastic and unbreakable, and then she sat and cried. I quietly said she did not think she could look at herself without adding on something like a crown, a necklace or a veil. Perhaps she did not think that I cared for her and that she was a princess or a queen. I added that pretending to be a princess or a queen was no good because she felt a useless handicapped one. She wished she could cover her face up to hide her Down's syndrome or throw it away.

'Why doesn't it go away?', she asked; 'Why is it here? Each time I look in the mirror it's still here and I'm a good girl.'

That really painfully brought home to me the predicaments of adolescence, as well as the pain of adolescents with a disability, because adolescents often look in the mirror wanting to see whether their sexual guilt and sexual desires are reflected by damage on their faces – pimples, spots and noses. Hatred of the nose – something that sticks out – being proof of some exertion, some sexual desire going on somewhere.

I think adolescence is a painful time when face values overtake a sense of worth, internal worth. Adolescents have these problems anyway, but handicapped adolescents have the extra problem that they are not just fantasising that they look different, they are different. And it does not go away. They are not going to be the frog that turns into the prince; they are going to stay the frog.

Carol's hope, that if she is good the handicap will go away, underlines the widespread unconscious fantasy that the handicapped individual possesses great destructive powers that have become linked to the bad destructive sexuality of the parental couple.

The mirror is not passive. It actively sends messages to us and affects our internal image of ourselves. Where there is an autistic blankness, the child turns to destruction and it was Maud Mannoni (1972) who first considered the plight of the child who feels danger when his parents look at him because the meaning of that mirror is the death wish of the adult towards him.

I think we can see this death wish communicated through the eyes in the myth of Perseus and Medusa, where, by not looking at Medusa directly, Perseus is safe. 'Looking' is sexually dangerous when the first mirror is a stony, castrating or dangerous one.

I think that one area where technique for me is different, is that the quality of looking which I do is not neutral in the way it is for some healthy patients, but has a far more engaged, interested look in my eyes. I have never allowed myself to feel sleepy. The moment that I get a sense of an attack that is making me sleepy, I fight it power-fully by refusing to be a mirror that is anything but concerned or interested. It has also meant that I have not been active in encour-aging the use of the couch because most of the patients I have seen are so traumatised that they need to see my eyes to know that I am not trying to kill them. That is one image from an adolescent.

SEXUAL ABUSE

Let me now give you an image from a children's group. This is a group for severely handicapped children, boys and girls, who had all been sexually abused. One theoretical issue I want to raise, one finding that has been the same for the children's group, the adult group and for individuals in therapy, is that their language changes dramatically.

In the first year of therapy before the secondary handicap, that is to say, before the death-feigning instincts have been worked on, there is usually a very tiny vocabulary. That is, patients who have verbal language usually tried superficial adjectives like 'nice', 'clean', 'good', 'pretty'. When you look at those words they're awful because, although they are cliché words, to think of a handicapped person using the words 'fast', 'quick', 'bright', 'nice', 'good', 'clean', really hurts. After a year in therapy, verbal language increases 500 per cent; receptive language infinitely more. Words like 'violent', 'jealous', 'unbearable', 'painful', 'terrible', 'smelly', 'unhygienic', 'depressed', 'suicidal', 'stained', 'devastated', 'slippery', 'ill', 'tracked', 'pathetic', 'disturbed', 'childish', 'spastic', 'retarded', 'stupid', 'dumb-head' are used.

I collected every single adjective from every patient of all ages to do a linguistic analysis. Swear words usually start after one year.

With ordinarily disturbed, conduct-disordered children who come swearing, therapy puts it back inside them.

There is a political meaning in language and I find it quite wonderful when severely handicapped patients start to swear! The main pattern of referral in England is that you are allowed, if you are handicapped, to bite yourself, self-injure, throw things at other people, be physically violent to other people, but you do not show direct rudeness to the super-race of normal people.

The commonest referral letter is: 'Please see X. He has a lovely personality and he smiles all the time. It is just that he knocks staff out and he bites us and so and so needed five stitches.' I find one aim is to allow direct verbal aggression in the sessions. I will actively elicit that in terms of verbalising the linked counter-transference I experience.

For example, one child, who cannot tell the time, came after a year in therapy with a toy watch and threw it at me one minute before the end of the session. This showed perfect unconscious and conscious sense of time, although he was thought not to have any. With an ordinary child I would have said, 'You're really fed up, you want to go.' With him, I said: 'Oh, this awful, terrible Mrs Sinason, when's she going to shut up, when can I get out of here, I can't stand this awful woman a moment longer' – with a slightly humorous inflection to make the anger allowed and not too frightening, and then he burst out laughing. The next session he could say 'shut up' when it was the end of time. I said that he was so cross that it was the end of time; it was as if I was shutting him up and he wanted me to know what that was like.

I think there is political censorship that goes on and for people without verbal language even more so. A lot of the boards for pointing to words and pictures have no swear words on them, sometimes not even the word 'hate'. You can have a rain cloud to be sad and the sun to be happy, but you have nothing to say 'piss off', 'hate you' or 'no'.

In one school, where I pointed out to the headmistress that there was no 'no' and there was no 'I hate', she said: 'This is a loving school. The children would never need to say "no" or "I hate".' I tried to explain that to say 'no' is one of the essential psychic organisers and how do you build a 'yes' and 'no' and choices in right from the start?

This is quite shocking language after a year of therapy and I am not going to bother you with details of the children, who were all between twelve and fourteen, other than to say that hardly any of them spoke when they joined the group. After a year the nature of their abuse and what has happened is vivid.

A group began. Lennox came in first and picked up my necklace asking what it was. Angela was carrying a huge handbag. She asked where Gloria was. Lennox asked Angela what was in her bag. She opened it proudly and showed him pictures of Michael Jackson. Lennox was very pleased looking at this, although he looked jealous. Angela said that her mother, whom she did not live with, had taken her shopping and had given her the bag. Then she cried, slapped herself round the face and said: 'No, mummy didn't give me the bag; my friend at school did.'

I said she was very pleased to bring her new bag full of nice things but there was a problem. She wished it was something good she had got from her mother but it was not. Perhaps she felt I did not give her anything good either. Angela nodded sadly. Lennox then showed his school bag with tapes in it. He took them out but he could not read the titles. He pretended he was reading, mumbling, too humiliated to speak. The words were too hard for him. I asked if he would like me to read them out. He nodded and I read out *Alice in Wonderland* and *The Little Mermaid.* He showed them to Angela and she said: 'You've got lots of things in your bag.' I said they were both happy that they had something inside them, even if they could not use it properly, even if it had not been given by the person they wished had given it to them. They both had something that they could appreciate in each other.

There was a knock on the door and John burst in and went straight for a giant teddy bear. He had an eroticised smile on his face and he started buggering the teddy bear immediately. Angela ignored it, but Lennox was worried. 'Don't hurt the bear', he said. 'Hello, Johnnie boy', shouted Lennox. 'Hello, stupid Johnnie; can't you do anything right, Johnnie, Miss Johnnie?' John ignored this and continued throwing himself on the teddy, bending it over the sink and then hitting the teddy's bottom ferociously. 'Oh, no', said Angela. 'He's gonna fuck the teddy again.' Lennox began again: 'Why don't you die, John? Have an epileptic fit; die, I hate you; just kill yourself, stupid Johnnie boy, Nancy boy, Miss Baking Tray.' Angela then joined him with the teasing 'Miss Baking Tray', the two of them mocking him.

I commented on this and the fear and anger his attack on the teddy had stirred up. John threw the teddy at the play house which then fell over. Lennox was devastated. He stood paralysed for a moment before screaming: 'Fucking bastard, bastard, bitch, pig.'

I told John to help me repair the house, while Lennox continued screaming. I said Lennox was really worried. He wanted to have a baking tray and manage the house, but he was scared he would be teased or seen as a girl and he was scared John would treat him like he treated the teddy bear. But now he was frightened; his teasing had worked and the house was destroyed. Gloria arrived, looked round the room and was upset. 'We tidied it up last week. Look what John's done, he's a bully.' John looked upset and said he was not. 'Yes, you are. He is just like my dad; he hurts the teddy, just like my dad hurt me', said Angela. I said everyone was either trying to turn someone else into Angela's dad or be the teddy bear. John either had to have a fit and die or be turned into a monster. The girls either had to tidy up or tease the boys. There was no choice for people with a victim or a bully.

The week after, everybody was there on time. Inside the room, Lennox and Angela went straight to the area where John and the teddy bear usually were. This time they attacked the bear. I said that without John here at the moment, someone else was expressing the group's need to fuck the teddy bear. 'Go on', shouted Angela, 'Kick his balls; kick the teddy; smash his face like happened to Tracy.' 'Who's Tracy?', I asked. 'My dad's girlfriend; he smashed her face in', burst out Angela, laughing.

Lennox hit the teddy but looked worried and then said: 'This is for her face, stupid thing ... stupid dumb handicapped thing. You don't know your alphabet. You don't know how to read and write, stupid, shit, cunt, handicapped pig.' Angela then said: 'I've got a friend called Leslie who knows how to kill people. Go on Lennox, you hurt the bear, fuck him to death.' Lennox looked worried, and then giggled and started bashing the teddy's head. They both poured abuse onto the teddy. Angela, in a completely different voice, said: 'You love him, you love that teddy.'

There was an electric pause in a long silence. And then they both sat down and agreed. I said that perhaps what made it so hard was that they loved the teddy and they wanted to hurt it and perhaps they were worried I loved them but hurt them too, just like their daddies and mummies.

I'm going to stop with the children's group at that point which is a shocking sort of extract to take in because the issues around the abuse are so much more powerful than the issues around the disability.

You can see the way that in the children's language their experience of being abused is primarily seen as a result of their handicap. In fact, when I did an audit of 200 referrals – the first 200 in one year – 70 per cent turned out to be because of sexual abuse. The extent of sexual abuse of the handicapped is absolutely enormous in England. The experience of the handicap and low self-esteem joining together makes the children infinitely more vulnerable.

What happened with that group as the last year went on was what happens in all groups. Because we could see in the group the way somebody took it in turns to be the one to sexually abuse the teddy bear, no one person held the guilt for the action. One of the key benefits of group therapy is that you can project into someone else your sadism, your perversion, and so long as it is interpreted, no one is scapegoated, no one is left feeling it is them. Those children were all practically non-verbal with no proper sentences when they started the group. To separate out the pain of the handicap, to handle the pain of the abuse, was one very important function of that.

CURIOSITY AND HUMOUR

In both individual and group work I have pointed out that a high level of emotional and physical tension is required from the therapist. I also think that where clients are functioning at infantile levels, you do have the function of aiding the development of thinking, filling in the joke, verbalisng the counter-transference until patients can speak more. There were two other areas that I thought were technically different. One is to do with curiosity.

Curiosity is one of the most precious things for a handicapped patient to express, because it is the most internally and externally attacked function. If we only think how hard it is in a peer group to say when we do not understand something for fear it will show us to be stupid. We know that if we ask we are actually likely to find we can understand the answer. What is it like to dare to ask a question when you do not know if you will understand the reply cognitively? To dare to be curious is extremely courageous when you have a handicap. Therefore, I will actually give reinforcement to curiosity. If someone asks: 'Where did you go at the weekend or are you on holiday?', instead of that poker-faced 'You are wondering what I am doing', I will say: 'You really want to know what I am doing; you are really getting brave; you are really wondering, am I with a man, am I with a woman, am I hurting a child?' Whatever it is, my voice will have an affect in it that is giving a reward for the question, even though it is an ordinary analytic answer.

This applies to abusers and patients suffering from other perversions as well. When handicapped people sexually abuse normal young children – and it is worth noting that handicapped sex offenders go for normal little children – they are attacking their own sense of self-hatred for not being normal. In terms of indictable offences, when it is peer-group rape, handicapped adults are raping handicapped adults.

James was under a section for sexually abusing normal children, anally raping them. He had been anally raped by his school teacher in his special school when he was eight. After five months in therapy, he started looking in a noticeable way under my chair. With a normal patient suffering from a perversion, I might have said: 'You're wanting to get inside my bottom with your glance.' With him, I said: 'You are really feeling braver in the room, you are really interested in what is under my chair.'

That, I have found, is a very important first step that could then lead to voicing more symbolic comments about perverse or sadistic wishes. More graphic interpretation at the beginning would, I feel, destroy those first attempts at infantile geography. There has to be a transitional interpretation space where the deepest level of meaning is held by the therapist until it is safe to mention. Anger, as I have said, also needs considerable holding, making it safe to be angry. Negative transference interpretations can be taken in best when they are said in a facilitating tone of voice, otherwise they are experienced as complaints from the therapist.

For example, in the sixth session when one patient said: 'I was violent to my friend Jane and I have to control my temper just like pills control my diabetes', I said it was very hard that bad tempers could not be cured by drugs. Perhaps the group felt I was a really bad doctor not having pills to make the bad feelings go away. Again, they all roared with laughter at me voicing the negative transference.

Slowly, as therapy goes on and you have an individuation and separation process, you also have the group being able to speak to each other. Let me take examples now from an adult group. In the beginning all conversation was directed at me, at the therapist. One person said: 'I had a dog that starved and was put down.' Another: 'I had a pet that went blind.' A third: 'My mother got cancer.' Another: 'When I was little, I had to go to Great Normal Street' – her term for Great Ormond Street Hospital. Yet another: 'I had a puppy that was put down.'

Terribly painful as always, the first session reveals the key issues, each of them verbalising images of death-making, as Wolfensberger (1991) calls it. There is the feeling that they are part of a species that is wrong and are unable to talk to each other. Then their language deteriorates and you have a lot of echolalic behaviour which then becomes available for meaning. For example, there was one woman who exhausted everybody in the group. She did the echolalia for everybody. 'I came in and said, "Good morning, John Smith." "Good morning, Mary Brown", said John. I said: "John Smith, would you like a cup of tea to drink?", and he replied, "Thank you very much, Mary Brown".' The whole group could give up their echolalia and be sick of it in her.

After a year, again on behalf of the whole group, she came in and said this: 'On Friday night, my dad, he banged his shoes on the table, he did, and he smashed all the plates he did, and he did shout at my mother and tell her to leave the house and he did throw things at my mother. My mother was crying and I did sit and cry and then I said: "Would you please, please, would you please like a cup of tea dad?" And my dad, he did say: "Thank you Mary, yes, I would like a cup of tea".'

I am just aware of feeling all prickly saying that again and feeling tearful, because I had never thought about echolalia properly before and it suddenly became noticeable then that the group was held in the face of unbearable trauma by the trite, courteous words of everyday life. All the group lost their echolalia at that point.

If you listen to your patients who are echolalic, nearly all of them are saying a sentence that is hurting in their heads and they cannot cognitively process it because they have not got an adequate thinking process and the words that hurt them are going round and round because the grief in them has not been picked up. The point at which a patient or a group lose it is nearly always after a year when the secondary handicap has been dealt with.

After a year, if one takes a time sample – the same weekend, the same month, the same period in the session to look at the linguistic change – there can be a pseudo-attempt at triangulation: 'A' saying while looking at me, 'I would love to know what it's like to get a job in a nursery, and me saying, 'You're looking at me wanting me to link you with "B". It's hard for the group to ask each other, but you are all beginning to be interested in what each other does and the fact that you could offer things for each other.'

Then 'A', very angrily said: 'I wonder, "B", what it is like doing your job in a nursery school', compliantly following my pathetic attempt which I was unable to resist at that moment of trying to keep them talking to each other.

It took three years before there was a real interest in the other, for example, in the post-pseudo politeness of 'A': 'I wonder why "B" isn't here today; I hope she didn't have a problem with her taxi; I hope her mother's not ill.' Then 'B' walks in late.

'Oh, "B", we were just wondering about you. We are so glad you're here.'

Four years for the therapist to be irrelevant, to be able to move really out and the group to show interest in each other.

One joke which I had to complete was at a point at Christmas where I had a South American co-therapist who was about to go on maternity leave and the group did not know consciously . They had not been told yet, but unconsciously they did know, and they brought two shabby Christmas presents wrapped in really damaged old paper – very handicapped looking presents – my Swedish friends have heard this incident before.

We were very surprised to get these presents. I opened them and for my co-therapist there was a shabby poetry book 'to a friend who is going far away'. I said they knew that Isabel came from South America and so they were preparing themselves for the thought that she might go. The one for me was *Every Woman's Health Book* and on the cover it had a slim athletic woman playing tennis.

I looked at it and they all had their heads down, trying to look handicapped with no expression on their faces and I thought, 'Is it?', and then, 'Of course, it is', and I said: 'Well, you really care about me and you want me to look after myself over Christmas and come back healthy.'

They lifted their heads up a bit and I said: 'And you're also pointing out that the only overweight woman in the group is the therapist.' And they all started roaring with laughter and again the joke would have all remained hidden if one hadn't verbalised their intelligence. I think the making of a joke together is a very precious thing where it is not laughing at, but laughing with.

I'm going to end with what was in fact my favourite. It is one where the making of the joke brought about healthy changes in the therapy.

It had taken four years to get to sexuality, adult sexuality and sexual feelings, and it turned out that some of them had been raped. There was a point where one woman started having very sadistic fantasies about mutilating the genitals of the men in the group and my male co-therapist. She had been raped very viciously and at one point when she was saying all these horrible things, the men in the group were putting their hands over their penises and there was a very uncomfortable atmosphere.

Then, a severely handicapped man said: 'I'd like to change the subject. I'd like to take the group somewhere nice, to the ballet, like to the "Nutcracker Suite".' We were all in hysterics for the next ten minutes, both therapists included.

So that was really wonderful and you can see that we absolutely enjoyed the beauty of that. It was like ordinary therapy. After four years the handicap is irrelevant. It is like ordinary psychoanalytic psychotherapy.

The last example is of an autistic woman, severely mentally handicapped, and it was after four years and on a rainy day. I had come out in sandals with no coat and in some omnipotent state of mind. I had two minutes before she came in, but I could not dry myself. There was a knock on the door.

In came an autistic woman in a raincoat, boots, gloves and with an umbrella. She looked at me really slowly, stared at my hair, looked all the way down to my feet, all the way round the room to see whether or not there was a raincoat. Then she took off her coat slowly, hung it up, put her umbrella down and had a sadistic little grin on her face. She looked at her boots and said: 'My boots are dirty.' There was a painful silence and I said: 'It's raining today. You came in the room and looked at me.' She lifted her head a bit. 'And you saw my hair was wet ... yes ... and my toes were wet ... yes. And then there was the beginning of a little smile and you looked all the way around the room to see if there was an umbrella. And there wasn't. Was there a coat? No, there wasn't. And then you looked at yourself and saw that you had everything that was right for this weather, the right coat, everything.' She nodded, and I said: 'And then you must have thought: what sort of an idiot is this, coming out on a day like this, dressed like that?' She burst out laughing and I said: 'You weren't allowed to feel you were more intelligent than me. So then you had to make your boots dirty and spoil them.'

The point of that was the preciousness of a joke in bringing out the unconscious hostility underneath. If we are willing to be the auxiliary ego and verbalise the counter-transference without taking over and putting words in the patient's mouth, that are not the patient's projection, then together we have the combined intelligence the patient was showing, but didn't dare to complete.

And since we are breaking taboos in working with these groups, putting the healthy side of humour on the map seemed a good way to end.

REFERENCES

Mannoni, M. (1972) *The Backward Child and his Mother,* New York, Pantheon.

Wolfensberger, W. (1991) *Der neue Genozid an den Benachteiligten, Alten und Behinderten,* Gütersloh.

Index

Index compiled by Sue Carlton